Saga of an Aviation Survivor

Howard John "Mike" Hunt
1922 – 2019

Howard John Hunt

Fathom Publishing Company
Anchorage, Alaska USA

ISBN 978-1-888215-85-4 (Hardback)
ISBN 978-1-888215-84-7 (Paperback)
ISBN 978-1-888215-86-1 (ebook)

Library of Congress Control Number: 2021919292

First edition January 2022

Author Disclaimer:
   These events are recalled as I remember them. Any errors or conflicts are mine alone.

Cover design and Cape Lisburne map by
   Jacques Polomé, Jacques Polomé Design, Perth, Australia.

Front cover image of BT13 and noted interior images of Howard Hunt and airplanes by
   Rob Stapleton, Alaskafoto, Anchorage, Alaska.

Other illustrations courtesy of the Estate of Howard John Hunt.

Publisher's Cataloging-in-Publication data

Names: Hunt, Howard John, author.

Title: Saga of an aviation survivor : Howard John "Mike" Hunt , 1922 – 2019 / Howard John Hunt.

Description: Includes bibliographical references and index. | Anchorage, AK: Fathom Publishing Company, 2021.

Identifiers: LCCN: 2021919292 | ISBN: 978-1-888215-85-4 (hardcover) | 978-1-888215-84-7 (paperback) | 978-1-888215-86-1 (ebook)

Subjects: LCSH Air pilots--United States--Biography. | Fighter pilots--United States--Biography. | Bush pilots--Alaska--Biography. | Airplanes, Military--Conservation and restoration--United States. | World War, 1939-1945--Aerial operations. | BISAC BIOGRAPHY & AUTOBIOGRAPHY / Personal Memoirs | BIOGRAPHY & AUTOBIOGRAPHY / Aviation & Nautical | BIOGRAPHY & AUTOBIOGRAPHY / Historical | BIOGRAPHY & AUTOBIOGRAPHY / Military

Classification: LCC TL540.A28 .H86 2021 | DDC 629.13/092--dc23

www.fathompublishing.com
Fathom Publishing Company
P.O. Box 200448
Anchorage, Alaska 99520-0448
Telephone / Fax 907-272-3305
Printed in the United States of America

Dedication

To my blended family who always supported me:
My wife, Ruth
My wife, Carol, "Queenie"
My children,
Nancy, Barbara, Diane, Dashelle and Howard

The Alaska Aviation Museum

Alaska Wing of the Commemorative Air Force

Table of Contents

Illustrations

Memories of Family and Friends

Foreword

The name "Hunt" is a common English word and simply means "to pursue, to follow game," and of course, long ago, the name could have applied to many people who hunted for food.

The name "Hunt" arrived in America as early as 1606. Robert Hunt, minister of the Church of England, came as a chaplain with Captain John Smith, who sailed from Blackwell, England in 1606 with a colony of one hundred and five men. Other Hunts followed and the name is well represented in the development of early American colonies. Although I was not able to tie my pedigree to those early settlers, I know my ancestors were in Maryland in the 1660s. The Hunt, Tipton, and Denton families lived together and intermarried. They moved west together from Maryland to Tennessee to Kentucky and points west.

My lineage came from Flemingburg, Kentucky. Rueben Hunt was a minister and had two sons who also were ministers. Ezekiel Hunt traveled west September 10, 1846, first stopping in Bonaparte, Iowa, then on to Camp Dodge, Iowa. Ezekiel had a son named James, who had a son named John V. Hunt who married Ada Schoff. To this marriage, seven children were born. Among them was my father, Harvey J. Hunt.

My mother's lineage is Harmon/Graeber and may be traced back to the 1700s in Germany. Through this brief sketch, you can see that although the name is English, a fair number of German was mixed into the bloodline.

I have only drawn this brief sketch to give you a background of how my fierce determination to do things may have evolved through some of this heritage or early nurturing from my peers.

Howard "Mike" Hunt
1992

Acknowledgments

I wish to acknowledge the contributions of my family, various friends and former colleagues who enriched the pages of this book. If it had not been for my family, Carol, Nancy, Barbara, Dashelle, Diane and Howard, these memories may never have been written. My children and friends insisted that I write a few things down. Daughters Nancy and Barbara offered to type the book if I would dictate the material. Barbara typed the first draft. The book was completed by Nancy and reviewed by grandson, Terry Braun. Dashelle and Diane provided numerous photographs from old scrapbooks to complete the story. My son, Lieutenant Howard M. Hunt, gave me the order, "Get it done now." He was, of course, interested in the military side of my career.

At first the project looked daunting as memories fade with age. A lot of my personal memorabilia of log books and personal papers were destroyed in a fire at the Amick Building, Anchorage International Airport, on January 11, 1979. As I started to recall memories, I opened the file drawers of my subconscious mind. At first there were a lot of blanks, but as I sifted through the dusty files in there, memories started to flow out. These memories are as I perceived them. As I look back, I wonder how I ever survived the many adventures where my life was actually on the line. It is not all skill and daring in survival, but mother luck also plays an important part.

This autobiography completes the *Saga of an Aviation Survivor*.

Howard John "Mike" Hunt

2019

Editor's Acknowledgments

A deep heartfelt thank you to Connie Taylor of Fathom Publishing Company for her expertise, positivity, diligence, and perseverance in shepherding this book through to publication. She spent countless hours researching, editing, and making sure all details were correct. If not for her, this book might still be languishing as an unfinished manuscript.

A special thank you to Wendy Kenny, editing assistant, Fathom Publishing. And to Becky McAlpine, Fathom Publishing, for proofing.

A special thank you to Jacques Polomé, artist, for his depiction of the front and back book covers as well as his creative illustrations.

Additionally, a warm thank you to Rob Stapleton, Alaskafoto, for his contribution of original photographs and overall support for the publishing of *Saga of an Aviation Survivor*.

Nancy Hunt Verlinde
October, 2021

Abbreviations and Acronyms

AEC – Atomic Energy Commission

AFB – Air Force Base

AFHQ – Air Force Headquarters

ATA – Air Transport Associates, Inc.

ATC – Air Transport Command

ATCF – Air Transport Command Ferry

ATC – "Allergic to Combat"

ATR – Airline Transport Rating

BIA – Bureau of Indian Affairs

BLM – Bureau of Land Management

CAA – Civil Aeronautics Administration

CAB – Civil Aeronautics Board

CAC – Canadian Air Carrier

CAF – Commemorative Air Force

CAM – Commercial Air Movements

CAP – Civil Air Patrol

CBI – China-Burma-India Theater

CIA – Central Intelligence Agency

CO – Commanding Officer

CPT – Civilian Pilot Training

DEW – Distant Early Warning

DOT – Department of Transportation

DR – Dead Reckoning

EDF – Elmendorf Air Force Base

EPA – Environmental Protection Agency

FAA – Federal Aviation Administration

FAR – Federal Air Regulation

FIDO – Flight Inspection District Office

GCA – Ground Control Approach

HP – Horsepower

HUFICO – Hunt Fike Company

IFR – Instrument Flight Rules

ILS – Instrument Landing System

LDA – Landing Distance Available

METO – Maximum power on engine for limited time

MK – Morrison-Knudsen Co.

MP – Military Police

NON-SKEDS – Non-scheduled airlines

NOPAERO – North Pacific Aero Trading and Transportation Co.

PNA – Pacific Northern Airlines

RCAF – Royal Canadian Air Force

RCC – Rescue Coordination Center

RON – Remain Overnight

ROPA – Reserve Officer Personnel Act, 1954

ROTC – Reserve Officers Training Corps

TR – Transport Request

USOA – United States Overseas Airlines

USSR – Union of Soviet Socialist Republics

V1 – Airspeed beyond which takeoff should no longer be aborted

V2 – Takeoff safety speed. Airspeed at which the aircraft may safely climb with one engine inoperative

VFR – Visual Flight Rules

VHF – Very High Frequency

VORTAC VHF – Omnidirectional Range/ Tactical Aircraft Control

WAC World – Aeronautical Charts

Part I

The Spring of my Life

Chapter 1   Farm Boy Aviator

The beginning of a survivor

It was a particularly hot, humid, June afternoon. The horses' tails flicked rhythmically side-to-side disrupting thick clouds of horseflies hovering over them. Side by side, the harnessed horses walked slowly down the cornrows dragging a heavy, one-row cultivator behind them. The cultivator carved a deep groove into the fertile soil. A young man walked behind the cultivator holding tightly to the old leather reins, trying to keep the cornrows straight while tripping over the churned up sod clumps and dancing around the recently deposited horse manure.

I was that young man; a thirteen-year-old kid doing the work of a grown man on the family farm in Iowa. During the 1920s and 30s, it was typical for young men to work on the family farm. The job was boring, hard, monotonous, and exhausting, but had to be done.

During the many trips up and down the cornrows, my mind would wander as I daydreamed about what my life would become. Frequently I was able to catch the glint of sunbeams glancing off the shiny metal skin of airplanes flying overhead as they made their way to destinations unknown. Then it hit me like a thunderbolt—that is what I wanted to do. That is where my destiny would take me. No more working on a farm for the rest of my life. I clearly visualized myself flying airplanes. From that day forth, I was captivated. Being an aviator became my lifelong passion and goal.

My interest in aviation actually started to take root when I was ten years old. My uncle, Jeanotte Harmon, my mother's younger brother, was my mentor. As a kid, he wanted to fly in the worst way. His father said, "Absolutely not!" In those days, you obeyed your parents. Uncle Jeanotte built model airplanes and read a wide variety of aviation books and magazines. He gave them all to me when he was finished. I read and reread every one of them; I couldn't get enough. Uncle Jeanotte continued to nurture my interest in aviation for many years.

I started building model airplanes; at first solid scale, and then large flying ones. Back in those days, models were built from a picture or from memory. No snap-together kits existed. It took a lot of ingenuity to come up with a look-alike model aircraft. Components were handmade—even landing gear casings were made from molten lead. The more I read about aviation, the more it increased my appetite to learn more.

One day my mother was preparing to wash clothes in her gas-engine-powered Maytag wringer washing machine. Lo and behold, the engine was missing. I had removed the engine and fastened it onto my coaster wagon. My wagon was powered by a pulley I'd carved from an old piece of wood. The pulley was fastened to one outboard rear wheel and a belt tightener. I didn't have any fear of the unknown or consequences of my actions, wading right into whatever I wanted to do with or without parental consent. Of course, I didn't have my transportation very long. It had to go back on the washing machine.

In my quest to understand how machines worked, I managed to con a local farmer out of an old abandoned Model T that was behind his barn. I figured out how to make it run and then used it around the farm without tires because I couldn't afford tires.

My brother Robert and I decided to use the coils off my old Model T to build a shocking device on the family car. I wired the coils up to the battery with an inside switch. To test it, I called the dog over. As his paws touched the door, he got a jolt and ran away yelping. Dad was close by and came over and in an angry voice asked, "What did you boys do to the dog?" He, too, touched the charged door and yelped. Of course, the last ones to yelp were us kids. We never used our shocker again, nor did we want to.

During the winter of 1937 when I was fifteen years old, I constructed an iceboat in our barn. After supper, I would light a kerosene lantern and head down to the barn to work on the iceboat. Nobody paid much attention to what I was doing. I found a 20-hp Saxon car engine lying around and

Ice boat built on the farm powered by old 20HP Saxon car engine, circa 1937.

mounted it on the back of the boat. I whittled a propeller from a 4" x 4" x 72" piece of wood. This propeller had too much pitch so I made another one from a 2" x 6" piece of wood. This was about right because it generated plenty of rpms. I fashioned a forward cockpit with a canvas covering to look as close as possible to an airplane and to act as a

Student pilot license, age seventeen, 1939.

windscreen. My engine was behind me so it was actually a pusher.

That same winter, my folks went away for a weekend. They left us kids home alone. I called up my cousin, Donald Harmon, who was a couple years older than me and asked him to drive over. We put the iceboat on a trailer and towed it behind his car. We drove to the Des Moines River where we fired up the engine and ran all around the river in the iceboat. We timed the boat's speed up to fifty miles per hour. The river had limited ice with running water channels, so we couldn't really reach maximum speed. When my parents came home and heard about this contraption and our escapade, they were horrified. I stoically listened to the lecture, understanding that we had undertaken a dangerous adventure.

The following summer, I put iron wheels under the iceboat. It wouldn't roll very well because of too much ground friction. I don't know why we weren't killed in this contraption. The propeller had to be hand-started and it was unguarded. At maximum rpm, the propeller was sending out a flurry of pinewood splinters from the tip of the blades. These mechanical contraptions were a precursor to my ultimate dream of becoming an aviator.

When I was sixteen, my parents occasionally let me drive the car to church-oriented, special functions. By leaving home early Sunday afternoon, I could get to the Ames, Iowa, airport, buy ten or fifteen minutes of flying time and still get to church on time. My folks always wondered why I never had money. I sold everything I owned to my brother Robert, or any willing buyer, to raise a little money for flying lessons. I picked up copper, lead, or whatever I could find and sold it to the junkman. I also helped my uncle put up hay for extra money. My weekly allowance did not go for treats, but for flying lessons.

In August of 1939 after a year and a half of flying lessons, I had accumulated over nine hours of airtime, and was ready to solo. Before I could solo, I needed my parents' consent on the license. Dad was furious with me. My mother, God bless her, was more understanding and finally convinced Dad to sign the consent to allow me to solo. I suspect Mom was still remembering her younger brother Jeanotte and how he didn't go into aviation because of his father. On August 15, I soloed at the age of seventeen. I managed to get in another hour and a half of flying but I was out of money and could not sustain the lessons any longer.

Everett Idle was a twenty-two-year-old man who lived around Slater, about thirty miles north of Des Moines, Iowa. Idle had an old J-3 Cub airplane. He was a little wild with it. He liked to fly or loop it under telephone and electric lines. I admired him and would occasionally fly with him. We'd climb up over the town of Slater and do a few acrobatic maneuvers; then he would shut the engine off. My job was to fly the plane as Idle put one leg out on the landing gear to reach forward and spin the propeller to restart the engine. This maneuver always attracted a lot of attention. He was a natural pilot and again had an influence on my development in the aviation field.

Family History

I was born January 16, 1922 on a tenant farm four miles north of Polk City, Iowa, and named Howard John Hunt. The following year, my mother, Ester Beula Harmon Hunt, gave birth to Robert Charles Hunt on February 10, 1923, and three years later, Virgina Irene Hunt was born May 3, 1926.

My father, Harvey John Hunt, was an ambitious, hard-working farmer. To supplement the farm income, he hauled various items for other farmers as well as gravel to put on the roads to maintain them. He worked extra hard to get off the tenant farm he was renting. My mother was an expert seamstress, artist, gardener and food preservationist. We lived off the land. We were poor but helped one another.

Early memories include swimming in Big Creek with my cousins. The creek ran a quarter mile from the house. My grandfather, John V. Hunt, was an expert carpenter and farmer. He could lay out big barn beams which were notched and pegged—no nails. The crew would stand the beams up and everything would fit. He was very busy building barns for other people. He also took the time to enjoy his grandchildren. He built a cut down pony cart for us that we hitched to our Shetland pony and had a great time riding around the farm. My grandfather could build anything from wood.

My mother's family was better off financially. They owned the brick mill and the bank in Polk City as well as a large farm. The family was very frugal and again self-sustaining. They were mechanically inclined and could make or repair anything made from metal.

Howard, Robert and Virginia Hunt, circa 1927.

We attended a small country school that had one teacher for the first eight grades. We learned very little as the one teacher had to teach all grades. There were about twelve students in the one-room classroom. Shortly after fourth grade, Dad rented a larger farm just one mile south of Sheldahl, Iowa, where I attended grades five through eight.

By 1935, my father had saved enough money to buy his own farm. The farm was a two-hundred-acre spread right on the south edge of Slater, Iowa. On this farm is where my aggressiveness got rolling.

Dad kept us busy helping out around the farm. We worked as men from age thirteen to sixteen. I would go out into the fields, pick a hundred bushels of corn by hand, and scoop the bushels into a corn bin. It was back breaking work. It took a lot of calories to work this hard. I would eat five times a day and cleaned my plate at every meal. Dad believed in using lots of manure on his land to make it fertile. I remember many a day spreading and hauling manure while other kids were playing ball at the schoolyard.

Around this time, I made up my mind I was going to become an Army Air Corps pilot. I knew I needed more education to do it. The minimum requirements were two years of college or pass an equivalent exam. I announced to my parents that I was going to Iowa State College that fall. They wanted me to work for a year and earn some money first. I wouldn't hear of it. I was a young man in a hurry. Again, it was probably my mother who convinced Dad to let me go. She knew that if they refused me, I would go anyway. They helped with my tuition and I also earned some of it by working at the Memorial Union at college. I worked in the dining

1939

C. R. Laughridge, Supt.
Willie Blaskovich
Edith Crnkovich
Leona Erickson
Arlene Estrem
Howard Hunt
Beverly McBride
Charles Peterson
Norma Peterson
Adriana Ryg
Wayne Severson
Maurice Stigler
Norma Sydnes
Sybil Walker
Rudolph Zagar

Slater High School graduation class of 1939. Slater, Iowa.

Civilian Pilot Training Certificate, Howard J. Hunt. Ground and Flight Course, Iowa State College, Howard Flying Service, Ames, Iowa, August 29, 1941

hall washing dishes, studied at night and attended classes during the day. Every night I took leftover food home to my boarding house to share with my roommates as we were all struggling to make ends meet.

I wasn't prepared for college. It was tough. I had signed up for mechanical engineering, a course that required a lot of math and physics, but I didn't have a solid math or science background to draw upon. I took Reserve Officers Training Corps (ROTC) and became better acquainted with the Army.

After two years in college, I became eligible for Civilian Pilot Training (CPT). War was a certain possibility. President Roosevelt wanted to have a reserve of pilots in case of war. I completed both primary and secondary CPT. About that time, an Army recruiting team came on the campus at Iowa State. I took the exam and was sent to Fort Des Moines for processing and then off to Army Flying School in California.

Chapter 2   Army Air Corps Flight Training

It was January 12, 1942, and I was finally realizing a boyhood dream of becoming an Army aviator. I boarded the train in Des Moines, Iowa, headed for Bakersfield, California. After the Japanese bombed Pearl Harbor on December 7, 1941, the urgency to defeat the enemy was real. Earlier, we were trying to stay out of the conflict and had only been sending weapons to England. As my train traveled west, a lot of thoughts crossed my mind. I felt lonesome and alone—a young man going on a big adventure without knowing any of the dangers, but still eager to experience the unknown.

After three days and nights on the train, a small group of recruits and I arrived in Bakersfield and were met by an Army truck in the middle of the night. We were hustled off to Minter Field where we were placed in tents. They told us not to bring extra clothes as we would be issued uniforms as soon as we arrived in California. The only problem was, they did not have much clothing to issue. It was cold and damp in California in January. I remember being very cold in our tent. Eventually, we did get most of our uniforms, but many of us caught bad colds as a result of this. I can remember getting up early in the morning to police the area around the front of our tent, and as I reached down in the dark to pick up what I thought was a gum wrapper or something similar, it was in fact someone's phlegm he had coughed up.

On February 23, 1942, we shipped off to Visalia, California, to start primary flight training. Sequoia Field was a nice little field surrounded by grape orchards. I was really excited now as I was an aviation cadet and a hot one, I thought. Since I'd already logged over a hundred hours of flying time from Iowa State College, primary and secondary Civilian Pilot Training (CPT), I was cocky and overconfident. After two and a half hours of dual instruction, my instructor, Mr. Neher, turned me over to the Flight Commander for a check ride. The Flight Commander was a gruff old guy. I hopped in the back seat of the PT-17 Stearman and started to take off.

Just as I was leaving the ground, he whacked the control stick and yelled, "You're slipping." Then he kicked the rudder and yelled into the gosport, "You're skidding." About the second time he knocked the stick out of my hand, I just let go.

He yelled, "Aren't you flying this goddamn machine?"

I shook my head and said, "No, you are."

Then he yelled, "Fly the goddamn machine," which I immediately did. I have always treated an airplane like a woman—very gently. I was disturbed that the controls had been knocked out of my hands.

We went through every maneuver I had ever done in CPT training— loops, snaps, rolls, spins, and forced landings. Since I wasn't used to doing acrobatics in the PT-17, I wasn't doing my best. I began to wonder if I was being washed out for being a cocky pilot. After an hour showing him everything I knew about flying, we went back to the airfield and landed. His only comment was, "You're ready to solo."

When new aviation cadets come in for flight training, they are called "Dodos." According to Webster, that is a flightless, extinct bird. The goggles are worn around the neck for all flight drills and other activities until you solo, at which time you can wear your goggles on your forehead. Since we'd only been flying for a week, I was signaled out as a hot pilot as I was the first Dodo in Class 42-H, Flight "L," to wear his goggles on the forehead as we marched back from the flight line to the barracks. The upperclassmen noticed this and started constant hazing and harassment. My attitude was a little cocky. I had been studying aviation since the age of ten, building model airplanes and reading my uncle Jeanotte's aviation magazines. Having soloed at age seventeen while in high school and having completed primary and secondary CPT at Iowa State College, I knew something about aviation.

For a month and a half, the upperclassmen tried very hard to break me down, but what they didn't know is that a Hunt doesn't break—we might bend, but never break. Many a time I would have liked to put a fist into the puss of an upperclassman who was yelling and screaming "attention," "hit a brace," "suck it in," "gut," "butt," "make your bed,"or "do pushups." The only thing that saved me was that in one and a half months, those upperclassmen who did not complete their training were shipped out to Basic Training. Those who washed out were processed for other branches of the Army Air Force. I found the training easy. It was more or less a review of the college CPT. Of the fifty-eight Dodos in my Flight "L," thirty-five cadets succeeded in standing up to the rigid requirements set down by U.S. Army Air Corps. That was a 40% attrition rate. I was happy. I gave the air corps my full attention as I was finally realizing a boyhood dream. I offered to help and render compassion to the other struggling cadets. This compassion built an "esprit de corps," and being with them was one of the best times of my life. Some of those brothers were my true friends for years.

Prop Wash 42H was a magazine published by the aviation cadets of Sequoia Field, Visalia, California. In an issue dated April 24, 1942, on page 26, there is a picture of me with the words "Overdue Mike" which I will explain at this time. Our home base, Sequoia Field, had hundreds of training planes. The field was not able to accommodate the activity. The instructor would check out several airplanes and assign them to outlying airports. My assignment that day was to fly one of the PT-17 Stearmans to another airport. After taking off, I ran into thunderstorms with heavy rain, which I considered not Visual Flight Rules (VFR). I did a 180-degree turn and went back to home base. Meanwhile, my instructor and the rest of the flight team had made it to the destination, but "Overdue Mike" never arrived. Since there was no telephone at the outlying airport, for several hours there was concern as to what had happened to me. When the instructor finally learned I was safe at home base, he was relieved and stated it showed good judgment on my part not to continue the flight in less than VFR weather.

How we kept from running into one another during the

August 27, 1942. Lt. Howard Hunt graduation, Class 42H, Victorville, California.

training, I don't know, as we would have up to one hundred and fifty airplanes at a time buzzing around like a swarm of bees. No radios, just a big pad where we could land a dozen ships at a time. There were many crashes, but I only remember a few deaths, mostly crumpled wings from low-level stalls and spins. You had to have a swivel head to avoid all the traffic conflicts, especially landing at Sequoia Field.

After flying thirty or more hours in the sturdy, well-powered PT-17 Stearman biplane, we were given a change to the lighter PT-22 Ryan monoplane, more or less reverently known as the Maytag Messerschmidt. We piloted the Ryan for another twenty hours. Uncle Sam needed pilots badly for World War II, so our primary flight training completion was moved up five days to April 24, 1942.

Much to my surprise, my cousin, Donald Shearer, showed up as an underclassman in Class 42-I. I was able to spend some time with him as his upperclassman. Of course, I gave him all the help and compassion that I could. Coincidentally, this was the last time I saw him alive. Donald went on to complete his training and was assigned to fly P-38s in North Africa. Unfortunately, he was shot down by a German pilot and crashed in the Mediterranean Sea as did so many of my classmates.

Basic Training

On April 25, we were sent to Lemoore, California, for basic training. Basic flight training was conducted in the North American BT-13, sometimes referred to as the Vultee Vibrator. This training was conducted by commissioned Army officers. Lt. Patterson was an instructor for five cadets of which I was one. One day I remember calling him "Pat" and he snapped me to attention by saying his name was Lt. Patterson.

At basic training, we were introduced to instrument flying by simulating flying in link trainers. We also flew the BT-13 under a hood in the back seat. We were introduced to night, cross-country and formation flying. One memory that stands out was a flight with Fellow Cadet Junior Klien on an instrument instruction training flight. We had decided to test the BT-13 in a spin, which, according to the flight manual, is an unauthorized maneuver. We entered the spin at about 8,000 feet and spun wildly down to about 1,500 feet, where we finally gained control by lowering the flaps. It frightened us very badly and gave us a healthy respect for what was written in the flight manual. The Vultee Vibrator was spinning so wildly that we couldn't even bail out. We never mentioned our experience to Lt. Patterson. The band of brothers stuck together.

The training was concentrated, fast and intense. We did not get hassled by upperclassmen, rather the regular Army flight instructors kept the discipline. The main push was training. The crusade was on. The U.S. needed fighter and bomber pilots to replace war casualties and to crew the many combat airplanes now in the construction pipeline. By now the non-aviators had washed out, and unless you really screwed up, like maybe an unauthorized spinning of a BT-13, we were going to be commissioned as officers and receive those silver wings. We finished basic training June 15, 1942. Next was advanced flight training.

Advanced Flight Training

My assignment was at Victorville, California, for twin-engine advanced flight school. Klien had a car and we drove down to Victorville from Visalia. It was now June 25, 1942. It was predictably hot in the Mojave Desert. It was here that we flew twin-engine airplanes. We flew the AT-9, known as a Curtis Bobcat, and the all-wood AT-17, known as the Cessna Bamboo Bomber. Our training consisted of instrument flights, formation flights day and night, and cross-country flights day and night. Night formation was the most difficult because you had to align five airplanes into a tight formation just by observing the tiny formation of lights on top of the wing. One errant slip could mess up the whole formation. Our instructor would lead and then we would join up with him and try to keep it tight. The instructor was uneasy about one cadet, J.E. Jones, so I rode with him for a few nights to try and help him get the hang of judging closure rates. Jones finally got comfortable enough so that he could judge distance at night.

Klien became a great friend and we gained rapport with one another. I guess our experience at Basic had cemented our relationship. On weekends we took trips into Los Angeles, and of course we were interested in girls, like other normal, healthy cadets. Years later, Junior was killed in a B-29 crash in Texas. His widow asked me to be a pallbearer, but because of other commitments, I could not make it.

The advanced training went well and graduation was upon us. There was some talk of not letting cadets under the age of twenty-one receive commissions. However, the decision was finally made that an exception would be made for flying officers. The following dispatch was sent out to affected local newspapers:

> Howard J. Hunt of Slater, Iowa, has been graduated from the U.S. Army Flying School at Victorville, California, as a pilot. He has been commissioned as a Second Lieutenant in the Army Air Force Reserve. Hunt graduated from Slater High School in 1939 and attended Iowa State College at Ames for two and a half years. He enlisted in the Army Air Force last January 12 and had his primary training at Visalia, California, and his basic training at Lemoore, California.

Some of the Harmon clan residing around Bakersfield, California, came down for the graduation. Also my uncle Jeanotte who kindled my desires in aviation was at the graduation ceremony. I'm sure my mom and dad were very proud, but they were unable to attend because of the distance and the cost. Nevertheless, it was a proud moment for me. I achieved my childhood dream of winning the silver wings and becoming an Army Aviator. The ceremony was brief and we all proudly stepped forward to accept our wings and commissions as Second Lieutenants. Handshakes were exchanged and soon we were all headed in different directions.

About half of the class, A to G, were sent to P-38 Lockheed Fighters. The rest of the class, H through Z, were sent to the Ferry Command. My assignment was

New Pilot

It was around 1991 or 1992 and Howard was back to Iowa and there was a get-together for him in Slater at the park cabin. I had recently just gotten my pilot's license and was visiting with Howard. I asked him what advice would he pass on to a new pilot. He paused and said make sure and not be complacent and use your checklist every flight. After almost thirty years of flying, I think of that every flight when I grab the checklist. He was an inspiration of perseverance and determination in his life and those wise words of advice have been passed on to others as well.

Memory of Nephew, Don Shearer

Long Beach, California. At the time, I was a little disappointed because I wanted to fly big airplanes, like bombers, but was elated to be an Army pilot as well as an officer and a gentleman. Half of Class 42-H were sent to P-38 training at Hamilton Field, California, and were then sent to North Africa where they suffered very high casualty rates. The Air Transport Command flew the whole inventory of Army Air Force airplanes to wherever they were needed, be it from the factory to training command or to overseas combat units.

Chapter 3   Army Pilot Lieutenant Hunt

My first assignment was at Long Beach, California, August 28, 1942. The first week was spent attending briefings and drawing equipment. I made one flight as a co-pilot in a Lockheed C-56E to Hamilton Field, Novato, California. The Army then decided I would be sent to Great Falls, Montana, where they were opening up a new Air Transport Command Base at Gore Field. Things were so new that the Army took over the civic center as a headquarters and we were billeted in the hotel across the street. New pilots received all the "nobody wants" jobs first, like "Duty Officer"and "Officer of the Day."

On September 13, 1942, after being at Great Falls for a week, another pilot, Hershel Patton, and I decided to fly a new AT-6 that had been sitting on the ramp. Neither of us had ever flown one, but we were hot pilots just out of flying school and could fly anything with wings. We took off and experimented with acrobatics for a while.

We spied a farmer plowing his field west of Great Falls and made a couple of passes at him that caused him to crawl under his tractor. We then disappeared behind

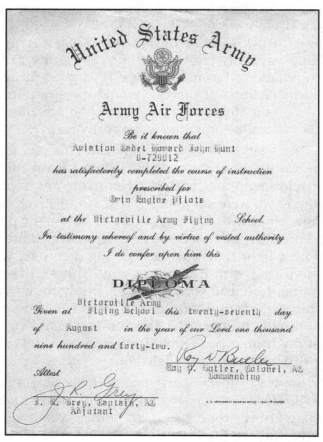

Victorville Army Flying School, United States Army Air Force, Twin Engine Pilots Diploma issued to Aviation Cadet Howard John Hunt, August 27, 1942

a knoll and flew to the river and followed it for some time. Unbeknownst to us, the farmer ran to a telephone and reported that an airplane had crashed on his ranch. The air base dispatched a rescue crew to the reported crash site. In the meantime, we had circled back to the air base and were calling for landing instructions. After landing, the tower told us the operations officer wanted to see us immediately.

We stood in front of the Major with our knees shaking. As he pointed to a big map behind his desk, he asked, "Were you guys flying over here in this area today?"

We answered, "Yes, Sir."

"Were you buzzing?"

"No, Sir, but we did make some simulated forced landings."

He smirked a little as he said, "That's good enough for me," and dismissed us. Had we admitted buzzing, we would have been peeling potatoes for the duration of the assignment.

By my twenty-first birthday, I had logged several hundred hours as a plane commander. I was checked out on the current aircraft inventory at Great Falls: AT-6, AT-9, AT-11, AT-17, C-60, C-47, A-20, B-25, B-24, P-39 and the B-17. The Flying Fortress (B-17) was my favorite. In fact, about that time I actually wrote a letter to the Army Air Force asking for a bomber command assignment. Maybe it's a good thing nobody acted on the letter as my chances of survival would have certainly diminished. It seems like when you are young, you think you are almost indestructible, but as we age we realize how fragile life really is.

The year 1943 was a happy time for me. I met and fell in love with a beautiful girl at Great Falls. When I wasn't flying, which wasn't often, I would spend time with her. Her name was Anabell Jensen. I remember one picnic we were on along the Missouri River near the city. I was showing Anabell how to fire my 45-caliber automatic pistol and how you also have to press the safety on the grip before it will fire. She was holding the pistol with a light touch, while pressing the safety with her thumb and pulling the trigger with her index finger. The 45 kicked back and put a nasty cut on her forehead which bled profusely for a while. I didn't make any love connections on that picnic. I guess I was too much in love with airplanes to put her number one. It was many years before I actually got that gal out of my thoughts. Maybe through other pilots she learned that I had other girlfriends along my flight routes. I guess I'll never know.

Anyway, she did marry one of the bomber pilots stationed at Malmstrom AFB. He was later shot down and killed in Europe. She attended Iowa State College for a year or so, probably as a result of my description of the beautiful campus. She then married another pilot from Malmstrom. After I left Great Falls for Wilmington, Delaware, for a new assignment, I lost contact with her. Many years later, I talked to her parents who still lived in Great Falls. Once I tried to make a dinner date with her, but the fact that she was remarried meant we could not rekindle our old flame. It would have been fun, years later, to discuss some of these old memories with her.

Ferrying B-17F from Assembly Lines

Boeing Airplane Company was now in full swing building B-17F Bombers. They were coming out the door, probably five per day. We were very busy flying them out to modification bases like Denver and Cheyenne. We then picked them up again after modifications and took them to bomber training bases all around the country. On a typical day, about a dozen of us would take off from Seattle's Boeing Field in the fog and rain, climb to 16,000 feet and head east. We knew 16,000 feet would clear Mt. Rainier. The scheduled airlines, United, Northwest and American, would try to get out of our way as our instrument flying was not very disciplined and the air traffic control had not yet been invented. The airlines basically provided their own traffic separation. The skies certainly weren't safe when a dozen of us launched out of Boeing Field. Why we didn't run into one another, I'll never know. I realized that instrument flying was one of our weak points and I used every opportunity to practice. If we weren't actually flying on instruments, we would put a map in the window to darken the cockpit so that flight would be by instruments only. We were rapidly gaining weather experience as well.

Flying B-17s out of Boeing Field, Washington, to training units and modification centers.

Right away, I was assigned as a co-pilot flying B-17s out of Boeing Field, Washington. The first pilot I flew with was Lt. Ely and after a few rides with him, I decided I would never survive the war. Lt. Ely was scared to fly and lacked confidence. It turns out he had been in combat and may have suffered with PTSD. However, I endured and after eighty hours was checked out as a plane commander of the B-17. Not yet twenty-one years old and now I was a Commander. Yes, the war forced you to grow up fast.

A curious incident happened regarding thunderstorms. One day around Rock Springs, Wyoming, we entered a cold front thunderstorm at twelve thousand feet. All hell broke loose—hail beat on the airplane like a thousand drummers, lightning struck the ship repeatedly. Turbulence was severe. One minute we were going up three thousand feet per minute, then down three thousand feet per minute. Airspeed would fluctuate from zero to two hundred seventy-five miles per hour. We were out of control. Then, just as suddenly as it had started, we were tossed out the top of the clouds at sixteen thousand feet. All the text books I read said, "Don't fly through cold front thunderstorms." This was a lesson that we experienced the hard way by actually experiencing it. Many an airplane has broken up in such turbulence or the pilot loses control and spins out the bottom to his death. An early airman who I looked up to, Everett Idle, was killed that way. His C-47 simply broke up in a violent thunderstorm and he crashed in Tennessee.

January 16, 1943, my twenty-first birthday, was spent flying a B-17 from Cheyenne, Wyoming, to a bomber command training base at Boise, Idaho. I had come a long way in just one year—from a wet-behind-the-ears cadet to a pilot in command of big bombers. I was becoming over confident as my over 400 accumulated flying hours was inflating my ego.

The Army wanted us to become proficient at instrument flight, so on March 10, 1943, we ran through a local course in the BT-13. We also ran through a regular airline-type instrument course at St. Joseph, Missouri. I now had the idea I could fly all weather, any time and place. On June 6, 1943, I was promoted to First Lieutenant after completing the St. Joseph instrument course.

Lend-Lease Program

July 1943 found the air base at Great Falls, Montana, behind in deliveries of lend-lease equipment, P-39s, A-20s, B-25s. These planes were being delivered to Russian pilots in Fairbanks, Alaska. A bunch of us four-engine bomber pilots were sent to help out. We delivered a few A-20s to Fairbanks.

Then they wanted some P-39s delivered. They showed us how to start the engines. We were to join up in a flight of five with a B-25 leading us to Fairbanks. "No need to waste fuel shooting landings around Great Falls," they said, "just follow the B-25 to Fairbanks and by the time you get there, if you do, you'll be all checked out." The Allison engine which powered the P-39 had a very small Prestone-cooling radiator, so right after the engine started, you had to be airborne or else it would overheat. Sometimes the P-39 would

Howard Hunt visited the monument to Lend-Lease Pilots in Fairbanks, Alaska.

be towed to the takeoff runway before the engine was started. We taxied out and launched immediately to join up with our five-plane formation.

About twenty minutes north of Great Falls at an altitude of 12,000 feet, my engine sputtered and quit. I fell like a flat rock out of the formation. During training, I remember them saying that "If the engine quits, pull the side door and bail out. We can always get a new airplane but it takes a while to train a pilot." My hand reached for the latch, but as I looked down, those snow-covered peaks didn't look too friendly. I immediately concentrated on the malfunction of my P-39. I changed fuel sources, put on a boost pump and just as I was reaching that critical altitude (1,500 feet above terrain) for bailout, the engine sputtered back to life and I joined my bewildered brothers in formation.

I analyzed the situation later on and realized what happened. In my haste to get airborne before engine overheat, I accidentally used the small reserve tank with a standpipe which lets the pilot know he had burned half his fuel—and it did just exactly that. The purpose of the tank was for a combat pilot to return to base after using all the fuel above the standpipe. It was a close call. I had another few seconds to bail out or ride it down, which would have been certain disaster. Pilots before me have said, "Flying is hours of boredom punctuated by moments of stark terror." I'd like to correct that to read, "Flying is hours of joy, punctuated by moments of stark terror." I had no more trouble for the rest of the flight. However, of the four P-39s that departed Great Falls that day, only two of us made it to Ladd Field,* Fairbanks. The other two dropped out for mechanical problems.

The Russian pilots who were taking over the planes in Fairbanks were seasoned pilots who had already been in combat and were quite experienced. They did not need any instruction from us ferry pilots. This turned out to be a good thing as there was a definite language barrier. Their mission was to fly the planes from Ladd Field, across Siberia, to the German war front.

We pilots enjoyed the Alaska flights. It gave us a chance to fire some of the armament aboard the plane. Of course, that didn't last long. The authorities simply plugged our barrels and took away all our ammunition. Even without ammunition, we could still do a little dog fighting and buzzing along the Alaska Highway. Many a truck convoy drove into the ditch to avoid a diving P-39 which would appear to the truck driver as if the plane were going to land on top of him. I'll have to say, I was no angel and enjoyed every minute of it. These antics seemed to go along with the fighter combat pilot image.

The P-39 had a very small cockpit. A person sat in front of the big Allison engine with a prop shaft housing between his legs. It fired a 37mm cannon through the middle of the prop shaft. The Russians really liked that 37mm as it made an excellent German tank buster on the war fronts. Aerial combat was not great, because the engine was not supercharged and could not sustain altitudes above 12,000 feet for combat. The engine was the weakest part of the whole machine. It has been said that you could navigate to Alaska just by following the wrecked P-39s. We carried a one hundred and fifty gallon, unbaffled, belly tank on the bottom for additional flying range, which gave it odd flight characteristics. It was difficult to keep the needle and ball centered as the unbaffled gas splashed back and forth in the tank. The tanks were dropped for combat duty. A lot of the belly tanks were also dropped on the ramps just before take off as the "red pull brake handle" was right beside the "red pull belly tank dump handle."

After we were current on lend-lease deliveries, I went back to B-17 deliveries. On July 26, 1943, I flew B-17F from Great Falls to Dyersburg,

---

* Ladd Field was established in 1939 as a cold weather testing station to test military aircraft, equipment and clothing in arctic conditions. It was named after a military aviator, Major Arthur K. Ladd, who was killed in an aircraft accident in 1935. The first Army Air Corps troops arrived at Ladd Field in September 1940. Ladd Field was renamed Ladd Army Airfield in 1942. In 1947 the name of the base was changed to Ladd Air Force Base. In 1961 the base was transferred to the Army and renamed Fort Wainwright after a World War II General, Jonathan M. Wainwright.

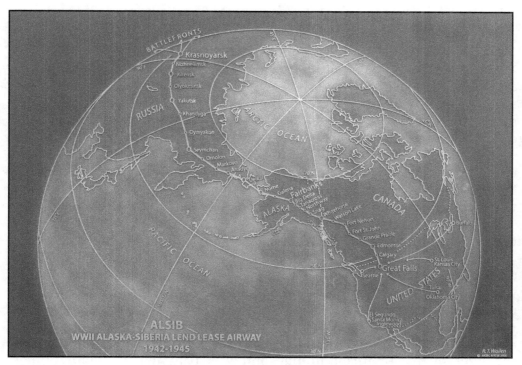

A Bronze plaque showing the lend-lease delivery route is part of the monument in Fairbanks, Alaska.

Tennessee, with a RON (Remain Overnight) stop at Des Moines, Iowa. A flight that I, or anyone around Slater, Iowa, will always remember.

It was a beautiful, clear day as we arrived over Slater—my hometown. We could see crews out threshing grain just west of town. What better time for a little airshow to show the taxpayers what they were paying for and to get a closer look at a B-17. We left cruise altitude for a few low passes over the threshing crews, scattering a little loose straw and frightening a few horses. The threshing crew stopped work for a while as they enjoyed the airshow. After all, just two and a half years before, I had been in that crew pitching bundles of oats into the thresher. I then made one pass at the farmhouse. My mother and sister stepped out into the yard to see the show. I suppose my dad and brother stood proud, as there I was in command of this big bomber.

Some large elm trees surrounded the farmhouse. We approached lower than we intended. We cleared the trees okay, but the sink rate of the big bird surprised me. Just because you pull the yoke back doesn't mean it will immediately respond. With a high sink rate, the climb response is slow, too slow. It shook me up a little. Shortly after that, we landed at Des Moines for the RON. Later that night while visiting with family and friends, I learned that I had scared my mother half to death. She cried out as I made the low approach, "Oh, my God, he has come home to die." Her fear touched me and I never ever put on an air show like that again—another lesson learned. My mother worried about my safety all the time anyway and I certainly didn't help with an air show just to inflate my ego.

On November 14, 1943, the lend-lease deliveries needed more help. We delivered some B-25s and A-20s. One very odd airplane we delivered was a B-25D. Where the co-pilot normally sits, a big 75mm cannon that fired through the plexiglass nose was installed. The cannon sat on a recoil track and the co-pilot sat in back of it. The co-pilot only had 75mm controls and a radio. The primary service he could provide for the pilot was passing him maps. The airplane was nose heavy and required extra power to get the nose up for landing as compared to other B-25s I had flown.

This particular flight turned out to be a merchandising flight. The ground crews who worked up and down the Alaska Highway were always asking flight crews to bring some booze. I invested in about a dozen cases of good whiskey. En route to Ladd Field, I made stops at Fort St. John and Fort Nelson, British Columbia, Canada, where I dispensed my merchandise. By the time I got to Ladd Air Force Base, I had a pocketful of Canadian money.

When I returned to Great Falls, the CIA, MPs and Commanding Officer all wanted to see me regarding my booze transactions. My only defense was that I was only being a Good Samaritan trying to please the ground mechanics along the Alaska Highway who were deprived of some of the pleasures of life. I did not profit from the transactions. After I brought in my receipts, it was proven that I had actually lost money. I had purchased the whiskey in American money and was paid in Canadian money, which was worth about 15% less. It was a good experience and got me thoroughly acquainted with all the high ranking officers at the air base. I guess the name Hunt must have stuck in their memories because on January 26, 1944, they promoted me to Captain. It could have only meant one thing—the alleged notoriety got their attention. Besides, I'd never planned on profiting from any of the transactions, but utilized unused cargo space aboard the B-25 to help boost the morale of the ground troops less fortunate than I.

My twenty-second birthday was spent delivering a B-24J from Lincoln, Nebraska to Valla, England. This was another merchandising trip where we landed in Boriquen, Puerto Rico and filled the bomb bay with cheap rum and untaxed whiskey which we delivered to various stops along the way. Again, this was at no profit but mainly to show a little compassion to the less fortunate. It also got a lot of extra mechanical service for the airplane and the crew. It was my first trip across the South Atlantic, along the coast of Brazil, across Dakar, then Marrakech and then on to England. The war was in full swing.

After a short visit around London and Piccadilly Square and a little fraternization with the English lassies, we headed back to New York on a commercial airline and then back to Great Falls for more B-17 deliveries. The airlines hated to see us arrive at a terminal because our A-1 priority to travel could bump a whole load of passengers. Our TR book (Transport Request) was a blank checkbook to pay for transportation tickets since most of our flights were one way. I've logged an equal number of hours riding the cushions back after an aircraft delivery.

Chapter 4   Wilmington Warriors

In March 1944, a new operation was getting underway at Wilmington, Delaware. It's purpose was to support the B-29s that were flying to India to bomb the Japanese in the Pacific Theater. They needed experienced four-engine pilots to start the "Crescent Caravan" to ferry all types of aircraft around the world to support the war effort. These aircraft included bombers, such as the B-17, B-25, B-26, and B-29; transport planes, such as the C-46, C-47 and the C-54; and even smaller planes like the A-26.

I was sent to Wilmington along with many others. After a check ride in the new C-54A, I made a co-pilot trip all the way to Abadam, India and then returned to Wilmington. We were now plane commanders of the four-engine C-54. The Crescent Caravan staged crews at the various stops so that there was always a fresh crew waiting to take the airplane on to its next stop. A typical trip would be out of Wilmington to New York, Stephenville in Newfoundland, Azores, Casablanca, Tripoli, Cairo, Abadam, Karachi and then back to Wilmington. Of course, there were many variations to this schedule. We hauled out people and logistics for the B-29 operation in India and brought back the wounded and other essentials for the war effort.

One memorable flight was transporting an iron lung patient from the China-Burma-India Theater (CBI) to Walter Reed Hospital, Washington, D.C. The 11,000 mile trip took sixty-five flying hours and five staging crews. I had the leg from Azores to Washington via Bermuda. It was a national news item.

During May 1944, we completed two weeks of very intensive instrument training at Homestead, Florida. It was the best training with the latest techniques from the airlines. After this course, you were confident that you could fly in any weather. It was comforting to have this knowledge as we flew all weather, day or night, across the North Atlantic, which is known for its bad weather. I don't ever recall a flight being canceled on account of weather. Maybe a diversion or a mechanical problem sometimes delayed us, but it was an "I can do that" organization and things got done. We were called ATC (Allergic to Combat) but, believe me, the Air Transport Command was a reliable, dependable part of the Army Air Force. It was a very professional organization and the expertise was getting better and better with the added experience.

Hunt Participates in Rescue Flight

Captain Howard J. Hunt, U.S. Army Air Force pilot with the Crescent Caravan, 2nd Ferrying Group of the Air Transport Command Ferrying Division, participated in the last leg of the dramatic rescue of a twenty-seven-year-old Army lieutenant struck down by polio while near the Tibetan border in China.

The rescue started when Second Lt. Robert Wesselhoeft, Jr., of Westwood, Massachusetts, part of a three-man mapping party in a remote area of southwest China, was struck with infantile paralysis. The party was in such a remote location that Lt. Wesselhoeft was forced to suffer through a two-day horseback ride to a missionary station, barely able to keep himself in his saddle. They arrived there on June 24, 1944. There his companions started twenty-four-hour artificial respiration, and taught the procedure to six Chinese who helped maintain the continual life-giving treatment for many days as they awaited rescue. As an Iowa newspaper reported following the rescue, "Sometime later a strip of canvas was tied across the patient's chest and manipulated by a lever as a substitute for normal administering of artificial respiration."

When it was determined that Lt. Wesselhoeft was too weak to be transported by jeep, Chinese coolies constructed a two hundred and fifty-foot airstrip on a small, flat island in the Lanping River. It only took them three days to clear the airstrip, but it would require a skilled pilot to land. An L-5 liaison-type plane flown by Maj. Fred G. Welsh of West Englewood, N.J., landed on the dangerous airstrip the next day. Everything that could be removed from the small plane was removed to make room for the lieutenant to be laid on his back with his head near the pilot. Maj. Welsh then flew the lieutenant out over one hundred and fifty miles of mountainous terrain and through rough weather that had grounded other planes. Maj. Welsh piloted the plane with one hand and at the same time he pumped the lever operating the makeshift iron lung every twenty-five seconds. He described the flight as "... the worst weather I have ever flown in. But I did not miss a single stroke with the respirator lever."[*]

After that three-hour flight, the lieutenant was flown over "the Hump" by the Air Transport Command to Calcutta, where he stayed in a British hospital for two- and one-half months. During that time, in a demonstration of American ingenuity, fellow officers and soldiers designed and built a home-made flying iron lung out of scrap parts from jeeps, planes, and tractors.

---

[*]   Air Force Magazine, John L. Frisbee, Dec. 1, 1996, https://www.airforcemag.com/article/valor-all-for-one/.

The Daily Monitor Leader* reported, "A 'masterpiece of junk' — a home-made iron lung — is credited with saving the life of Lt. Robert Wesselhoeft ... when he was stricken with infantile paralysis in China some months ago, according to Army engineer Lt. David B. Conard ...." The ingenious iron lung was installed in a giant C-54, and preparations were made for the Crescent Caravan's record-breaking eleven thousand mile relay of flights to bring Lt. Wesselhoeft safely to Walter Reed Hospital in Washington, D.C.

The C-54 Skymaster carried Lt. Wesselhoeft in his iron lung from Calcutta in five legs, stopping in Karachi, Cairo, Casablanca, the Azores, and Bermuda, with a new flight crew for each leg of the journey. Lt. Wesselhoeft was accompanied by the India-China division surgeon of the Air Transport Command, Lt. Col. E. A. Abbey. In the Azores, they were also joined by Flight Nurse Lt. Mary E. Hoadley.

The Iowa newspaper reported, "Capt. Howard J. Hunt, of Ankeny, Ia., piloted the giant Skymaster from the Azores to Washington, D.C., the last leg of an air trip requiring only sixty-five hours and ten minutes. . . . After getting the patient to Washington, Captain Hunt flew the plane back to New Castle Army Base."

Lt. Wesselhoeft's amazing journey ended on Thursday, October 5, 1944, when he was admitted to Walter Reed Hospital in Washington, D.C. Three days later, on October 8, an Evening Star article reported that doctors at Walter Reed classified his condition as good, and stated that he was able to spend twelve to thirteen hours at a time out of the iron lung.[†]

The Evening Star[‡] reported on October 9, 1944, "Mrs. Wesselhoeft arrived by plane from her home in Westwood, Mass., to see her husband for the first time in more than a year, and to hear in person the story of how he was kept alive by artificial respiration, carried many miles by coolies, and flown to the United States in an iron lung made from parts of jeeps and planes."

What could have ended in the tragic death of one American soldier on foreign soil, ended in life, and became a story of humanity, ingenuity, determination, and a band of brothers working together to save the life of one of their own.

*   The Daily Monitor Leader. [volume] (Mount Clemens, Mich.), Nov. 16, 1944. Chronicling America: Historic American Newspapers. Lib. of Congress, https://chroniclingamerica.loc.gov/lccn/sn96077289/1944-11-16/ed-1/seq-17/.

†   Evening Star. (Washington, D.C.), Oct. 8. 1944. Chronicling America: Historic American Newspapers. Lib. of Congress. https://chroniclingamerica.loc.gov/lccn/sn83045462/1944-10-08/ed-1/seq-37/.

‡   Evening star. [volume] (Washington, D.C.), Oct. 9, 1944. Chronicling America: Historic American Newspapers. Lib. of Congress. https://chroniclingamerica.loc.gov/lccn/sn83045462/1944-10-09/ed-1/seq-17/.

In November 1944, we started flying into Paris. The German armies were being beaten back and our Air Force was destroying their ability to produce weapons. German soldiers had broken out of the bulge, but we quickly contained them. During one RON in Paris, we attended a fancy nightclub. It was customary for the French to have a woman in the men's room to hand out towels for drying hands after washing. The officer I was with, after using the towel, started to leave and the woman wanted a tip for the use of the towel. She said, "Oui, oui, Monsieur." The officer replied, "No wee, wee," and walked out. The French clubs and hotels were very cold as heating fuel was scarce. There must have been a shortage of hot water for bathing as well since the ladies were heavily loaded with perfume.

In between my trips coming and going from Wilmington, Delaware, I met and fell in love with a beautiful young lady by the name of Ruth Elizabeth Gadow. On February 21, 1945, we were married in the base chapel at Wilmington. She was from a small farm in Preston, Maryland. We took about a week's honeymoon and set up a small household off base. Then I went back out on the line again flying the North Atlantic.

On May 8, 1945, the Germans were defeated and President Truman and Prime Minister Churchill declared V-E Day. On that particular day, I was on a flight in a C-54 between the Azores and Stephenville, Newfoundland. The mighty German Army was defeated—her industry bombed to rubble. It was an air victory.

Howard Hunt on the left camel near the Great Pyramid, Cairo, Egypt, during a layover on an Air Transport Command trip, circa 1944.

In June 1945, Ruth and I had a chance to buy a surplus Fairchild PT-19 military primary trainer. Ruth drove me up to Readington, New Jersey to pick it up. After I took off, Ruth drove back to Wilmington. It was supposed to be a short flight of a little over an hour. After familiarizing myself with the PT-19, I took a heading that should have been towards Wilmington. I pulled out my World Aeronautical Charts (WAC) to do a little navigation and nothing looked right. I couldn't figure out my location. Finally after an hour, I began to realize I'd better land and find out where in the world I was. So I landed at an airport and an operator came out and asked what did I need. I said, "A quart of oil and fifteen gallons of fuel." I then strolled into the office where there is

Captain Howard J. Hunt, circa 1945.

always a map hanging with a smudgy center showing where you are. To my surprise, I'd landed at Lancaster, Pennsylvania, a good forty-five degrees off the course I'd intended to take. So without asking, I had found out where I was, paid my bill and took off again. Now I knew my magnetic compass was forty-five degrees off. I flew on to Wilmington after dark and about three hours overdue. Ruth was really getting worried as she had been home for hours.

On my days off, I would do acrobatics or give instructions. One of my students was Harold Shearer, a marine, a cousin, and the brother of Don who was killed in a P-38. Harold was stationed at Quantico, Virginia.

On June 26, 1945, I had two weeks leave, so I loaded Ruth in the back seat of the open cockpit PT-19 and took off for Des Moines, Iowa. I wanted my parents to meet my new bride. Ruth was airsick the entire way, hanging out over the side of the plane, vomiting, and trying to keep it off the airplane. By the time we arrived in Des Moines, she was wind burned, airsick and not quite the pretty bride I wanted to show my parents. We had a nice visit with my family. I gave most of them a ride in the PT-19 including my eighty-year-old grandmother Hunt, who loved it.

One day I asked my dad if he wanted to go for a ride and look at farms from the air. He agreed, so we flew out and looked at farms, including his mother's. She came out in the yard to wave. That seemed like all the audience I needed to put on an airshow. I did a few hammerheads,

Ruth Elizabeth Gadow, age 21, and Howard John Hunt, age 23, following their wedding, February 21, 1945, Wilmington, Delaware.

wingovers and other acrobatics. As I looked in my rear view mirror, I could see that my dad's cheeks were starting to swell. I sensed airsickness. I asked him through the gosport if he wanted to go back to the airport and land. The answer was affirmative by a headshake. Dad laid down on the couch at home for several days before he was normal again. The acrobatics had really upset his equilibrium. It was a beautiful vacation trip and one that was long remembered by all our friends and relatives.

We left the PT-19 parked at the Des Moines airport when we went back to Wilmington. A few months later, a student pilot taxied an airplane into the PT-19's left wing. Four feet of its plywood wing was chopped into toothpicks.

Chapter 5   WW II Flight Assignments

The war was now shifting to the Pacific. On August 5, 1945, the B-29 "Enola Gay" dropped the first atomic bomb on Hiroshima. On August 9, another bomb hit Nagasaki. Then, on August 15, the Japanese agreed to an unconditional surrender. On that day, the Air Transport Command (ATC) launched the Purple Project. I took a Sunday call at home and the Operations Officer told me to report the next morning for a flight to Okinawa. All four-engine pilots and airplanes were going to Okinawa to haul the occupation troops to Tokyo. I only had time to pack a bag. It was up to Ruth to run the show on the home front and she was eight months pregnant. The ATC was able to assemble three hundred C-54s at Okinawa for the airlift.

On August 30, we started the massive airlift. Airplanes were taking off every thirty seconds and flying at staggered altitudes to Tokyo. By September 10, we had completed the airlift. Why we didn't have some mid-air collisions, I don't know. The weather wasn't visual flight rules (VFR), nor was it daylight all the time. General MacArthur concluded the formal Japanese surrender aboard the battleship Missouri, riding anchor in Tokyo Bay, on September 2, 1945.

My first child, Nancy, was born September 5, 1945 while I was flying occupation troops into Tokyo. It would be several months before we would meet one another.

Ruth, Nancy and Howard Hunt, Vallejo, California, in 1946.

The ATC was then called upon to supply the airlift to move Chinese occupation troops into China. On September 14, 1945, I received my orders to proceed to Kurmitola, India, to fly the China-Burma-India Route over the Himalaya Mountains. The route was called "flying the Hump." During the war, more than three thousand allied transports and tactical aircraft had been lost among those jagged peaks. The Hump was never closed by weather, despite the monsoon weather conditions. The crashed airplanes made an aluminum trail all the way over the Hump.

A typical flight would take off from Kurmitola, climb over the Himalayas and land at Luliang or Liuchow, China, with a load of fuel. We would load the plane with eighty or so Chinese soldiers, complete with weapons, kitchen and personal gear. We told their officers that if any of them got airsick, we would throw them off mid-flight. They were the best-behaved passengers I had ever flown. We then took them to places like Kunming or Shanghai. After dropping the Chinese soldiers off, we went back to India for another load. This project ended in November 1945. I was then sent to Hamilton Field, California—my next duty station.

I returned to Wilmington in November for a few days and then flew an ATC flight back to Hamilton with Ruth and Nancy aboard. We rented a temporary war housing unit in Vallejo, California, with very spartan furnishings. We obtained some mattresses and other furnishings from the air base, but most furnishings were homemade. We used an apple box for a dressing table, whiskey bottle table lamp and a mattress for a davenport. Within a few days, I was back flying the Trans-Pacific route to Manila and Tokyo. Pacific flying was very peaceful weather-wise as compared to the North Atlantic or "the Hump" flights.

My brother, Robert, had been instructing aviation cadets at Santa Ana, California. When the military closed the school down, he joined the ATC at Hamilton. When he arrived, Robert was eight hours short to draw flight pay for two months. I said, "No problem." On the evening of March 10, 1946, I got permission from base operations to fly a VIP C-47. Right after we took off, the bay fog rolled in and Hamilton was closed. We cruised around all night between Hamilton and Fairfield. As the sun came up the next morning, the fog broke up and we landed at Hamilton—eight flight hours later. Only problem was we had taken a General's VIP airplane and had run it out of time and fuel. The C-47 required a maintenance inspection before another flight could be made. The general raised hell with everyone concerned. Meanwhile, my brother got his flight pay before departing for Manila, which was the next place I met up with him.

On April 22, 1946, the Commanding Officer at Guam, Colonel Knight, set up a special mission flight (Army word for shopping trip) with many of his base personnel. Since the Colonel wasn't current in the C-54, I went along as Safety Pilot. On the leg from Tokyo to Shanghai, the weather turned nasty. We were shooting a ground control approach (GCA). The Colonel was having a little trouble holding onto the glide slope. At 100 feet we started breaking out and the Colonel pulled the power to land. About then, a row of parked C-46s appeared directly in front of us. The Colonel could kill himself, but I wanted no part of it, so I rammed the throttle forward to full power and pulled the yoke back for the missed approach. On the next approach, I helped him to stay on the centerline and glide slope and we landed safely. The Colonel thanked me for saving his ass and the passengers. Some high-ranking officers don't like lesser ranking officers (Captains) taking command away. There was no time to argue or coach—I acted instinctively.

Fairfield Air Base (now called Travis AFB) was open and we started using it instead of Hamilton. I started giving pilot instruction and was a check pilot at Fairfield. On a return flight from Honolulu, the crew had gone through the checklist while I was on board as the check pilot. It was a gusty evening so the crew had left their gust lock on, which meant the controls were locked. They pulled onto the runway preparing for take off. I said, "You guys aren't going to take off with your controls locked, are you?" Boy, three guys, the flight engineer, pilot and co-pilot, just about melted right there. I loosened the strap that had their controls locked. Leaving the controls locked would have been a fatal error. It was my job to make sure they did all their crew duties. It's on the checklist, "controls free and easy before take off." They would have crashed that night if I hadn't been there.

I had been studying to get my Airline Transport Rating (ATR) from the Civil Aeronautics Administration (CAA). One day, I dismissed all my students except one. We took off for Oakland, picked up the CAA examiner and took the check ride for the ATR. This was the highest rating a pilot could obtain and was required if you wanted to fly for commercial airlines. By now, September 1946, a number of my flying friends had left the Army Air Force to fly for the airlines and I was vacillating pro and con. Actually, I think I had decided to stay in the Army Air Force. I liked my job. It was satisfying. There was a stigma of being "only" a Reserve Officer as they could boot you out at anytime. I had met the board requirements for a regular Army commission, but had not been chosen. Meanwhile, all these good commercial airline jobs were getting filled.

The Army Air Force at this time did not look like a steady career choice. Had I been selected for a regular Army commission, I would have stayed. I went to San Francisco for an interview with Pan American Airways. I took their aptitude tests and physical exam and was told to go home. "We'll call you later," they said.

It was about this time that I met Amos Heacock, another ATC pilot and a brilliant man, who was trying to form his own airline with runs to Seattle, Anchorage, Fairbanks, and points west. I listened to him talk and looked at his prospectus. It sounded exciting. Greed got the best of me, so it was then that the decision was made to become the "big American businessman." Years later, I regretted this move but there was no turning back. A week later, Pan Am called and said, "Come to work." Greed and excitement of the business entrepreneurship won. I declined the Pan Am job offer.

On January 3, 1947, I said so long to the Army and put my efforts into making a new company, North Pacific Aero Trading and Transportation Co. (NOPAERO), successful. During my five years in the Army Air Force, I had logged 3,100 hours. I had also collected a few ribbons: Asiatic-Pacific Campaign, European-African-Middle Eastern Campaign, World War II Victory, Bronze Star, Air Offensive-Japan, China War Memorial Medal. It was a good record to be proud of and I was still alive—a survivor.

Chapter 6   NOPAERO

Amos Heacock met Jack O'Neill, an old time Alaskan with business interests and an entrepreneurial spirit. The seeds of North Pacific Aero Trading and Transportation Co. (NOPAERO) developed from this meeting. The original business was to be an airline flying from Seattle to Anchorage and Fairbanks, then extending westward to tie into the Union of Soviet Socialist Republics.

This original plan became sidetracked when the equipment we bought from the War Assets Administration was located in Honolulu and Guam. Heacock and some of the other eleven partners had already gone to Honolulu to start the operation. Partners contributed varying amounts. Heacock owned 22%, I owned 19%, O'Neill owned 10%, Wilber Fitch and Duncan Miller both owned 10%. Some partners owned as little as 1%. The total investment was $46,600 to complete the monumental task of certifying three C-46s and two PBYs.

Ruth, Nancy and I arrived in Honolulu in February 1947. We set up housekeeping in temporary quarters at John Rodgers Airport. NOPAERO was rapidly depleting its assets, so we had to get an income started. We rented two big, double-deck Quonset huts from the Territory of Hawaii. These buildings had formerly been Navy Officers quarters at the airport. We cut doors between two rooms and rented them out as one-bedroom apartments that promptly brought us $3,200 a month in income.

The War Assets Administration was now selling all kinds of war surplus. The island was loaded with surplus equipment because it had been the Pacific staging area. We only knew about airplanes, so we avoided the heavy equipment, which was cheap in Hawaii, but valuable after you shipped it stateside. We bought two PBY amphibious aircraft, work stands, aircraft tires and paraphernalia. We hauled the equipment to an open nose dock on John Rodgers Airport, Honolulu, Hawaii, which we shared with the CAA. Work started on licensing one PBY.

Our big problem was how to get three C-46s off Guam, which had been hit by a typhoon. The control surfaces had been bent and destroyed. We already had one mechanic and partner named Jack Hovermale who was working hard, but he needed help. Fitch and I caught a ride on a Navy dependents' ship heading to Guam.

We set to work with a positive "can do" attitude. We decided to cannibalize one of the aircraft to rebuild the other two. They were new planes with only eighty hours of ferry time. Guam was another big storage area for aircraft and parts. We peeked in a lot of boxes trying to find needed parts. The Air Force and Navy were actually disposing of a lot of aircraft parts by burying them in coral pits. We had resolved our problem down to hinge fittings and surfaces for one airplane. Then it happened—a C-46 coming in from Manila one night undershot the runway and collapsed its gear by forcing the drag strut through the rear spar. The next day, the Air Force dragged the damaged C-46 into a revetment next to our work area. That turned on a light bulb for me. Hovermale was game, but Fitch was reluctant for the midnight exchange of good surfaces and hinge fittings for damaged and broken ones. By morning, we had solved our monumental problem and the ship was now ready for a test hop.

I had never flown a C-46 before, but after working on them for over a month, I knew how all the systems worked. On July 6, we test hopped one C-46. She flew just fine. We continued to work on the second plane and on July 13 and 15, we test hopped the other C-46. It, too, flew nicely. We installed long-range fuel tanks on both planes by cannibalizing the six wing tanks from the third airplane. We then started loading aboard spare engines and a lot of other valuable parts. We did not bother to weigh anything. If there was space, we put something in it. Believe me, a C-46 full of iron weighs more than the 48,000 pounds it was certified to carry. I needed another pilot to fly the other C-46, so Heacock agreed to do it. I checked him out. He'd never flown a C-46 either. Heacock wanted me to teach him celestial navigation as we didn't have any navigators on board. I told Heacock, "I can't teach you celestial navigation overnight. You're just going to have to follow me." That's how we left Guam. On July 25, 1947, Heacock and Bud Myers showed up to help us fly the C-46s back to John Rodgers Airport in Honolulu.

On July 27, we did a take off for Kwajalien, which is an island between Guam and Hawaii. I'll never forget that take off. We rolled and we rolled and as we approached the very end of the 10,000-foot runway, I pulled her into the air. I swear the palm trees just laid down so we could get over them. The ship was on the verge of a stall as I was fighting to get on the front side of the power curve. We staggered along at wave-top height for twenty miles at max power before she ever started to fly. Heacock did better as he was not so heavily loaded. Heacock didn't understand Loran or celestial navigation so he followed us to Kwajalien Island—which was a ten-hour flight. At Kwajalien, we opened the cowling and found the firewall green with gas stain. This was part of our problem. We tightened up the intake manifold which really improved engine performance.

Another incident happened en route. We had fifty-five-gallon barrels of gas aboard. Hovermale went back to transfer gas from a barrel into the long-range tank. He struck the barrel bung with a hammer to loosen it and the spark caused a small explosion with some raw gas on the top of the barrel. We heard the explosion as Hovermale came running forward to the cockpit scared to death. Thankfully, we survived again.

On the morning of July 28, we took off for Johnson Island and landed nine and a half hours later. Next was the final leg to John Rodgers Airport, where families were waiting for us after the twenty-five hour flight from Guam. The following day we landed in Honolulu and unloaded the C-46s. It was obvious why they wouldn't fly. In our greed to salvage everything possible, we estimated we overloaded 5,000 pounds on each aircraft.

We didn't have the engineering yet to license the C-46s so we went to work on the two PBYs. We were getting one almost finished, as Swanson and Fowler had been working on one PBY while we were in Guam.

We were now having all kinds of personnel problems. We were each only drawing $100 per month from the company and some partners wanted more. A liquidation of the company would be made on the basis of cash investment at risk. Some partners wanted more salary—some had invested less than $1,000. The arguments grew louder and our cash balance went to zero. We were cash poor, so the decision was made to sell the PBYs and liquidate the partnership.

Heacock was also trying to promote fish hauling and merchandising in the Islands. The other partners were skeptical. We had lost our original plan of operation. Since we were out of cash, we decided to sell everything, including our apartment lease.

On August 6, 1947, Ruth presented me with a brown-haired, pretty little girl. We named her Barbara Jean. Our little one-bedroom apartment without windows was starting to get very crowded with a family of four, but it was cozy.

Paul Mantz, from Burbank, California, learned that we had a Navy PBY for sale. Mantz was a World War II military pilot, whose post-military career included air racing and work as a movie stunt pilot.

He flew over to Hawaii to look at the PBY. He wanted it because it was unmodified, just like the day the Navy left it, including mess kits lying on the floor. He wanted the airplane for some movie work. I was elected to make the deal with Mantz. We met at his hotel where he had a pretty blonde by his side. We started negotiating. As he poured me drinks, and the blonde sweet talked me, the price was coming down. I think I started out at about $10,000 and finally settled for something over $6,000. My partners thought I sold out too cheaply. Maybe the blonde and the booze softened my brain?

Mantz had his mechanic go over the airplane to ensure it was ready for flight. Just Mantz and the mechanic were ready to leave for Burbank. He asked me to go along as a navigator, but I didn't like the looks of things so I said "No." The next morning, they took off, buzzed Waikiki Beach and Pearl Harbor. When the tower said he was in restricted airspace, Mantz replied, "What the hell, I'm a taxpayer and I have a right to see what I'm

PBY-5A on runway in Honolulu, Hawaii. This plane was one of three we sold, circa 1947.

paying for." He then headed to San Francisco and landed there eighteen hours later. I know the plane made it to Burbank as I saw it there a few months later.

We finally made a deal to sell the two C-46s to Slick Airways. We were to deliver them to Burbank. Part of the deal was to get engineering rights to the licenses so we could use it later for our next corporation. On October 13, 1947, Fitch and I took off for San Francisco. We aborted after twenty minutes as the engines were torching and running rich flames back toward the tail. Adjustments were made to both carburetors and we took off again the next night.

Since I knew celestial and Loran navigation, Heacock followed me. During the night he kept calling, "make a 360-degree circle with landing lights on so I can find you." His landing gear kept falling out. Fourteen hours and five minutes later, we landed at San Francisco. We arrived in the early afternoon, so we decided to fuel up and go on to Burbank. We calculated the exact gas we needed to get there, because any extra gas would belong to Slick Airways. But what we didn't calculate was the evening sea fog rolling into Burbank. It's a two-hour and forty-five-minute flight and I knew it was going to be close. En route, I had Fitch go back in the cabin and unstrap the long-range tank from the floor and hold up one end so as to get out that last drop of fuel. On approach over Burbank all the tanks were reading empty—what a predicament. The control tower gave me immediate let down and we made a short-approach landing. The next day when Slick Airways went out to drain fuel from the wings before the plane was moved into the hangar for disassembly, they couldn't find any gas and wondered why. I decided after that trip that I'd pay for gas out of my own pocket rather than go through that again. Later on, I would carry a few extra gallons just for the family. Heacock was also close to empty, but not as close as I was. We caught United Airlines back to Honolulu the next day.

We finally sold the second PBY to Air France who took it out to the Islands. The PBY was full of corrosion. We tried to paint over a lot of it, but every time we would use a rivet gun somewhere on the ship, the vibrations would cause white corrosion powder to fall out on the ground. We had to correct a lot of things to make it airworthy for the sale. I think we eventually got $32,000 for it. We sold off our surplus C-46 parts to Slick Airways. Flying Tigers bought a bunch of C-46 tires we had. They went to Hong Kong. We sold our apartment lease to a Japanese businessman for $27,000. As near as I can figure out, the new terminal building at John Rodgers Airport now sits where NOPAERO apartments once stood. Liquidation was now complete and I realized a return of 110% on our investment of $9,000.

We had an argument with Bud Myers regarding a $2,500 note he had tendered to NOPAERO for the balance owed on his investment. Since he never actually put the money to risk, the partners voted that his investment was only the $2,500, which he had put up originally. The

Ruth, Barbara, Howard and Nancy on Matson Steamship leaving Honolulu heading to the mainland, March 1948.

final dissolution agreement was signed December 31, 1947, by all eleven partners. Approximately $130,000 was distributed on a percentage based on initial investment. NOPAERO was no more.

On March 17, 1948, Ruth, Nancy, Barbara and I boarded the Matson Steamship for a boat ride back to Los Angeles. Everyone was having fun on deck as we pulled away from Honolulu. Dinner was announced so we all went down to the dining room. Ruth and the girls ordered sumptuous meals, but before the waiter could deliver them, Ruth became terribly seasick. She spent practically the whole trip sick in the cabin. I suspect that Nancy and Barbara had sympathy sickness. After arriving in Los Angeles a week later, we unloaded our luggage and spent a few nights with my uncle, Jeanotte Harmon, and family in Hayward, California. We bought a used car and trailer to haul our meager possessions to my folks' place in Ankeny, Iowa.

It was a time of reflection—where was I going from here? I missed my Army Air Force flying. I made a trip to Des Moines and actually applied for a call to active duty. The Berlin Airlift was now in full swing because of the Russian blockade of Berlin. They considered me, but did not call. Bud Myers, one of the NOPAERO partners went back on active duty. I envied him. I went to work for a couple of months with a local contractor as a carpenter, but I wasn't happy. I wanted back into aviation. In June, Heacock and family showed up in Ankeny and we started planning Air Transport Associates (ATA); just the three of us—Heacock, O'Neill and myself. We would incorporate and launch a new airline.

I had been a ramrod for NOPAERO. I had a "can do attitude." I pushed everybody as hard as I pushed myself. Our mission could have failed many times except for that added effort. I was a stern taskmaster and had many arguments with Heacock. He was a brain stormer, but had trouble putting things into a working plan or staying on course.

Chapter 7   Air Transport Associates

Air Transport Associates, Inc. (ATA) was really the operation Amos Heacock had planned back in the fall of 1946, but he got side tracked in the Islands and blown off course. We incorporated ATA and then leased three C-46s from the Air Force at Fort Pyote, Texas. Joe Halsey and I flew the first C-46 out July 19, 1948 from Texas to Boeing Field in Seattle. We had a small maintenance facility at Boeing Field run by Ted Vosk. A few days later, we delivered the second ship from Texas. We immediately licensed N1301N and N1302N and made our first cargo flight August 5, 1948 to Anchorage, Alaska.

Since we didn't have a passenger interior in the ships yet, we were only hauling freight. There was a large volume of northbound freight at fifteen cents per pound, but we needed some southbound freight to make money. Because Alaska was a place of sales and service, it was difficult to find southbound freight other than seasonal seafood. We offered a rate

Air Transport Associates C-46, "City of Cordova," Merrill Field, Anchorage, Alaska, 1952.

southbound of eight cents per pound and got some limited business. We had to have more revenue.

In one ship, we installed military bunks along with about thirty gougler seats down the center for passengers to occupy during take off and landings. A gougler seat is a rigid metal-structure seat—not very comfortable. The thirty gougler seats and the bunks along the inside walls of the plane would accommodate a full passenger load of forty-five people.

It was now "Sleep to Seattle for $70.00." The promotion attracted a lot of attention. We were now in the passenger business. The ships were still not insulated, so the passengers had to keep rotating on the bunks as the walls were very cold. In 1948, there were approximately twenty-four different non-scheduled (non-skeds) airlines operating to Alaska, mostly all with the smaller C-47. We were one of the first to use the larger C-46 airplane to haul freight and passengers.

In the fall of 1948, Heacock got the idea that we could be the worldwide distributor of whale meat. We could even can it in a meatloaf fashion and sell it to hungry Europeans and third world countries. We flew one C-46 up to Port Hardy, Alaska, where there was a whale processing station and brought down a load of whale meat. We distributed it to various meat markets all over the U.S. Everybody was willing to try it. It was cheap and red in color. We even hired a Norwegian woman to write recipes and cooking instructions.*

Ivars Seafood in Seattle featured whale meat on their menu. A lot of people tried preparing the whale meat at home, but then the backlash happened. The average housewife didn't know how to cook it. She dropped it into a hot skillet and it caught on fire or smoked violently. She ended up throwing the meat and the skillet out the door. Properly prepared, it was delicious as demonstrated by Ivars. In just one planeload, we had flooded the whale meat market. The remainder of our load was finally donated to the Seattle Zoo. There was no demand for our whale meat. Meanwhile we installed seats and airline interiors into our C-46s. The northbound loads were combination loads—cargo up front with passengers seated behind.

Fitch and Miller joined ATA, which was an excellent move as Heacock was hard to deal with. During the winter of 1948, we prepared three C-46s for the Alaska business and stateside charters. I remember once having a crew of workmen trying to decide where to place extra windows in the C-46. Disturbed by their indecision, I grabbed a fire ax and said, "I'll show you where they go." I walked up the inside of the fuselage slamming holes in the skin of the airplane. Then work began in earnest.

My family rented a little apartment in Lakewood, Washington. When I wasn't flying, I was working on airplanes or trying to generate some more business for the company. On November 21, 1948, Diane Raye was born, our third daughter. We had a close circle of friends: Vosk, Heacock,

---

*   Appendix 2.   Air Transport Associates, Inc., Whale Meat Recipes

Interior of a C-46 awaiting passengers. Notice the narrow aisle and lack of overhead storage bins.

Passengers aboard ATA "Kenai Trader" being served coffee by a stewardess.

Interior of a C-46 loaded with fresh produce for Alaska.

ATA offered first class sleeping accommodations on their C-46 bound for Seattle for the low price of $70. Rest in comfort on the twelve-hour flight to Seattle. Triple bunk accommodations were available on selected ATA flights to and from Seattle.

ANCHORAGE TO . . .

Seattle	$ 60.00*	Miles City	$100.00*
Baltimore	159.00*	Minneapolis	139.00*
Bismark	125.00*	Newark	159.00*
Burbank	98.50*	New York	159.00*
Chicago	139.00*	Omaha	129.00*
Cincinnati	149.00*	Philadelphia	159.00*
Cleveland	151.95*	Pittsburgh	159.00*
Denver	129.00*	Portland	67.80*
Detroit	148.00*	Salt Lake City	105.00*
Evansville	148.00*	San Diego	103.50*
Everett	60.00*	San Francisco	85.00*
Great Falls	85.00*	Spokane	68.70*
Kansas City	139.00*	St. Louis	139.00*
Miami	202.74*	Washington, D.C.	159.00*

*All Fares Plus Tax

FOR RESERVATIONS CALL COLLECT

ATA AIRCOACH

213 - 4th Ave.   Anchorage 4-5555

ATA AIRCOACH 419 - 2nd Avenue Fairbanks, Alaska Fairbanks 5001	ATA AIRCOACH 730 - 14th ST. N. W., WASHINGTON, D. C., NATIONAL 3955	ATA AIRCOACH Frye Hotel ELliott 2900 Georgian Hotel SEneca 0436 Seattle, Wash.
ATA AIRCOACH Coeur d'Alene Hotel Spokane, Wash. TEmple 2574	ATA AIRCOACH 109 No. Clark St, Chicago, Illinois CENtral 6-4928	ATA AIRCOACH 120 West 44th St. New York, N. Y. JUDson 2-5305

Air Transport Associates, Inc., is not a regularly scheduled carrier, but is operating on a non-scheduled basis.

NOW

Deluxe

ATA AIR COACH

TO ALASKA AND THE EAST

FARE SCHEDULE

GATE PASS

Please show this number to pass through gate

Flight _____   Date _____

Destination _____

From _____

Number _____

Please be guided by this . . .

IMPORTANT INFORMATION

1. Passengers are requested to check in at airport at least 30 minutes before departure time.

2. If your plans change, have us cancel your reservation so some other person may use your space.

3. Reconfirm reservations for continuing or return space by telephoning local office at least 6 hours before scheduled departure time.

4. For future reference please retain Passenger Coupon of your ticket.

5. 55 pounds of baggage carried free on each ticket, Seattle to Alaska; 40 pounds East and West; rates vary for excess.

LEAVING _____   AT _____

ATA AIR TRANSPORTATION FOR EVERYONE

ATA Aircoach

SERVICE TO ALASKA and EASTERN CITIES

A.T.A.'s fine equipment and personnel flew 41 million safe, passenger-miles in 1951. A.T.A. provides the most comfortable and speedy air passage between

Eastern U.S. Cities, Seattle, and Alaskan cities—de luxe air travel at coach fares, on convenient non-scheduled flights. A.T.A. fares are low.

Inquire at any travel service or A.T.A. passenger office in all major cities, where you can get exactly the information you want, and help in planning your trip.

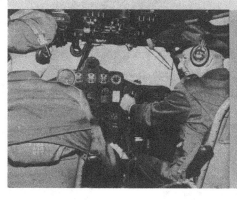

Responsible A.T.A. Captains all hold the highest certificates of competency —Airline Transport Rating, rechecked every 6 months by CAA inspectors on competency and in flight emergencies. Also, A.T.A. minimum requirements for Captains are 3500 hours, plus entire winter operating on A.T.A. routes.

There are A.T.A. offices or agents in all major cities throughout Alaska and continental United States. Whether traveling on business or pleasure, there are only a few hours between Alaska, Seattle, and the East.

SAFE AIRCRAFT OPERATION . . . WITHOUT FRILLS AND UNNECESSARY EXPENSE

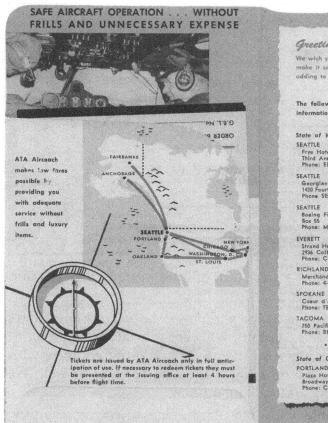

ATA Aircoach makes low fares possible by providing you with adequate service without frills and luxury items.

Tickets are issued by ATA Aircoach only in full anticipation of use. If necessary to redeem tickets they must be presented at the issuing office at least 4 hours before flight time.

Greetings . . .

We wish you a pleasant flight and will do all we can to make it so. We want you to call on us for any service adding to your comfort and enjoyment.

—Employees of ATA

The following offices will give you all flight and rate information by

ATA AIRCOACH

State of Washington

SEATTLE
Frye Hotel
Third Ave. at Yesler St.
Phone: ELliott 2900

SEATTLE
Georgian Hotel
1420 Fourth Avenue
Phone SEneca 0436

SEATTLE
Boeing Field
Box 55
Phone: MOhawk 4200

EVERETT
Strand Hotel
2936 Colby Street
Phone: CEnter 1212

RICHLAND
Merchandise Mart
Phone: 4-1226

SPOKANE
Coeur d'Alene Hotel
Phone: TEmple 2574

TACOMA
750 Pacific Avenue
Phone: BRoadway 0411

State of Oregon

PORTLAND
Plaza Hotel
Broadway & Wash Street
Phone: CApital 9367

Alaska

ANCHORAGE
213 Fourth Avenue
Phone: 4-5555

FAIRBANKS
419 Second Avenue
Phone: 5001

JUNEAU
181 South Franklin
Phone: 844

Eastern Offices

CHICAGO
109 North Clark Street
Phone: CEntral 6-8155

NEW YORK
King Edward Hotel
120 West 44th Street
Phone: JUdson 2-5305

BALTIMORE
110 W. Baltimore Street
Phone: LExington 6524

WASHINGTON, D. C.
720 14th Street N.W.
Phone: National 3955

Canada Office

VANCOUVER, B. C.
901 Robson Street
Phone: TAtlow 8264

Fitch and the Millers. We spent a great deal of time working together and socializing.

In order to attract business during the winter, we slashed passenger fares to $60.00—round-trip fare was $120.00. We were now attracting a lot of passengers. The other non-skeds with their C-47 could not compete with us. The scheduled airlines gave up a lot of their traffic to us as well. We were now red hot and rolling and making money.

We'd been having trouble with our Anchorage manager regarding collections of airbills and remitting passenger fares. It all came to a sudden end when the FBI arrested Pop Strickland, alias Hobletzell, our manager,

Left to Right, unidentified, Amos Heacock and Howard Hunt standing in front of Trade Winds Bar, Fourth Avenue, Anchorage, Alaska, circa 1950.

on a fugitive warrant from Los Angeles for dealing in stolen property. It was at this time that I took over as the Alaska Manager. We opened a new ticket office in the Trade Winds Bar in Anchorage.

We opened a Fairbanks office with Grace Kennedy in charge. We also opened many other small offices around the state. We offered every cab driver 10% if he would bring us a passenger. I set traps all over Alaska to generate more business.

We hired publicity agent, Herb Hilcher, to keep our name in the local Alaska papers with positive news articles. We ran radio spots and newspaper ads to increase business. If I knew that one of my competitors had a delay in departing, I would infiltrate the passenger boarding gate and tell them I knew how they could get out immediately—on ATA. Once the airlines saw they were losing the passengers, they were more than happy to turn over the entire load for a commission. One night, we promoted a whole load of thirty passengers away from Alaska Airlines.

Bill and Virginia Clark were two clever ATA employees. Virginia ran the office and Bill did a lot of undercover work for us. We even started a little bar game whereby you would slide a whiskey jigger down the bar. If it went all the way, it was "ATA all the way" and if it fell off short, it was "PNA, half the way." Pacific Northern Airlines (PNA) only offered service to Juneau where they connected with Pan American. It was good publicity and in a short while we became well-known—Alaskans were all for us.

The freight business was growing, too. We bought delivery trucks and hired Ralph Givens to run our freight department. He did an excellent, around-the-clock job. Our service was reliable, the merchants could order something one day and get delivery the next morning. We had a "bull by the tail." Now we had to hang on and keep it on course. The company bought me a red Buick station wagon. I'd smoke a cigar now and then to display that successful airline image. The sky was the limit.

Seattle Crash

On July 19, 1949, tragedy struck.[*] One of our C-46s, N5076N, crashed on take off from Boeing Field into a Georgetown residential district. The pilot, Merle Edgerton, had lost an engine on take off. He sliced through power lines, then through the third floor of an apartment house. The plane wiped a brick house off its foundation. There was an immediate fire on board. Heacock, who was a passenger aboard this flight bound for Chicago with twenty-eight service personnel, was the hero. He assisted most of the passengers off the plane. Then he entered the cockpit to find the crew jammed under the controls with the radio rack and other paraphernalia piled on top of them. The flames were singeing his neck as he threw Edgerton, reserve pilots Jim Adams and Anthony Gjessing out of the cockpit and to safety. Two soldiers occupying the two front right-hand seats were overlooked as they were knocked out cold and covered in debris. They perished in the flames as well as five occupants of the apartment house. Heacock's wife, Dorothy, was the stewardess on the flight. She, too, was a heroine, directing passengers off the burning plane.

Of course, an investigation was started right away. The pilots used "V" numbers for take off. Any loss of power before V1 was an abort, and after V1, was continuation of flight. We did not dwell long on the crash as a few hours later our Alaska flights were taking off through the smoke of the crashed flight.

Heacock immediately put the Airport Authority to blame by saying, "If you hadn't allowed that power line to be built so close to the airport, the airplane wouldn't have crashed into it." The power lines should have been underground. The real truth was that the pilot was at error. He made two decisions: first to stop, the second to go. The altitude and speed he lost from his first decision doomed him when he tried to continue the flight. Merle Edgerton never flew for us again. However, Jim Adams did

---

[*]   Seattle Post- Intelligencer, Vol. CXXXVI, No. 142, July 21, 1949.

and eventually became a Boeing test pilot. The insurance company took care of the claims and the loss of the airplane. Later we had to conduct extensive tests to prove that a C-46 would fly on one engine at a gross weight of 48,000 pounds.

CAB Problems

The Civil Aeronautics Board (CAB) was now going after the non-scheduled airlines for providing too much service. We were destroying the scheduled airlines who had a mail subsidy supporting their operations. Non-skeds had discovered a new air transportation market, "Air Coach." They had opened up the low-cost passenger and freight market that had been untouched by scheduled airlines. Since the CAB regulated the subsidized carriers, something had to be done to eliminate this competition.

With our six airplanes, we were running two and three trips a day between Seattle, Anchorage and Fairbanks. We tried departing from Everett, Washington, which was another point of departure. The CAB ruled that was a subterfuge because in effect we were providing transportation from Seattle to Everett. Then we tried departing after midnight, which would be another day. We were boxed in by the CAB with no viable solutions. We hired attorneys and went to court. As you know, an attorney only fights as long as he's being paid. Finally, our attorney said, "You boys really have a good case going here and I'd like to keep representing you, but I have to have money up front." We were running out of resources and ATA was on the verge of going belly up.

Heacock, by now, had organized the non-scheduled airlines into the National Independent Air Carriers. He accused the CAB of harassing air progress by subsidizing the scheduled airlines and not allowing competition. He was also appealing to Congress to stop the CAB from acting to enforce these economic regulations onto the non-scheduled airlines. Because of Heacock's aggressive attitude against the CAB, we became an immediate target for enforcement proceedings. We were actually forty years ahead of our time. Under President Reagan, many years later in 1980, the airlines were deregulated and it was survival of the fittest. If you could show financial responsibility and your airplanes were airworthy, you could fly. Competition made the next guy do better or else he perished. After all, wasn't that one of the things we war veteran pilots had just fought a war for—freedom of competition and not to be enslaved by some bureaucratic government agency? Freedom is really a shallow word when you look at all the protection given to big business. We were combative and vocal against the system. This attitude would later cause our demise. We had Alaskan public opinion on our side, however, the CAB was now out to get our scalps.

In Alaska, business was booming. In order to get a favorable ticket office location on Fourth Avenue in downtown Anchorage, we bought an entire bar along with entertainment—The Hanger Lounge. We had a grand opening with free drinks. Jayne Lowe played her accordion and sang. We packed them in that night, but the bar never was a moneymaker. The airline carried it. Anytime you see the cash register open in a bar, there is a good chance the bartender is sticking the bar receipts into his pocket instead of ringing them up. It was a management-intensive job and I couldn't find the time to catch those dishonest barkeepers.

It was, however, an excellent traffic location. One night while sitting in the bar talking to a friend, Phil, and his wife, one of our pilots, Clarence Chapman, walked in and sat down on my other side. Clarence kept eyeing Phil's wife and Phil was getting angry. He wanted to fight. I asked Chapman to leave, which he did. I then cautioned Phil that he did not want to fight Chapman as he had been a Golden Glove boxer in his youth.

Phil said, "I know how to handle him."

I said, "How?"

Phil said, "I'd use jujitsu on him."

I said, "He wouldn't sit still for that."

Phil said, "Fold your arms, Mike, and I'll show you."

He then slammed me with his fists, knocking me from my barstool. I immediately got up and grabbed him by the shirt in preparation for a fight. Then he said, "I didn't mean to do that, Mike, I'm sorry." I'm sure the booze had something to do with the incident. The moral to this story is, don't sit on a barstool with your arms folded.

The Great Clam Adventure

We needed more southbound cargo for our airline, so Heacock thought we could harvest razor clams on the beach at Polly Creek on the Kenai Peninsula. We would barge them to town and then fly them live to Seattle. I was skeptical, but had the job of setting up and running the operation. Heacock would handle shipments of clams when I got them to Anchorage.

One morning, I set out for Polly Creek with a chartered landing craft, a dory, a jeep, trailer, tents, food and about twenty clam diggers. We went ashore and set up camp. We organized the diggers for the next low tide. Fortunately, I had a few experienced clam diggers who could teach the city drunks how to dig clams. Some would dig with their hands like a dog after a bone. I had a barge anchored on the clam bed so all I had to do was pick up the clams in boxes from the diggers, load them onto my jeep-pulled trailer, unload boxes onto the barge, and from there, the landing craft would float up at high tide. After a couple of tides, I'd collected a planeload of clams. The landing craft chugged into Anchorage with about 10,000 pounds of clams on board.

Heacock didn't know what to do with all those live clams. He found some paper bags, but the clamshells cut the bags and they leaked. We finally had to put the razor clams into burlap bags and put the bags on a big tarp on the floor of the airplane. What a mess we had when the airplane took off for Seattle. After finally arriving at a Seattle cannery, there was nothing left but shells—the clams had died.

Meanwhile, my diggers had dug another 20,000 pounds of clams, which were sitting on the barge waiting for a lift to Anchorage. During the night, a big wind came up and the barge drug anchor and disappeared up Cook Inlet. We finally found it several days later and hauled it to Anchorage. This load didn't even smell good, so I arranged to freeze them at Castors Cold Storage, shells and all. It became obvious we didn't know what we were doing so we canceled the clam operation.

It took thirty days and $10,000 to find out we couldn't fly live clams to Seattle. The clams should have been shucked on the beach and frozen or canned. Using this method, you didn't need an airplane to move them to market. A surface ship would do the job nicely. Anytime Heacock mentioned seafood after that, we became very skeptical and refused to go along unless we had a working plan.

Of the stored Anchorage razor clams, I took some out to the Vanover Hog Farm to see if the pigs would eat them—even they refused. Vanover felt sorry for me and said, "Go ahead and bring your clams out here and put them in that gully. I'll cover them up with the dozer for you." My freight handlers hauled them out and, after handling those rotten clams, the men smelled like skunks for the better part of a week.

During this clam escapade, I was involved in an airplane crash. Ray Jones, a friend, offered to fly me, Red Wolfson and Jack O'Neill to the Polly Creek Beach in his Stinson Gull Wing if I would buy the fuel. Not being an experienced pilot, he stalled out a hundred feet above the ground and we cartwheeled and rolled down the beach with gas soaking everything. It is a wonder the plane and passengers didn't catch on fire. We scrambled out with only cuts and bruises. Jones was humiliated by the experience. He walked the beach kicking rocks. We were picked up by another plane and flown to Anchorage. We returned the wreckage to Anchorage with our chartered landing craft. The Gull Wing was never rebuilt—it was a total loss.

A funny thing happened while clamming. I'd gotten my jeep stuck out on the clam beds and the tide was now starting to come in. Salt water was up to the hubcaps. I carried a coil of rope just in case something like this happened. I rounded up all my clam diggers to pull me out. As the rope uncoiled, a couple of assholes (Navy term for knot) formed in the rope. I was up on the Jeep hood yelling, "Keep those assholes out of the rope." One southern boy walked back, tapped me on the shoulder and said, "Sir, if you want to get this jeep unstuck, let's not be calling anybody an asshole."

We continued trying to develop a seafood back-haul for our airplanes. We had unlimited freight to move northbound, but little to move southbound. Whoever could load both directions would have the key to success.

We developed a fish tub made of aluminum about two-feet wide and three-feet long and two-feet high with a rolled edge for carrying with two pieces of pipe to move the tub like a stretcher. The tubs were tapered so they would basket one inside the other. We made one hundred twenty-five of these reusable containers, which was about enough for three planeloads. Today, those fish tubs are scattered from Kodiak to Anchorage. People would steal them from us as they were useful for a variety of purposes.

We set up a fish-buying operation as well as a butchering operation in Kenai, complete with a forklift and cold storage. We enjoyed limited success, but the project was seasonal and came in floods or famine. Fishermen wanted to be paid with cash, not an I.O.U.

Then what do you haul when the fish run is over? We hauled king crab out of Kodiak, Dungeness crab from Cordova and Yakutat, but again, this was seasonal. The canneries in Seattle where we flew our fish were always trying to beat us down for a deal. They fought amongst themselves all the time, but when a new kid on the block tried to join the party, they banded together to give him a bad time.

The idea we had back in 1950 was sound and, with modifications, is the way lots of fish are handled today—flown to canneries stateside and within Alaska. We even considered putting into service a big four-engine flying boat we had purchased surplus: a PB2Y that was an Admiral's VIP airplane during World War II. It would be a flying tender picking up fish from the scows that were anchored in the fishing areas. We eventually decided against it. The main reason was weather and rough seas that could have prevented pick up and then again the transfer problem from flying boat to the next mode of transportation.

Manager and Jack-of-All-Trades

When I first came to Alaska to manage the operation, I did everything. I was the pilot, the deliveryman, the mechanic, and the ticket salesman. I was spread so thin I wasn't effective anymore. When we had a malfunctioning machine, I changed mags, starters and other items sometimes holding a flashlight in my mouth. You name it—I could do it. I decided if the operation was to grow, I would have to delegate good people to run the various departments, and if they didn't do it to my satisfaction, they would be fired. I would still fly an occasional trip when I had bulky cargo or an overtime pilot.

One night, freezing rain was a problem and the pilot didn't want to fly. We had a load of passengers to fly from Anchorage to Seattle. I judged the weather flyable, so off we went. I didn't do this often because usually when the pilot canceled he had a valid reason. This particular night, I was determined to complete the flight. The weather was bad, the plane bounced around, freezing rain was a problem and the passengers were sick. I learned a lesson that night—when the captain cancels the flight, I should listen. Unlike flying the Hump which never closed to weather, this wasn't World War II and I should have respected the captain's good judgment.

I remember one night bringing a flight into Merrill Field where the turbulence was so severe that a child's leg was broken. The child was flung to the ceiling, and then slammed to the floor. We also scrambled a lot of eggs in our cargo load that night.

I now started to become more of an executive—promoting, planning and getting involved in politics. It became obvious to me that if we were to survive, we would have to change the political structure back in Washington, D.C. The people in Alaska were 100% in favor of ATA's survival and responded by sending thousands of wires and letters to the CAB, our delegate to Congress and other government officials.* Heacock was now full time in Washington, D.C., trying to unshackle the noose that was tangled around our necks. The CAB did not like the attacks from Heacock and our lawyers, so we became number one to remove from airline operations.

We were making money in our Alaska business, grossing one million dollars annually. We had something worth saving. We hired some expensive attorneys to win favorable recognition and respect from the CAB. I accumulated a footlocker full of court briefs and petitions that our main Washington attorney, Warren Miller, filed on our behalf that attest to the fight. I have a scrapbook full of newspaper clippings of the various rounds we fought with the CAB until the last knockout round.

Family Life

As you read this, you are probably wondering why there is very little family involved in this venture. It's because I was all engrossed in making this airline succeed. I only came home occasionally to change clothes and I was off again. Ruth did a good job raising the family, making decisions that perhaps we should have been making jointly, but she never complained.

Now and then, we would take short trips and I'd carry my gold pan and Geiger counter, as I was interested in prospecting. Ruth would also take an occasional trip to Seattle for shopping with the girls. Ruth sometimes acted as a stewardess on a flight if we needed one. Mostly, she liked our little homestead and did a lot to help develop it. She was a great gardener, seamstress, cook, and mother to our three girls. She instilled a "can do" attitude in the girls that exists today.

Airline Business Booming

By 1951, our passenger traffic was really starting to grow. Alaskans were giving us their business. Because of southbound passenger increases, we dropped some of our southbound seafood operations. After all, a passenger was three times the revenue and it walked on and off the airplane. It was also a time to reorganize the company so as to cut down on corporate income tax. We set up three corporations: ATA (the airline), ATA Sales Company, and Airline Services, Inc. The idea, of course, was to balance out the profits that ATA was earning. ATA Sales Company charged a commission for the traffic it sold the airline. Airline Services charged a fee for the maintenance

---

*   Appendix 1.   Veterans of Foreign Wars of U.S. Press Release, October 1951.

provided to the airline and, of course, the charges could be varied. It was a modern organization that was quite common in airline-type operations and it also limited the amount of liability for which one corporation was responsible.

We had planned to put a four-engine DC-4 on the Alaska run, but the Korean War created a demand for this type of transport, so the supply was nil.* We bought one DC-4 in Louisville, Kentucky, that was used as a hamburger stand. It was called the C-54 Grill. It had both wings cut off at the fuselage and the interior was fixed up as a diner. The cockpit had a thin layer of concrete covering the floor and was used as the restroom. We gave away all the hamburger and beer, jacked it up and loaded it onto three railroad flat cars. We shipped it to Palmdale, California, where we planned to rebuild it into a flyable airplane. We started a worldwide search for parts.

I made a trip through Asia to Cairo, Egypt, procuring parts. The center section, wings, and tail came from Albuquerque, New Mexico; the engine and other parts came from a mountaintop above Anchorage. More parts came from a DC-4 that crashed in Yakutat, Alaska. Other parts came from a plane that crashed on a mountain in Montana. Anything we could find for a DC-4, we sent to Palmdale. I located crash sites by checking with the Rescue Coordination Center (RCC). We then hired a couple of good mechanics to start rebuilding the DC-4. We expected to be able to have this airplane flying to Alaska by the fall of 1952 for less than $500,000 in rebuilding costs. During the Korean War, DC-4s were selling for $750,000. After World War II, DC-4s sold for $20,000. It's all about supply and demand.

In order to meet the cooling temperature needed at METO (maximum takeoff power), we converted all the engines to super C-46s, which cost us about $30,000 each. The modifications installed augmenters on exhaust pipes, added a quicker retracting gear and made propeller adjustments. The airplane then met "T" category certification and was legal for 48,000 pounds gross passenger take-off weight. The C-46 was a proven airplane that had served the airline industry well and won fame for flying men and supplies over the China-Burma-India route during World War II.

The CAA started an effort to reduce the gross takeoff weight of the C-46 from 48,000 to 45,000 pounds. This would have been an economic blow because losing 3,000 pounds could have taken the profit out of flights. So on April 18, 1952, we took one of our C-46s, loaded it with 48,000 pounds of sand bags and proceeded to demonstrate to the CAA and CAB at Friendship International Airport, Baltimore, Maryland, that we could fly on one engine with this load. Newsreel and television cameras were there to record this bit of history. Heacock was aboard. Captain Bernasconi was the pilot. As the C-46 reached V1 speed (approximately eighty-six miles per hour), Heacock feathered the right engine. The pilot continued accelerating to V2 (approximately ninety-five miles per hour), rotated and

<hr>

*   Appendix 3.   Air Transport Associates, Inc., Letter to Under State Secretary for Aviation Affairs, December 10, 1951.

climbed out and flew around for two hours in front of media cameras before coming in for a perfect landing. Although the test was successful, it was not scientific enough for CAA since the pilot knew it was going to happen and was ready for the engine cut.

CAB Attempts to Force ATA Out of Business

ATA had now been ordered out of business by CAB and were to cease operations by October 21, 1952, for violating economic regulations of the CAB. Our next legal move was to appeal this decision to the U.S. Circuit Court of Appeals. After a few months, the Circuit Court upheld the CAB's plan to revoke our certificate. We then filed our appeal to the U.S. Supreme Court. Meanwhile, we asked the District of Columbia Court of Appeals for a stay of execution of the CAB order until the Supreme Court could review the case. The noose was beginning to tighten. Joseph Adams, of the CAB, made a fact-finding trip to Alaska in July, 1952. He gathered a lot of supporting evidence from Alaskans who wanted to retain our airline, but Adams was only one member of the board and a politician. The response from Alaskans was 100% for ATA.

Our only hope now to save the airline from certificate revocation was a political one. In August 1952, Senator John Sparkman was chosen as a Vice Presidential running mate for Adlai Stevenson. Heacock was the first person on the convention floor to congratulate the successful Democratic nominee for Vice President. Sparkman had been a Senate leader in the campaign for Alaska statehood and was in favor of protection for non-scheduled air carriers serving Alaska. Along with Bob Bartlett, delegate to Congress from Alaska, we had some allies. If we could only get Democrats Stevenson/ Sparkman elected, the political climate would change for non-scheduled airlines.

Heacock garnered further publicity when he put out a paper fire on the convention floor with his coat and suffered minor burns on his left hand and wrist. We even flew George Ahgupuk, famed Alaskan artist, to present Sparkman with a pen drawing on sealskin. The drawing was inscribed "In grateful appreciation for service to the

George Ahgupuk, left, and Howard Hunt.

Eskimo Girl Carries Petition to President Truman

Clad in a fur parka and mukluks, Pearl Ittigish, a six-year-old Eskimo girl, accompanied by her mother, left the northern Arctic village of Minto, Alaska, December 5, 1951, on a six-thousand-mile flight to Washington, D.C., courtesy of ATA. The purpose of her trip was to present President Truman with a petition signed by twenty-five thousand Alaskans asking that the order of the CAB closing down ATA flights between the U.S. and Alaska be lifted. The petition urged the President to make it possible for more milk, fruit and vegetables to be flown into Alaska at an affordable price.

Pearl, the daughter of an Athabascan chieftain, first flew to New York City, landing at LaGuardia Field. She was met by a group of admiring New York children who presented her with six quarts of milk. Pearl brought along a sack full of Christmas toys donated by the Veterans of Foreign Wars which included authentic Eskimo dolls, baskets and toy sleds for children in New York and Washington, D.C. While in Washington, she went sightseeing and made television appearances. She then flew on to Key West, Florida where President Truman maintained his "little White House."

ATA officials pointed out that the little village of Minto had received only occasional shipments of fresh food and vegetables in recent years. Many of the villagers were suffering from tuberculosis, which is partly due to improper diet. Pearl herself was treated for a minor case of tuberculosis. The villagers selected Pearl to fly "outside" from Minto to show Americans how many Alaskans depended on air transportation for the necessities of life.

people of Alaska."   Bartlett was supporting the Vice President and praised the Senator for his campaign on votes for Alaska statehood and his vigorous defense of non-scheduled carriers serving Alaska.

In September 1952, because of political pressure, the CAB launched a full investigation of non-scheduled airlines. Hearings were expected to take several months and would be held at various towns around the country. The biggest problem was the frequency of non-scheduled operations between two points. In the case of ATA, we tried to comply by altering our departure times. As mentioned earlier, we departed after midnight so as not to get two Mondays in a row and two Tuesdays in a row. Then on the third week when we couldn't give any service at all, we moved our operation to Everett, Washington, which was fifty miles away from Boeing Field. It was an impossible situation. We had many customers to serve and we needed to do it the best possible way.

The frequency regulations as defined by the CAB would not work for a large carrier such as ourselves. We had applied to become a scheduled air carrier, but the CAB was not going to give honor to bootleggers if

Alaska Freight Delays

On September 21, 1951, after several years of legal battles, the Civil Aeronautics Board (CAB) issued an order to revoke Air Transport Associates' (ATA) Letter of Registration. ATA was given thirty days to cease operations. Hunt was quoted as saying, "Under terms of the ruling, we're allowed thirty days—until October 21—to put our affairs in order. Actually, we have already ceased operations." Some contract obligations had to be filled, so during the thirty-day period, only contract flights were made. At the time, ATA had 145 employees and did a $2,000,000 a year business flying passengers and cargo between Seattle and the Alaskan communities.

This curtailment of cargo, particularly fresh produce, became a big problem for Alaskans as 75% of the fresh food products brought from the Lower 48 was flown in by ATA. When the CAB order was received by ATA, 20,000 pounds of fresh produce scheduled for shipment to Anchorage were left behind. ATA had operated four C-46s on an average fourteen flights per week between Anchorage and Seattle. At least seven flights per week were solely cargo-carrying operation.

At the same time, Northwest Airlines had placed an embargo on cargo in order to catch up on the backlog piling up in Seattle. Some backlog was due to the Korean War ramping up. The United States government was using commercial airlines to fly troops and equipment into Korea. Simultaneously, Alaska Airlines' flights between Anchorage and the Lower 48 were temporarily halted due to repairs being performed on three C-54 cargo ships at their California maintenance shops. The timing created a major hardship on all Alaskans.

In an effort to address the CAB's order to comply with frequency and regularity regulations, ATA immediately enacted a 30% reduction of its Alaska operation as a demonstration of its willingness to cooperate with all valid orders of the CAB. While reducing frequency of flights, ATA filed an appeal of the order to the courts. One member of the CAB, Joseph Adams, dissented with the opinion of the board. Adams stated:

> I dissent, however, from the decision to revoke the letter of registration of ATA summarily stopping its operation without first issuing an order to "cease and desist" from continuing violations of the board's regulations. ... I find no justification for taking a short cut in this case.

The Senate Small Business Committee had recommended that the CAB take no action against non-scheduled carriers. Their report stated that the irregular air carriers had made a major contribution to air transport and "have managed to survived since 1948."

Excerpt from
Future of Irregular Airlines in United States Air Transportation Industry
Hearing before a Subcommittee
of the Select Committee on Small Business
United States Senate[*]

May 4, 1953

The CHAIRMAN. You may proceed.

Mr. HUNT. I am just a simple Iowa farm boy, whom Uncle Sam taught to fly during World War II, and like a lot of other veterans, we organized veteran airlines. We saw an opportunity in it and we went ahead, but now after working 5 years to build up a legitimate business in Alaska that was encouraged by the same government I fought for, I now find I am prevented from continuing in business because an agency called the Civil Aeronautics Board says that it's a crime for me to compete with their pet carriers. If the boys in Korea felt the shock of this injustice as I do, they would believe as I do, that they were fighting for a bunch of bureaucrats and not the free United States.

We chose Alaska as our operation because it was the last frontier and stood on the threshold of a large development. I went to the territory 5 years ago just to organize the Alaska operation, and I have been there ever since.

I never did get the job done to my satisfaction. I have gone sour and I have no dough, so I guess I am a true sourdough.

I live in Alaska and I know their problems. ATA's complete operation was built on the demands and needs of the territory. Whatever service Alaskans have asked us for, we have complied with. Ours has been a personal one. People have come to me and said "Mike, how can I move this?" And I have given them an honest answer.

We have developed special techniques for handling perishables, especially insulated and heated trucks for the delivery of perishables in 40-below weather. Our arrivals are planned for early morning so that produce may be sold that day.

We pay off any damage claims immediately so as not to cause any undue hardship on a small-business man. Our service has become the standard of the industry, and as our competitors have found out, one of the chief complaints they hear is "Why don't they do it like ATA does?"

Seventy-five percent of the people of Alaska today, if they had their choice, would say, "Please ship it ATA." Alaskans are very fearful of what will happen to their freight rates and passenger fares now that the competition has been throttled by the Civil Aeronautics Board.

---

[*]   Appendix 5.   Howard J. Hunt Statement before a Subcommittee of the Select Committee Small Business, United States Senate, May 4, 1953

they could help it. The CAB was promoting and protecting the scheduled airlines with subsidies: Pacific Northern Airlines, Northwest Airlines, Pan American, Reeve Aleutian Airways, Alaska Airlines, Wien Airlines, Northern Consolidated Airlines and many others. We were staying the CAB Revocation Order by filing appeals to the courts.

Bob Reeve, the owner of Reeve Aleutian Airways, decided to run for Alaska delegate to Congress as a Republican and opposing Democrat Bob Bartlett.* We turned our efforts to minimizing Reeve's influence. While campaigning around Alaska, Reeve would usually show wildlife slides or movies. So, at one such meeting in Juneau when the lights were out, we had handbills distributed that challenged Reeve to debate the issues with Bartlett. When the lights came on, everybody had one of these handbills.

Reeve was furious. He stomped over to the Baranoff Hotel to punch it out with Bartlett. Bartlett was innocent. He didn't even know about the plot. A lot of nasty words were exchanged and finally a debate was scheduled. Republicans wanted the debate as far out in the boonies as possible so the media couldn't cover it. We were there and we recorded it. As predicted, Reeve lost his temper as opposed to Bartlett's factual responses to issues. We then played excerpts of our recording on the radio station a dozen times a day. After the voters heard this recording, even the Republicans voted for Bartlett. They didn't like their own man. The vote was

Political cartoons published in various Alaskan and national newspapers describing the plight of Air Transport Associates (ATA) 1951–1953.

---

*   Appendix 4.   Air Transport Associates, Inc., Letter to Amos Heacock dated September 17, 1952.

Wreath announcing the closing of the airline was mounted on the ticket window.

Republican for President Eisenhower/Nixon. Reeve spun, crashed, and burned. He never ventured into politics again.

We decided to hold off the CAB by filing briefs. The Supreme Court in November, 1952, issued a stay order keeping ATA flying and then on March 12, 1953, the Supreme Court refused to review the CAB Order revoking ATA's certificate. Again, we filed a motion for leave to request a re-hearing by the Court of Appeals. We won a stay while the court considered the motion. The motion was again turned down by the Court. We were now given until April 24, 1953, to wind up our business. However, in order to dramatize our position, on March 30, 1953, I announced we were ceasing operations immediately in Alaska and thanked everybody for their continued support.[*] The results were dramatic.

Then forty-eight hours later, after a meeting with the directors, I went to the media and announced that we would continue fighting. Miller announced from Seattle, "We'll never quit—they'll have to drag us out feet first."[†]

We were still hoping that we might somehow win another reprieve. But, on April 24, 1953, the trapdoor opened and the noose tightened, eliminating ATA as an air carrier. I appeared before the Small Business

> After working five years to build a legitimate business in Alaska that was encouraged by the same government I fought for, I find I am stopped from continuing in business because an agency of the Federal Government says it is a crime for me to compete with its pet carriers. Sir, if the boys in Korea felt the shock of this injustice as I do, they would believe as I do, that I was fighting for Bureaucracy and not the free United States. In a few words, I am the small American business man who has been forced out of business—because I made good.
>
> *Howard Hunt,*
> *Aircoach Transport Association, Inc.,*
> *Press Release, May 4, 1953*[*]
>
> ---
> [*] Appendix 7.   Aircoach Transport Association, Inc., Press Release, May 4, 1953.

Committee on May 4, 1953 in Washington, D.C., but it was to no avail.[‡] I received a lot of sympathy, but the CAB had won. We had another application to be recertified as a scheduled air carrier to Alaska, but trying to prove need and necessity when you've got all the scheduled carriers on one side of the table saying, "We can do better," we were beat.

We were out of money. We had spent a small fortune in attorney's fees trying to win all the way to the Supreme Court. Believe me, the government had far more resources than we did and can simply outlast anyone.

All personnel in Alaska were discharged[§] and all the support ground equipment sold. A burial wreath was attached to the ATA office door.[¶]

---

[*]   **Appendix 8.**   Air Transport Associates, Inc., Interoffice Communications, March 30, 1953; **Appendix 9.**   Air Transport Associates, Inc., Interoffice Communications, March 30, 1953; **Appendix 10.**   Air Transport Associates, Inc., Interoffice Communications, March 31, 1953.

[†]   **Appendix 7.**   Aircoach Transport Association, Inc., Press Release, May 4, 1953.

[‡]   **Appendix 5.**   Howard J. Hunt Statement before a Subcommittee of the Select Committee Small Business, United States Senate, May 4, 1953.

[§]   **Appendix 11.**   Air Transport Associates, Inc., Interoffice Communications, April 22, 1953.

[¶]   **Appendix 6.**   History of Air Transport Associates, Inc.

Oil Lease Adventure

While ATA was shutting down, I found time to get involved in a group of oil leases on the coast of Alaska. During the days that Kennecott Mine was operating back in the 1930s, there were shallow, oil producing wells at Katalla, Alaska, about twenty-five miles south of Cordova. The deepest well was about eight hundred feet. They produced a light crude that could be burned in an engine once it was warmed up on gas. Some of this oil was shipped to Kennecott, Alaska. There was a fire at the refinery at Katalla, about the same time as Kennecott was having a miners' strike and the mine shut down. They never rebuilt Katalla after the refinery burnt to the ground.

A group of Anchorage investors, including myself, acquired oil leases in southeast Alaska. We held sixteen sections of land at Cape Yakataga, Icy Bay and Yakutat. Phillips Petroleum struck gas and rumors of an oil strike abounded, but no official announcements were ever made. I've personally visited the well at Yakutat. If you strike a match around the old well, it will cause the match flame to increase. When we read these announcements in the paper, we were naturally excited thinking we were going to become millionaires. We planned to lease the land from the Bureau of Land Management (BLM). Then a group of us would unitize our holdings and lease the units to the oil company. Of the four deals we were involved in, we always made our money back plus some. But they never announced commercial oil, so we never received that one-eighth barrel royalty we had written into the leases.

These opportunities made living in Alaska exciting. Where else in the world could the average citizen lease ground from the U.S. Government at twenty-five cents an acre? I still think somebody is going to get lucky down there and strike it rich. After all, Katalla did produce oil from shallow wells and now is an abandoned ghost town.

In 2019 the Alaska Department of Natural Resources issued a limited Gulf of Alaska Oil and Gas Exploration License to Cassandra Energy Co. of Nikiski, Alaska, to explore for oil and gas on 65,733 acres in and around the Katalla area. The company is required to complete at least twenty-five percent of the exploration work within four years of receiving the license or the license will be terminated.

Chapter 8   Homesteading in Alaska

Ruth and the girls had joined me in Alaska within a few months after the birth of our third daughter, Diane. In February 1949, we bought a little house in Woodland Park located in Spenard, adjacent to the city of Anchorage. Shortly after settling in, I learned about a land lottery being conducted by the Federal Government. The lottery focused on land that had been taken over by the federal government from the territory of Alaska during World War II. The land had been incorporated into a section of the Fort Richardson Army Base. Four years after the war ended, the land was reopened for homesteading via a lottery drawing.

Some eight hundred people were hoping to obtain land in the lottery conducted May 13, 1949. I was fortunate enough to be drawn and allotted forty acres. The land was approximately five miles east of the city of Anchorage, but completely remote. It literally was a moose pasture. During this timeframe, approximately six hundred and fifty acres of surplus government land was allotted. The land was inaccessible and undeveloped. Just getting to the homestead was a challenge as no roads existed.

One of the requirements to obtain a homestead was to "prove up" on the land. This meant a person had to clear ten acres, build a structure, and live on the land for seven months. After seven months, the homesteader paid a $16 filing fee to record the homestead patent. At that point the title to the homestead was secure.

I immediately purchased a beat up war surplus truck to get back and forth to town. The surplus war vehicle was a four-wheel-drive weapons carrier capable of traveling over rough terrain. Once we established a trail to the homestead, we used it to commute to town weekly to buy groceries and other supplies. The weekly trip into town was quite an adventure for the girls as they had to sit behind the cab of the truck on eight foot long folding wooden bench seats under a torn camouflage canvas-covered metal-framed canopy. They were tossed to and fro as the weapons carrier bounced off downed spruce trees and lumbered across muddy ruts in the roughly-hewn trail that finally, after several miles, converged with a proper road. I kept a company vehicle parked in a turnout on Oil Well Road. We used this company vehicle to drive the rest of the way into town and back.

After clearing land for the cabin, we constructed a simple two-room 16' x 24' structure. In 1950 we moved from Woodland Park and began living on the newly minted homestead. We had no electricity, water, or telephone—almost nothing. Within a couple months, with a lot of hard work, persistence, and cooperation, we had electricity, water and a 10-party telephone line.

Two other homesteaders, Dick Turpin and Vince Huebsch, lived adjacent to our land. Dick Turpin owned several pieces of heavy equipment including a D-6 bulldozer. I hired Turpin to carve out a driveway to our home. In short order, Turpin had completed the rudimentary driveway by simply bulldozing trees out of the way and smoothing out the road surface. The driveway contained no gravel, just dirt. Depending on the time of the

---

Set Net Fishing off Bird Creek in Cook Inlet

In the mid-1950s, our family had a set net in Cook Inlet near Bird Creek. Back then, it was legal to put a net out to catch salmon during the salmon run. Of course, the net had to be checked at every tide, which occurred every twelve hours around the clock. Mom, Dad, my sisters and I (ages nine, seven and six) drove to Bird Creek on the Seward Highway, parked by the railroad tracks, and hiked down about a quarter of a mile to the silty waters of Cook Inlet where the set net was located.

Checking the fish net in the middle of the night was not pleasant, especially for three little ragamuffin girls who would rather sleep through the night than go hiking down a steep embankment to retrieve stinky fish. The Inlet was muddy and treacherous. Several times we slipped out of our boots in the wet clay. We struggled to pull our boots free and stick our muddy feet back inside them. We would haul out approximately fifteen to forty salmon on each tide. We would drag the fish up the steep banks in containers, then along the railroad tracks to our car. This endeavor went on for weeks until we had a plentiful supply of salmon, at which time we removed the net.

Once we arrived back at the homestead, Dad cleaned the fish while Mom prepared a salt brine for smoking—reluctantly, we grumpy little girls helped out. Dad modified a smoke house that was a converted surplus "one-hole" outhouse. Dad constructed chicken-wire racks in the old outhouse to hold the filleted, brined fish. A fire pit was set up a few feet away with a stovepipe capturing the smoke and sending it into the smokehouse. The smoke from the alder wood filtered up through the hole in the seat wafting through the chicken-wire racks loaded with salmon. The design of the smoker was perfect until one of Dad's friends (after a few too many beers) suggested the fire needed to be hotter, so Dad added more wood to the fire. A short time later, the smoke house went up in flames along with about one hundred pounds of salmon.

Memory of Daughter, Nancy Verlinde

year, the driveway was either four-inches deep in a powdery dust that billowed and floated around, coating everything in its path when driving on it; or during spring breakup, the driveway was a foot deep in mud. Many vehicles became stuck up to the running boards when the driver attempted to negotiate the driveway. At times like that, the farm tractor came in handy to drag out vehicles that were stuck in the mud. If the tractor couldn't do the job, the D-6 bulldozer was called into service.

Barbara and Nancy Hunt stand with the ATA jeep on the homestead in the 1950s.

The new road Dick Turpin was punching through, Turpin Road, connected the remote homesteads to established roadways several miles away, namely, DeBarr Road.

Since I had airplanes coming and going at all hours of the day and night, I spent a good deal of time in town at the Lane Hotel or at the ticket office where I had a telephone to keep track of things. Ruth and the girls lived on the homestead while I spent most of my days in town running the airline. We had planned to prove up on the land, and then move back into town. As it turned out, we liked our remote surroundings in the woods, even with all the inconveniences.

Hauling water in jerry cans to the homestead was an unwieldy proposition. One of the first orders of business was to dig a well. Using an old tractor and a shovel, I spent many long hours digging the well. The water well was about fifty feet deep and was encased in a wooden crib to keep the dirt from sliding in. A well pump was installed about six feet inside the well crib. On a few occasions, during the winter months, the well froze over. In order to get the water to flow again, someone had to climb down in the well crib on a makeshift ladder with an ax to chop through the ice to reach liquid water. Since I was gone so much of the time, Ruth would crawl into the well to accomplish this task. I remember a time or two when she discovered frozen mice embedded in the ice. That did not go over well to say the least.

We kept adding to the house until it became a small, three-bedroom home. The additions consisted of a cold weather enclosed porch, a 16' x 16' surplus building that was designated as the living room, and a galley kitchen which was constructed between the original cabin and the surplus building. The cold weather enclosed porch served as a chicken coop for

Bounty from Ruth's garden. Daughters, Barbara holding large turnip, Nancy holding a forty pound cabbage, and Diane holding a large potato, circa 1956.

a time and then was turned into a bedroom. After a couple years, the entire house was raised to put in a cement-block basement, which eventually housed the furnace, laundry room, and root cellar.

Ruth tended a big garden in the summer months. She canned and preserved vegetables of all kinds, including turnips, cabbage, carrots and potatoes, which we consumed during the winter months. The girls, although young, were a big help to Ruth. Our food supply was supplemented with moose, caribou, sheep, and goat as well as plenty of salmon. We also raised chickens. When the chickens were fully grown, Ruth would butcher them, dress them out, and sell them to local businesses, bartenders and grocery stores. She sold a lot of fresh chickens by word of mouth as well. Most women would have walked away from this lifestyle, but Ruth was a trooper and did whatever was necessary to help feed the family. We mostly lived off the land.

We didn't have an indoor toilet when Heacock and his wife, Dorothy, visited one day. Dorothy wanted to know where the bathroom was. I replied, "Just pick a tree." Dorothy was not amused. We used a slop bucket and dumped it every day. Eventually a toilet and proper bathroom were installed.

After gaining a homestead patent to this forty-acre homestead, I made an entry on another homestead on the Kenai Peninsula a few years later. My idea was to get a floatplane and commute back and forth to Anchorage. When I tried to move Ruth and the girls to the Kenai, Ruth rebelled and wouldn't move. Ruth said, "I've made enough sacrifices." One homestead was enough. Years later, oil was discovered on that Kenai homestead land in the Swanson River Field. We would have been unitized under that discovery and received oil royalties, which would have made us very wealthy. Ruth was sorry she had put her foot down and not proved up on the second homestead parcel. However, we were fortunate to have proved up on the forty acres outside of Anchorage. The homestead eventually became part of the city of Anchorage. In the late 1990s, the homestead was subdivided into 158 lots and became known as "Huntwood Subdivision."

Chapter 9   House Builder/Prospector

After Air Transport Associates shut down, it was time for reflection. I had put all my efforts into making ATA a successful airline. I had promoted and won 100% support from Alaskans. However, the CAB had prevailed in the end. Now we were broke. All our assets were depleted from paying attorneys and key people. The four-engine DC-4 in Palmdale, the hamburger stand conversion, was a forced sale to Kirt Kekorian for $140,000. Kekorian finished the project and the plane flew again. I felt very discouraged, but the Hunts don't break, they just bend. I needed to eat. I had a wife and three young daughters to support. I decided to learn something about construction. Maybe I could become a contractor and besides, aviation had burned me out. I would be a family man and stay at home and play with my wife and kids.

A seventy-six-home project was starting up in Anchorage called City View Horizon. On May 15, 1953, I went there and asked for a job. The foreman put a shovel in my hand and I went to work as a laborer digging plumbing sets and setting septic tanks. The ditches I dug were immediately noticed by the foreman as being perfect. They were straight, the right depth and accurate. I always put my best into whatever I was doing—110%. I wasn't getting any other experience, so one day the boss came over to talk as I was setting a septic tank. I told him I'd come to work to get some construction experience. At that point, I had been so far underground that I couldn't even see the project.

The foreman asked what else could I do.

I replied, "I'm an excellent carpenter."

He said, "We'll see about that."

He put me to work as a carpenter and I worked extra hard to prove my worth. I became a full Journeyman Union Carpenter. My attitude was one of an intensive young man in a hurry to get things done and to do them in a professional manner. I had pride in everything I did, regardless of how menial it was.

After the homes were built and all construction people dismissed, I was made project manager. This job involved settling sub-contractor contracts, selling homes, and other duties. I did everything from fixing appliances to starting a furnace in the middle of the night.

It was in my role as project manager that I met Carol Pierce. She had purchased some drapes from the management company. I agreed to hang the traverse rods. After I hung them, Carol walked into the room and said, "Isn't one end higher than the other?" Sure enough, I'd made a two-inch error, which I quickly corrected.

By this time, I'd moved Ruth and the girls into the model home office where she could run things while I was involved in other jobs on the project. Since none of the seventy-six homes had telephones, when phone calls would come into the project office for families in the subdivision, Ruth would write the message on a slip of paper. For ten to twenty-five cents a trip, the girls would jump on their bikes and deliver the messages. While we lived in City View, we rented our homestead house to a military family.

One very spectacular thing happened that I must mention. On July 9, 1953, we were working building homes when the sky became very dark, like a gigantic thunderstorm. We didn't know what was happening. Then a fine ash started to fall and we learned that Mt. Spurr, a volcanic mountain eighty miles west of Anchorage, had blown its top. It was about noon. We quit work and everyone went home. You needed lights to drive around it

Prospecting

In August 1992, Grandpa and I flew in the Piper Cub to the Collinsville Mine. About one hundred air miles northwest of Anchorage, Collinsville has a dirt airstrip and an active placer gold mine operation.

Years ago, Grandpa had stashed two off-road quad ATVs near the airstrip. We transferred our overnight gear to the quads and then dragged the gold grabber and freshwater pump out from under a tarp. We bungeed the pump to the handlebars of my quad while grandpa set the six foot long aluminum sluice along the axis of his quad. He straddled the sluice while I wobbled my steering of the quad up the dirt road to the Boulder Creek cabin where we would spend the night.

We reached his mining claims and Grandpa set up the pump and gold grabber in the creek. He then handed me a shovel and gave me a general sense of where to start digging. The prospecting was for entertainment purposes only. No nuggets in the box and a few pennyweights of gold flakes in a vial was all we had to show for three hours of work. We loaded up the quads and spent the night in his Boulder Creek cabin. Grandpa checked the weather in the morning. We learned that a volcano, Mt. Spurr, had erupted a second time. We cut our trip short and flew back to Anchorage under gray, ashen skies.

Memory of Grandson, Terry Braun

was so dark. Before it stopped, about a quarter inch of gray ash had fallen on everything. Many birds and animals suffered in the ash fall. We only had to dust off our garden with a water hose and we were mostly back to normal, except for all the ash that was tracked into the house. Evidence of the dust can still be seen. If you dig a hole, you will notice a light gray color near the top of the layers of soil. That's the ash from the 1953 Mt. Spurr eruption.

Prospecting

In my spare time, I studied prospecting. The Atomic Energy Commission (AEC) came out with a study that suggested a certain area in Alaska contained radioactivity. The closest area was Medfra, located near McGrath. Mel Tipton and I flew there. Right away my Geiger counter and

---

Fishing

Grandpa often flew family and friends in his Cessna 180 to go fishing. The typical trip for an out-of-town guest would start in Grandpa's garage with finding hip boots that leaked only a little bit. He then grabbed his Trapper Nelson wood-frame-canvas backpack and the fishing trip was officially underway. The backpack contained the tackle box, salmon-egg bait, lunch, and bug repellent. The best bug repellent contained DEET and he always had some army surplus supply of the good stuff loaded with DEET.

Weather and rumors of good fishing determined the destination for the day. After landing on an open body of water and taxiing to the shore, you unloaded the fishing poles and backpack and followed him into the brush.

"Make noise," Grandpa would say, "it keeps the bears away," as you pushed alder branches out of the way and wondered where the trail and the bears were.

Once you reached the fishing spot, he would unload the backpack and assign the fishing poles based on who needed a fishing license and who did not. He would spread out the salmon-egg bait on a log and remind you how to secure the bait on your barbed hook. Then the fishing began in earnest. Our luck would vary but we were seldom skunked.

We would stop for lunch. The backpack always included peanut butter and jelly sandwiches wrapped in aluminum foil made the night before by Grandpa. We sat on the ground or a log, attempted to dry our feet, and enjoy our meal. Depending on weather and our success in fishing, the day would end with taking a few group photos, cleaning the fish and then jumping in the plane for the flight home. A great time was had by all.

Memory of Grandson, Terry Braun

scintillation counter started registering high radioactive emissions. I was so excited. I didn't know whether to make camp or stake claims. I tried to identify the radioactive rocks but was unable to do so as I was on top of a grandodiorite dome, which gave off a high background reading. By packing my suspicious ore rocks about six miles away to a shale rock area, I was able to identify the ore. We staked four claims and then came back to town.

Analysis of ore at the lab showed it was not commercial quantity or quality. The old claims are still in the archives, as one time in Fairbanks in the 1980s, I ran across the claims located in Paradise Gulch. The other radioactive area described by AEC was in southeast Alaska. The claim was staked by a pilot from Ketchikan. He made millions of dollars off the claim as it was commercial grade ore. However, it is no longer worked. Uranium, like all metals, must compete on the world market.

I prospected in other areas in Alaska—Dan Creek, near McCarthy, and various highway cuts. But, again, I had a young family to support and, unless some large company backed you, you could starve before you made a strike. I even organized a small company with Bill Fike called HUFICO for Hunt Fike Company, but my backers could not come up with the money I needed to sustain a summer working in the field.

Home Again

Since I was home every night now, I was starting to bond with my family. We did a lot of things together that year such as camping and fishing on the Kenai Peninsula. Skiing and ice skating during the winter months was another family activity.

One event that stands out was a late season moose hunt with Fike. We flew out to Seventeen Mile Lake. The lake is named this because it is seventeen miles southwest of Skwentna. Fike showed my partner and me some moose from the air. He then landed on the frozen lake where we hurriedly set up a camp. We took off walking cross-country through the snow to intercept the moose. In November, the days are quite short and twilight comes on about 4 p.m. The moose had moved a little further out and when I finally made my shot, the moose didn't fall down. We started tracking the blood trail and saw moose tracks everywhere.

We tried to follow our tracks back to camp but we couldn't see them in the dark. We realized we were just wasting our energy. The tendency is to panic and walk until exhausted while trying to find your camp. I came to an area with some dry downfall timber and decided that would be a good place to build a fire and sywash (quick set up of a temporary camp) for the night. We had dressed in light jackets and were not equipped for a sywash in zero degree weather. We started a fire. As the campfire lit up the area, we could see other dead wood and so we dragged the dead wood to our makeshift campsite. Nights during November are fourteen hours long, so I had some time to think about our problem. My mind was fighting panic as I imagined reading the Anchorage newspaper headlines: "First day of search was negative" and "Nothing second and third days." We were not exactly lost, we just didn't know which way to walk back to our camp.

Morning came and an airplane flew overhead. We flagged him in and he lifted us to our lake about a mile away. Fike showed up a few hours later ready to start hauling our moose meat to town. He could hardly believe our night of suffering out in the cold woods. If there is something to be learned here, it is to take a tail bearing from your camp so that when you are ready to return, you will know which way to proceed. Of course, don't panic and make sure you have a way to start a fire. If you can start a fire, you can survive just about any winter situation in Alaska, even if you are wearing inadequate clothing.

Family bonding, home building, prospecting, hunting and fishing were memory-making for me, but aviation was like a magnet. It was pulling me back to my first love—flying.

Big Lake Cabin

At a very young age, I learned that when Grandpa asked you if you wanted to do something, he wasn't truly making an inquiry. He was letting you know what you were going to be doing, because he knew you would be successful at whatever adventure awaited you.

When he said the fish should be biting at Weenie Lake, he was really saying go get your waders, choose your favorite old hat from the collection hanging in the garage, and pack a lunch for two; toasted peanut butter and jelly on wheat and two apples.

If he mentioned it was a nice day for flying, that was your queue to get your shoes on and be ready before he drove off without you. Expect to chase his truck down the driveway to remind him that he forgot you. Once in the truck, you couldn't wait to get to Lake Hood, for Grandpa drove as if he were soaring in the clouds. Automobile lane lines were merely recommendations and if he dropped something on the floor while driving, he would bend over for seconds at a time searching for the dropped object, as you discreetly grabbed the steering wheel and pretended it was normal behavior.

I was fifteen years old when he proposed that we needed to get a new dock hauled to the Big Lake cabin. It would be easy he explained; "we'll just stick an outboard motor on the dock, drop the dock into the water at Burkeshore Marina, then ride the dock to the cabin." He helped prepare my dock commander kit, which included the standard brown bag lunch, rain jacket, crate seat, full gas can, and one wooden oar. Once the dock was in the water, he tossed my provisions aboard, gave me a hug, and said, "Head to the right and I'll meet you at the cabin in a couple hours."

Shortly after dusk and after several rain squalls, wrong turns and many hours later, I arrived at the cabin unscathed. He wasn't surprised when I pulled up with the dock. I honestly think he lost track of time because he was busy salvaging old nails from rotting boards that were laying around the cabin, and completely forgot about me.

Every adventure with Grandpa was pure joy and filled with a sense of accomplishment. He gave me confidence when I had none, believed in me when I didn't believe in myself, and trusted me when I know he shouldn't have. Though a tremendously accomplished aviator, businessman, veteran and more, to me, he will always be my "Gramps."

Memory of Granddaughter, Denise Chinchilla

Chapter 10   Back in Aviation

It was now 1954 and I had a lot of time for reflection. I wanted to get back into aviation. Working for a living was tough. My expertise was aviation. I asked for active duty again as the Korean War was just winding down.

Miller, Fitch, and Heacock had been struggling with some Commercial Air Movements (CAMs) which were strictly military charters—and doing it on the certificate of Air Cargo Express,* a company which we still owned. Heacock was head of Aircoach Transport Association, Inc., which was responsible for handling military loads for all non-scheduled carriers. Fitch was back in Washington state doing the bidding and Miller was controlling crews from Seattle, but with no common carrier certificate. Our maintenance facilities, Airline Services, Inc., at Oakland and Baltimore, were struggling to keep our financial head above water.

When my partners asked me to join them in an aircraft rebuild project, I was ready. In January 1955, I left the family in Anchorage, packed my tool box and headed for Columbus, Georgia. I took along a young sixteen-year-old fellow named Gordon McCrary, who was on probation from the courts in Alaska at the time. His folks were one of the original homesteaders in Eagle River. Mac McCrary, Gordon's father, was a free-lance airplane mechanic.

In 1953, one of our C-46s, N1302N, had crashed at Columbus, Georgia. The airplane was making an approach to Lawson Army Airfield at Fort Benning in a severe thunderstorm with a load of troops. The pilot saw the airport through a break in the clouds, and thinking it was Fort Benning, he

---

*   Air Cargo Express, Inc. was incorporated in New Jersey, November 21, 1947. Air Cargo Express concentrated its cargo service between the Pacific Northwest and Alaska as well as overseas service. The base of operations was Boeing Field in Seattle, Washington. The company operated between 1951 and 1955. Its busiest year was 1952 with 147 flights in inter-state commerce and twenty-eight flights in overseas commerce. Air Cargo Express was closely affiliated with Air Transport Associates (ATA). The shareholders, officers and directors of both corporations were one and the same.

The Civil Aeronautics Board (CAB) had revoked the Operating Certificate of ATA on March 25, 1953. Because the shareholders, officers and directors were the same for both companies, the Board found that the carrier could not be entrusted with operating authority and that its license must be revoked. The company went into receivership June 17, 1955.

Columbus, Georgia, rebuild of ATA's C-46, the "Kenai Trader."

canceled the IFR flight and landed. It was Columbus, Georgia's Municipal short runway. The airplane hydroplaned off the end of the runway into a thirty-foot ditch. Both engine nacelles were bent up, landing gear knocked off and the belly flattened from nose to tail. No one was injured. We, the ATA partners, bought the airplane from the insurance company for $5,000 of our own money. We called the new company Black Diamond Enterprises. The pilots on the N1302N crash were Bernasconi and Paul Palmer. Bernasconi had been our test pilot on the one-engine demonstration at Baltimore, Maryland. He was a good pilot.

The three of us, Miller, McCrary and I, showed up at the airport and told the airport manager, Guy Kilgore, we were going to rebuild N1302N and fly it out. Kilgore couldn't believe it as over the years, the airplane had become a derelict. Kids had smashed all the instruments and cut various components from the airplane. We had very little money, so Kilgore let us stay in a spare, upstairs, unfurnished room next to the furnace. We set up our three canvas army cots; and that was to be our home for the next five months. We went to the YMCA once a week for a shower and took our meals in a little café in the terminal. We hired a couple of good southern sheet metal men and went to work—from can't to can. We put up a little shelter around our work area as it is very cold in Georgia in January.

We had a lot of spare C-46 parts in Seattle that we needed in Georgia. Fitch shipped us a railroad car load, including a wing. One of our biggest problems was the replacement of both engine nacelles and a forward and rear belly. We found these in Norfork, Virginia. Miller and I hauled them to Columbus via back roads, as we had a rather strange load aboard our little sixteen-foot stake truck. More of the belly was hanging over the back of the truck than was on the truck. We moved all the parts in three loads.

At Fort Benning, the military was using a couple of C-46s for fire drills. We managed to get into them and remove certain landing gear casings, spar extrusions, and parts that we needed for the rebuild. One day while Miller was cutting parts out with a torch, the MPs looked at the still smoking center section of the airplane and drove off. We held our breaths hoping they wouldn't ask us any questions. Actually, we were just recycling some valuable parts for our rebuild that the Army was reducing to aluminum ingots for fire drill.

We had to splice and repair front and rear spars as the landing gear had been ripped out on the right side. It was during this repair that I finally gave up trying to smoke a pipe. I would be inside the center sections, bucking rivets and my pipe would be on the other side of a wing rib. It was interfering with my work, let alone with my health. I threw all my pipes away and never picked them up again.

After our hired help had put in their eight hours, Miller, McCrary and I would continue working, sometimes until after midnight. The impossible project was taking shape. We riveted the new engine nacelles onto the center section and the front and rear belly onto the bottom of the fuselage—lots of tough metal work and riveting.

In the spring, you could see that we had succeeded. On May 13, 1955, we flew the C-46 from Columbus, Georgia, to Wildwood, New Jersey, to have radios installed. We flew this route without radios, following the coastline all the way to New Jersey. The local residents of Columbus didn't believe such a project was possible. As we told Kilgore, all we needed to start the rebuild was the aircraft's serial number. We would build an airplane around it. N1302N had been resurrected from the dead and would fly again. As a matter of fact, N1302N "Kenai Trader" eventually made it back to Alaska. Reeve Aleutian Airlines was flying it when a cargo load of cement shifted. It crashed in the water after take off from Driftwood Bay, Unalaska, Alaska.

Chapter 11   Ice Floe Rescue

Just as I emerged from the Columbus, Georgia, project, a new drama was unfolding in the Arctic. In May 1955, a United States Overseas Airlines' (USOA) DC-4, returning from a supply flight on the DEW Line, passed up Coral Harbour on the way to Fort Churchill, Canada, and ran into strong head winds. It actually ran out of fuel about forty miles north of Fort Churchill. Hudson Bay was frozen over at that time of the year so the pilot decided he could safely land on the ice. He was counting on a dog sled team to get some fuel out to him so he could fly the plane back to Fort Churchill. He set up for his landing, and just as he was flaring, he struck an ice pressure ridge. The landing gear collapsed. The plane went down on the right wing tip. The right gear was knocked off and some other damage occurred. This left the big DC-4 sitting out on the ice. What a sight that was!

The insurance company paid USOA for the airplane. My partner, Amos Heacock, and I got an idea that maybe we could salvage this DC-4. We bought the airplane from the insurance company for $5,000. We then went to USOA and said, "If you will finance this operation, we'll get it off the ice for you." Ralph Cox, the owner, agreed.

We set the project in motion. In May, Arctic weather starts to warm up and there was little time left to get the plane off the ice. Our idea was to insulate this piece of ice where the airplane was sitting with hay and sawdust. We would then tow the pan of ice to shore and slide the airplane onto the beach. We would have the plane safely home.

Just in case that didn't work, we had a second plan. We procured thirteen surplus Army pontoon inflatable boats which we placed underneath the airplane. We had hay and sawdust delivered by rail car into Fort Churchill. From there we flew it out to the ice using DC-4s. We had a helicopter and two Super Cubs brought in so that we could support our logistic operation. We had twenty-five DC-4 loads of hay and sawdust to drop on the site. The DC-4 came in low over the downed DC-4 and salvoed its load of sawdust or hay. I was out on the ice to supervise the operation. I felt they weren't dropping the hay and sawdust bags close enough to the airplane. I picked up my walkie-talkie and told the pilot, "Come in closer." On his next drop, he salvoed them right on top of me. I could see the bags plummeting

DC-4 on Hudson Bay ice floe sitting on the pontoon boats.

down at me. I tried to get out of the way. One hit me right on the bottom of my leg and sent me skidding on the ice for fifty feet. I picked up my walkie-talkie and said, "That's close enough."

When the thirteen Army pontoon boats were air dropped, they bounced like big basketballs. The pontoon boats would go bouncing, kaboom, kaboom, when they hit the ice. We placed twelve of those boats under the wings and fuselage of the DC-4. The other one we put inside the plane in case the ice ripped everything off, we could still save the airplane. The airplane might be in the water, but that one pontoon inside the fuselage would keep it afloat.

I hired a crew of native villagers to help prepare the airplane. The two engines on the left side were still in good shape. Part of our plan was to use those engines for power to help propel our pan of ice to shore. We painted the airplane black with Perroxotone, which is a saltwater preservative. By the time we had the airplane ready to float, open water was all around us.

As we were working on the ice pan, one of my workers fell through a hole in the ice. I happened to hear him yell for help. I immediately grabbed a piece of rope and went running to his aid. I got to him in time and drug him back onto solid ice. We placed him inside the airplane, removed his wet clothes and stuffed him into a sleeping bag along with dry clothes. The man was in shock so we airlifted him back to Fort Churchill for medical aid. The water was so cold that survival time would be minutes at best. My workers were afraid while out on the ice and would not come out unless they had their canoes.

I lived out on the ice for about three weeks. One night, I remember a very fierce storm causing the ice to crunch and grind all night. I spent that night in a life raft by the back door of the airplane. Every once in a while a big chunk of ice would break through a soft spot in the surface ice and come up as big as a house. It was terrifying and, had one come up under us, it would have destroyed our whole airplane camp.

After we got the airplane ready to float, it was only necessary to keep track of it from the air. When we had enough open water around the plane, the plan was to pull the pan of ice to shore with the airplane resting on it.

This is also the first time I became genuinely interested in helicopters. The helicopter provided a ton of logistics for our project. It was dangerous flying, however, as the Arctic sky was hazy with little to no definition between the sky, the horizon and the ice field. Immediately after take off, the helicopter pilot noticed the variation on the directional compass was off by sixty-five degrees. This phenomenon occurred due to our close proximity to magnetic north as opposed to the geographic North Pole. Not only that, but vibrations in the helicopter engine itself caused the directional compass to spin around which presented additional problems with navigation. Whenever the helicopter was airborne, we had to fly out ahead of it in a Super Cub, where we could navigate by taking a directional heading from the surrounding icebergs. By using this method, we were able to fly a pretty straight line.

The helicopter pilot we hired was fearful of flying under these adverse conditions. If he could not see where he was going, he would turn around and head back to Fort Churchill. His fear of flying out over the ice eventually caused him to quit. When I think back on it, he was smart. However, that put more of a burden on me to do the mission with the Super Cub since I didn't know how to fly a helicopter yet.

One day I started up the chopper, but I didn't have the guts to pull in the collective because I was afraid it would get loose on me. From what I know about helicopters now, it is a good thing I didn't pull back the collective that day. I would have wrecked that helicopter for sure. I used the Super Cub instead. The Super Cub was a fast way to get out to the ice. When we first started the operation, it was solid ice. When the ice started breaking up, there wasn't much to land on anymore. We had about a football field piece of ice around the airplane.

The Rescue Coordination Center (RCC) at Fort Churchill warned me about flying over the ice pack in a single-engine wheel plane. They said, "If you don't come back someday, we're not even going to look for you. That's dangerous work."

I said, "I know it is but I have a bull by the tail and I can't let go. If I let go, the project is gone." Those were sobering words, but what were we to do if I didn't continue the project? The project would collapse and we would lose all our investment. If you keep your name on

A DC-4 Cargo plane dropping bagged sawdust.

the damn-fool list long enough, there is a good chance you will get called by the Grim Reaper.

After we got the airplane ready for floating, the main objective was keeping track of it. The ice floe drifted around in Hudson Bay. Some days I couldn't even find it while flying in the Super Cub. I would fly out looking for the DC-4, but I couldn't locate it. I would think, Oh, my God, I wonder if it sank. I would keep looking and eventually I would find it. Navigation is quite a problem that far north. If you fly in that Arctic haze over the ice in Hudson Bay with a lot of open water and a magnetic compass and you dip the wing of the airplane, the magnetic compass does a 360-degree turn. When this happened, I would wonder if I was still headed in the right direction. I would try to navigate Indian fashion. I would pick out an iceberg up ahead and try to maintain a straight line heading toward it. The magnetic compass wasn't of much value.

More open water appeared around the DC-4. I went to the harbormaster and said, "I want to rent your big harbor tug to go out in the bay and hook onto that piece of ice and start pulling the airplane to shore."

He said, "No way." It was too dangerous. He wouldn't go out there.

I then located several villagers with boats. Between them, they had two old whaleboats and three canoes. We went out with that armada and hooked onto the piece of ice and started to pull it to shore.

The whaleboats were in terrible shape; it took one man on each boat bailing to keep them afloat. We hooked on and for three days we pulled on this big piece of ice. It was such a massive ice chunk that we couldn't get it to move very fast. It would move in one direction and then would collide with other pieces of ice. Bits of ice were chipped away from the ice pan under the airplane. The morning of July 3, 1955, the whole pan of ice came apart and floated away. The airplane settled on the pontoons and stayed afloat. Now we had a lightweight piece of cargo that we could maneuver. On July 4, we reached Fort Churchill with the airplane on the pontoon rafts.

Fort Churchill had a large platform slipway to launch boats. We made arrangements with the harbormaster to run this slipway out in the water. Then, at high tide, we floated the plane on top of the platform and tied onto it. When the tide went out, the plane was sitting on this railroad-type platform. In order to get up over the abutment, we had to collapse the nose wheel and jack up the landing gear to elevate the airplane tail to clear the shore abutment. Once we got the airplane ashore, we disassembled it and loaded it on seven flat rail cars for transport to Wildwood, New Jersey.

The plan was to rebuild the airplane at Wildwood, but the rebuilding was too complicated for the United States Overseas Airlines' crew, so the plane was shipped from New Jersey to Brownsville, Texas. The PAN AM maintenance facility there finished the repair and eventually the DC-4 flew again.

Our job was finished when we got the airplane to Fort Churchill. Our compensation was to be 25% of the salvage value. We didn't have anything in writing. Everything had to be done so fast that the little Scotsman, Ralph Cox, who owned the airplane to begin with, ran up a lot of expenses on us. He charged us $500 per hour for dropping hay and sawdust. We had over $25,000 in hay and sawdust bills and then we had to pay $32,000 for helicopter usage. We also wrecked one Super Cub. By the time we added up all the expenses, there wasn't much left. I got good wages out of it, but considering the risks I took, it was hardly worth it. There were times I would have liked to be back on the mainland at Fort Churchill.

The project required a lot of imagination, vision and energy. We had to make do with what we had. We couldn't do it in accordance with Federal Air Regulation (FAR) or anything like that. Once you have a project moving, you must make it go or else you are going to fail. I was much relieved to be back on the mainland with the DC-4. My adrenaline glands were all hyped up as I was already planning our next adventure.

This salvage operation was written up in Life magazine, June 27* and July 18,† 1955, and in Calvalier magazine.‡ These stories include actual photographs of the mission.

Family Travels Alaska Highway

It was now July 1955. Ruth and the girls had not seen me for over six months and some of the stories in the Anchorage media regarding the Hudson Bay salvage operation were pretty wild. Ruth decided to load the family into our little Hillman Minx station wagon and drive the Alaska Highway—4,070 miles to Ankeny, Iowa, where my folks lived. Ruth had four flat tires en route, as well as numerous bouts of an overheated radiator, but the little car made it all the way before collapsing in the driveway in Iowa. The car was so small and so packed that two girls had to lay prone on top of a mattress in the back of the car while the third girl sat in the front seat with Ruth. The girls rotated taking turns in the front seat. In those days, if you got 15,000 miles out of one of those throw-away English engines, you were lucky.

I called Ruth after getting the DC-4 off the ice. I planned to work my way to Ankeny after a little prospecting around Canada's Great Slave Lake. We had one surviving Cub we hadn't crashed during the ice floe operation. In early July, Heacock and I took off for Great Slave Lake. We looked at a few uranium properties, but at this time, there were restrictions against Americans staking mining claims in Canada.

---

* Life, June 27, 1955, pages 61-62, The Sawdust Airdrop on Hudson Bay, https://books. google.com/books?id=qlYEAAAAMBAJ&pg=PA61.

† Life, July 18, 1955, pages 34-35, https://books.google.com/ books?id=11YEAAAAMBAJ&pg=PA34.

‡ Cavalier, March 1958, pages 36-41, 87-92. "The Great Ice Floe Gamble" by George Scullin.

We took off for La Pas, Manitoba, Canada, and then Winnipeg, Manitoba. Heacock was flying and I was navigating from the back seat. As we approached the small village of La Pas, the weather was down to treetops with rain and fog. We couldn't turn around to go back. This was wild wilderness country with no roads. I navigated okay to La Pas, but the airport sat on a little knoll that was covered by the fog. Strangely, we couldn't get high enough to land. We found a little country road and, as we were landing, the right wing caught a road sign and we ground looped into the ditch, damaging the Cub, moving the front spar back, and bending the fuselage. We patched it up a little bit and hunkered down for the night. The next day we took off from the road heading for Winnipeg. We left the Cub at a repair shop to be rebuilt. It flew kind of sideways after the crash.

Heacock and I split up in Winnipeg. Heacock went his way and I went to Ankeny where I tried to make it up to the family for being gone so long. I suppose in the back of my mind, I was planning my next adventure. The Iowa stay was short—about four months. We traded the Hillman for a red Ford station wagon in preparation for traveling westward. Then we drove to Seattle where we rented a furnished home.

I took off again on August 4, 1955 to pick up N1302N, the plane we had resurrected from Columbus. We had a contract to fly the military's Commercial Air Movements (CAMs). We tramped all over the U.S. in and out of different military bases. The military wanted to move troops at night so they wouldn't lose any working days. It was a tough way to make a living. Fly all night, the next morning check into a hotel, get a little sleep and be ready for the next night's flight. We lived out of our suitcases.

On September 23, 1955, since I had demonstrated a lot of "I can do that" attitude on the ice floe project, United States Overseas Airlines asked me to come to work on their DC-4 flying CAMs and contracts. We made trips across the North Atlantic all the way to Casablanca and back. We also criss-crossed the United States and made trips across the Pacific to Tokyo. It was a replay of the kind of flying I had done for the Army Air Force back in the forties. The only difference was we had a four-man crew in the United States Overseas Airlines.

We never got off the ship other than to refuel or do maintenance. While two pilots flew, the other two pilots were in crew bunks resting. Talk about jet lag. Over time, this kind of operation will really upset your system. The contract with the military ended November 30, 1955, as somebody else was low bidder and got the contract for military flying.

The military usually made awards to the lowest bidder, everything else being equal. I went back to Seattle for a few weeks and introduced myself to my family again. 1955 was a fast and furious year. I think I ran on adrenaline the whole year. I helped pull off some fantastic salvage jobs, but here I was thirty-three years old and living by my wits, nothing was secure. I felt like the Army aviator I was back in the forties.

Chapter 12   Arctic DEW Line

January 1956, I once again left Seattle to crew Air Cargo Express's "Kenai Trader," N1302N, C-46 flying CAMs for the military. This continued until April when we secured a sub-contract with Maritime Central to fly the Distant Early Warning (DEW) Line. The U.S. Military was building a large number of radar sites across Alaska and Canada. The Canadian Air Carrier (CAC) won the bid on the contracts, but didn't know how to fly the bush with a big transport, so CAC awarded sub-contracts to Americans who had airplanes and the expertise in the Arctic to use the planes. Miller and I took N1302N on this mission. We operated mostly out of Frobisher Bay to fly to the DEW sites. Every three or four days we would schedule a trip down to Mont-Joli, which was Maritime Central's main office and a staging area for many of the DEW Line materials.

Duncan Miller and I planned our strategy well before leaving. We took heaters, a good aircraft mechanic, Swede Axelson, a big box full of C-46 parts and six cases of whiskey. When we went to Mont-Joli and Frobisher, we met with Maritime Central's mechanics, loaders and gas people. The word spread that when you see airplane N1302N land, come immediately and give service—after which we generously handed out whiskey to all the help. They treated us like kings. Any time we landed, they dropped what they were doing and gave us immediate service. They would have taken a wheel off their own airplane if we needed it. They gave us the best loads. As a result of all this service, we outflew everybody by hundreds of hours. In fact, for the month of May, we logged over 330 hours with one ship—eleven hours per day—using two crewmembers. That was unheard of. Miller and I would fly three days in a row without sleeping. After one of these three-day binges, we started back to Mont-Joli for some R&R. Miller was exhausted, so I told him, "Curl up in the corner and go to sleep. I'll fly." He did, and sometime later I became wide awake when empty barrels were rolling and popping in the cargo area due to the changing air pressure. We were in a deadman's spiral. The airspeed was pegged, the wind was screaming around the windshield, the altimeter was unwinding and the horizon indicator was on the vertical.

I quickly recovered my senses and for the rest of the trip was wide awake. In fact, even now, when I get sleepy in an airplane, all I have to do is think back to that memory and I'm wide awake. How close we came to the ground I do not know, but many a crash I'm sure has been caused by the same circumstances. There is a good reason for the FAA to limit flying to eight hours and then have twenty-four hours of rest. But on this project, nobody had jurisdiction over us, so greed took over. We were paid by the ton/mile delivered and we planned on making a bunch of money.

Another trip from Frobisher Bay on the Arctic Ocean north to one of the DEW sites convinced me that somebody up there may be looking out for me. We were an hour and a half into our flight and should have been close to our site. We were IFR at eleven thousand feet and receiving no beacon signal yet. I added another half hour to the flight, but still no beacon. We decided we must have crossed our site and should now be over water in Baffin Bay. Not wanting to take a load back to Frobisher without pay, we started a slow let down. At nine thousand feet, rocks started passing right under the belly of the airplane. My God! I rammed full power on and climbed back to eleven thousand feet for another half hour. We started another let down, this time we were over water as we broke out of the clouds at about seven thousand feet. We visually turned around to locate our site so we could land and unload. We found out later that the reason for the beacon not being on was that it was interfering with the site's radio, so they had turned it off. I gave them a lecture as to how important it was to leave the beacon on.

What happened was, we had run into unforecasted strong headwinds and, being IFR, we did not know our ground speed. The mountains we just about struck were called the Cumberland Highlands, a mountain range in the Canadian Arctic near Baffin Island, Nunavut, Canada. Not many pilots get a break in the clouds to avoid a rock contact in a letdown. Navigation in this area is tough, variation was up to 65 degrees West. We had set up three gyros on the ground at Frobisher Bay and tract out on them. We compared our tract with Frobisher's radar for course and speed for about seventy-five miles. Then we were Dead Reckoning (DR) or visual until we picked up a low-powered beacon at the site—if they had turned it on.

We were one of the first ships into Site #42 on the DEW Line. They had taken apart a D-6 bulldozer. We hauled it to the site in pieces. We landed in a fjord on the sea ice and they skidded the parts down planks onto the ice where they re-assembled it. It took three trips to get the D-6 delivered. They drove it ashore and started building the site including another airstrip. We had many such trips and some were quite hairy. With pilot skill and a little luck, we survived the DEW Line flying. By the middle of June 1956, it was getting too soft for ice landings and our contract was finished. We took the ship back to Seattle for maintenance and to get reacquainted with the family.

While Miller and I were flying the Arctic DEW Line contract, the Civil Aeronautics Board was conducting hearings in Washington D.C. regarding the revocation of our operating certificate. After lengthy hearings the operating certificate was officially revoked and a receiver was appointed to handle the disposition of assets. Air Cargo Express was placed into receivership on June 17, 1955. The receiver, Samuel Steiner, determined that there was no path to rehabilitating the airline as no assets existed and the liabilities amounted to $60,000.

After we lost the "Kenai Trader," N1302N, in the creditor's lawsuit, it was sold to Cordova Airlines in 1956. Cordova Airlines flew it for a while and then in 1957, sold it to Reeve Aleutian Airways. Reeve pilots were taking off from Driftwood Bay, Unalaska, Alaska, with a cargo load of cement when the load shifted and the airplane crashed. The co-pilot swam to shore, but the pilot drowned. That was the last flight for N1302N. It saddened me, as we had not only salvaged it from Columbus, Georgia, but I had spent a lot of time in its cockpit on the Canadian DEW Line, Alaska DEW Line and other places. The "Kenai Trader" looked out for me and kept me alive more than once.

Back to Alaska

After completing the six-month DEW Line contract, Miller and I headed back to Washington State. We had a wrecked C-46 sitting in Seattle that had crashed at Annette Island, Alaska. It was dropped a second time by a crane operator in Seattle. We also had a large 40' x 80' unassembled Quonset building, so we decided if that building was assembled, we could rebuild the C-46.

I took on the project of assembling the Quonset building. Miller and Fitch were to help, but when I needed them, they were usually busy doing something else. I put in the footings, got the bows all bolted together. Then the time came to start standing them up. I was using a forklift with a pallet and stepladder attached to get the height needed. I was doing pretty good by myself and had about six bows standing when one of the infamous Seattle rain squalls came through with accompanying strong winds. I was up on the ladder attaching braces when I felt the structure shaking and then start to collapse. I jumped from twenty feet in the air as the steel clattered down on top of me. Miller and Fitch heard the noise and came running to my aid. I checked into the emergency room. Besides bruises, I had two broken ribs. Since it was a non-revenue project, I told Fitch and Miller where they could put the building. I was going back to Alaska. Several years later, we did rebuild this airplane but it was done inside an air bubble tent.

We secured a contract flying for the Morrison-Knudsen Co. (MK) in Alaska. MK was building White Alice installations and DEW Line radar sites. I loaded Ruth and the family aboard one of our planes to fly back to our home in Alaska. Heacock stayed in Seattle. This time my co-pilot was Duncan Miller and the other crewmembers were Walt Keith and Jim Osborne. No more of this three-day flying without rest as we were back under the jurisdiction of the FAA. Ralph Schletch was our mechanic and general manager. Flying was tame and routine as compared to flying in Canada. Our reputation to deliver the goods was a legend by now.

Chapter 13 Salvage Job at Cape Lisburne

During late summer of 1956, the C-46 owned by Alaska Airlines, N1244N, crash landed and ended up in the ditch off the runway at Cape Lisburne. The right landing gear was knocked out from under it. My business partners, Miller, Fitch, Pierce and I decided we should buy it so we could own and operate another airplane. Since the name of the plane was *Barter Island*, we called the partnership the Barter Island Co. I excluded Heacock because he was greedy during the ice floe project and took the lion's share from the USO settlement and only paid me wages. I was the driving force in getting the DC-4 off the ice and I took the most risk. I should have had an even split. Heacock wouldn't agree to it, so I said, "I don't get mad, I get even." When he asked for a piece of the action in Barter Island Co., I said, "No. Remember the ice floe?"

We bought the plane with a bid for $27,000. Fitch and Axelson traveled to Cape Lisburne to start the rebuild operation while I continued to fly the MK contract. A lot of MK trips were to Cape Lisburne so I was able to haul aircraft parts to them. On one of those trips, it was foggy with a strong

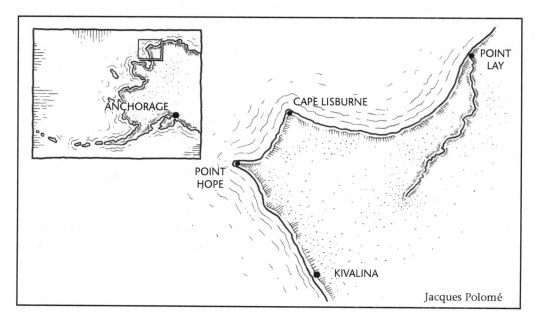

Jacques Polomé

crosswind of about thirty-five knots. Those conditions were probably the same conditions that caused *Barter Island* to crash the first time—strong cross winds. I had some parts Fitch and Axelson needed for the rebuild so I was very anxious to get in to Cape Lisburne. I made two attempts. On the last attempt, I had my wheels on the runway, but when I decreased power on the upwind engine, the airplane started to turn into the wind. I had to finally give it up and carry the load back to Anchorage. Fitch and Axelson were watching those landing attempts from the ground. I think I received a telepathic message from Fitch, as he said to Axelson, "I hope he doesn't try to land again, or we'll have two planes to rebuild." The C-46 has a crosswind landing limitation and we had found it.

When the *Barter Island* landed, the nose bent up and the belly flattened. One of the problems, after it finished gyrating around, was that the plane ended up with fourteen feet of wing sticking out onto the runway. The Air Force, which was based there, sent firemen out and they chopped off the wing that was blocking the runway. There wasn't anything wrong with the wing. It could have been unbolted instead of being chopped off. The firemen were not thinking like airmen.

The main problem was how to get a replacement C-46 wing to Cape Lisburne. I contacted Bobby Sholton, a C-82 Boxcar owner, and made a deal with him to haul a wing to Cape Lisburne from Anchorage. By putting the wing on a diagonal inside the belly of the plane, we were able to get in all but thirteen feet, which was still hanging out the rear end of the C-82. The FAA was watching when I was loading the wing and they wanted to know what I was doing.

They asked, "Who are you working for?"

I said, "Well, I am just helping to load this wing."

They wanted to know who owned the wing.

"Well," I said, "I don't know."

They finally reached Sholton and told him if he took off with this wing in the back of the C-82 Boxcar, the plane was going to crash and burn, and if it didn't, they were going to take his license. Sholton was scared. He told me he couldn't do it. I said I would have to do something else then.

Through friends at MK and the Air Force, we contracted a trip to Cape Lisburne to pick up some heavy equipment for MK the next day. Since the Air Force C-124 would be going up empty, I could use the space. I then unloaded the wing from the Boxcar onto a stoneboat, hooked it up to a dump truck and drug it down International Airport Road to Tudor, turned on Boniface and hauled it to Elmendorf AFB. I called ahead and they opened the doors on a C-124. We winched it aboard. At that time, you could hire a military airplane to move outside cargo if no one else could do it. We flew the wing to Cape Lisburne.

This wing presented a bit of a problem because it was a "D" wing and we were trying to put it on an "F" C-46. We had two different sizes of aileron control cables to match up: a quarter inch and three-sixteenth inch. The only way that could be accomplished was to put the two cables together and clamp them. We clamped the aileron controls together and bolted the wing onto the fuselage, and covered the nose up with canvas, tin, Duct Tape and anything else we could find so the wind wouldn't whistle through.

Since the right landing gear had broken off, we had to make repairs to the spar. We found some angle iron that was actually from some iron cots that had been thrown in the dump. We bolted the angle iron on the spars to hold them together.

People were betting that we would never take off. Well, we fooled them. We did take off. It was the day before Thanksgiving. The crew consisted of myself, Roger McKenzie and Swede Axelson. Fitch had to go back to Seattle on business, so McKenzie acted as my co-pilot. It was getting cold and dark in the Arctic. Working conditions were miserable and a strong wind was blowing, lowering the chill factor considerably. We worked with flashlights stuck in our parka coats or in our mouths. We finally took off and flew south to Nome. We only had a few hundred gallons of fuel on board, so we stopped to fuel up. We actually aborted the first take off after the engine quit—probably from contaminated fuel. The second take off was okay, but rough.

We took off again from Nome in the dark. By the time we crossed over Farwell, two hundred miles west of Anchorage, we were running out of gas in our center tank. I tried to select a new fuel source. The C-46 has a control cable on the side to control the fuel selectors. The wreck had damaged the cable drum and I couldn't find another source of fuel.

When landing in Anchorage, we came in on empty tanks. I called air traffic control as soon as I could get ahold of them and told them I was out of fuel and I needed to land as soon as possible. The weather was awful that night. As I came across the Susitna Flats, turbulence was bad. In fact, they had abandoned Merrill Tower because of the wind gusts so we headed to Anchorage International Airport. In my mind, I could see this scrap iron we had bolted to the front spar. I could see those stove bolts working loose and I hoped and prayed they wouldn't shear off. I wondered what I had done to myself now. The only thing I could do was to slow down to eighty-five miles per hour—just enough to stay in the air and wallow along.

I made it in safely and landed in spite of the airplane having no brakes. We taxied up to the tower at International Airport. As I parked under the tower, the right engine quit. It was completely out of fuel. Remarkably, the left engine was still running. It was Thanksgiving Eve. I went home that night, grateful that I had once again survived.

The next day, I had Thanksgiving dinner with my family, which was a nice respite. The pleasant interlude was short-lived, however. After Thanksgiving dinner, I filled the C-46 full of fuel and took off for Everett, Washington. The right engine had a bad shake all the way down the coast but we landed successfully. Months later we learned that one of the prop blades was unbalanced by more than one pound. The prop shop admitted to making a mistake. We had a contract with Alaska Airlines to rebuild the C-46. The airplane later came back to Alaska and Wien Airlines in Fairbanks flew it.

The C-46 airplane, N1244N, had quite a history. The plane was a large cargo or passenger airplane with two engines that could carry almost the same load as a DC-4. It was one of the most efficient, early planes in Alaska. The C-46 was built by Curtis as an assault transport plane, but it was first proposed to be used by the airlines. The plane was designed with a tricycle landing gear. Then the military decided they wanted to use it as an assault transport. They put a tail wheel on it and took the nose wheel off. The C-46 was now a very efficient load-packing airplane. It was built very strong and was a good airplane for what it was used for. The C-46 came into fame by flying the Hump into China because of its altitude capabilities. The plane could go up to 21,000 feet if it wasn't too hot outside. I never flew one at that high altitude, but came very close.

I have always been a shaker and a doer and it seems like I always end up doing the shaking. My best advice is be careful and calculate your odds. Don't keep your name on the "Damn Fool Seniority List" any longer than you have to because sooner or later, you might get called to meet your Maker.

Chapter 14   New Start

The winter of 1956 was a cold one. I didn't have any regular employment. The MK contract ended in mid-December. We flew the ship back to Seattle where it was seized by a group of old creditors from ATA. An attorney named Fred Paul, Jr. had gathered some of the old creditors together and brought suit against ATA. The end result was that we lost the airplane we had resurrected from Columbus, Georgia, N1302N, worth $125,000.

Discouraged, I went back to Alaska. I had put forth a lot of effort and failed. Ruth had grown a bumper potato crop that year, so we ate potatoes and moose meat all winter. On January 27, 1957, a C-124 Globemaster took off from Elmendorf Air Force Base one night during an ice storm. Right after takeoff, the plane lost two engines and had to turn back to Elmendorf. Although the pilot was able to turn the plane around to head back, the plane had lost too much altitude and crash landed on the ice pack in Cook Inlet several miles from the Elmendorf runway. It stayed afloat until the plane was beached with the help of helicopters and tow ropes at the end of Fourth Avenue in Anchorage. The Air Force salvaged a few easy things, like wings, flaps, ailerons, cockpit seats and engines, and then asked for civilian bid salvage of the ship. R.J. Stevenson won the bid and disassembled the plane in Bootleggers Cove. He then hauled it to Merrill Field. I tried to figure out how I could make some money from this project. I figured I would watch the salvage yard and when the stuff the Air Force had taken off appeared, I would buy it and then sell it back to Stevenson for a profit.

Sure enough, I bought all the salvage they had taken off except the engines. Of course, Stevenson needed my parts as he announced plans to have the first C-124 civilian transport. We made a deal for $10,000. Stevenson could never come up with the cash, so I kept all the salvaged parts. That was how a pair of C-124 wings ended up on our homestead.

Fred Klouda and Huey Younkins, good friends of mine, were helping Stevenson with the salvage operation. Stevenson went belly up and the whole C-124 project ended up as scrap aluminum, as he couldn't pay the freight bill to Foss Barge after it was towed to Renton, Washington. I kept thinking somewhere, someday, somebody will need those wings and the price will go up. They don't make C-124 wings anymore. Cliff Everets called me from Fairbanks wanting to buy them. He had heard they were C-46 wings. But since they were C-124 wings, he didn't need them. The wings eventually found new homes; one went to the aviation school and the other was melted down.

During the winter of 1957, I met Col. Alex Elmore. The Air National Guard was getting out of the F-86 Sabre Jet business and into C-47s for the Alaska mission. He needed some good, experienced transport pilots. He agreed to hire me as a Captain. This was something I really wanted to do and I was excited about this new opportunity.

He took me for a check ride in a C-47. I also added some T-33 sub-sonic jet training flight time with Col. Elmore. All was well. I went out to Elmendorf to take my physical. He sent my paperwork into Air Force Headquarters (AFHQ). In about a week, the disappointing news came back. I was no longer eligible to be hired since the Reserve Officer Personnel Act of 1954 (ROPA) had passed me over twice for a promotion because of inactivity in the reserves. I was being discharged. I protested to our delegate to Congress, Bob Bartlett, and to the Air Force. Despite all my aviation experience, rules were rules. They wouldn't change the rules for me. Only an act of Congress could make the changes. So, I was shot down in flames. Col. Elmore couldn't hire me although I was certainly over-qualified otherwise. We remained good friends.

Through the Rescue Cordination Center (RCC) and talking to Alaska Natives, I had learned of a World War II C-54 crash around Iliamna, Alaska. In April 1957, I spent time in the area trying to find it. When I started talking to the Natives, they were very vague. They would say, "I think my cousin Joe knows about it," and when I found Joe, it was somebody else who knew about it. It was like a turning wheel after a while; what goes around comes around. I was chasing my own rumors. After a couple of weeks flying, searching and talking, I decided that airplane must have been removed years ago. It supposedly was intact, but I never actually located a trace of it, not even a slide mark in the tundra.

On April 13, 1957, I went to Fairbanks looking for work. Bob Rice, the chief pilot of Interior Airways, gave me a check ride and a route check. He wanted to hire me, but his boss, Jim McGoffin, was trying to save some money so he wouldn't hire me. I came back to Anchorage.

Bob Sholton wanted someone to help him fly a wrecked C-46 off Granite Mountain near Nome. We got her off the mountain and delivered her to Seattle for rebuild. After getting back from that trip, Cordova Airlines, Mud Hole Smith's company, won a contract with Morrison-Knudsen (MK), the same contract that Air Cargo Express had the year before. But now we had no airplane. I went to work for Mud Hole. Smitty was a bandit at heart. One day, after I'd put in my eight hours, he had another trip scheduled.

He said, "Mike, will you fly this extra trip? We won't log it, but I'll pay you extra."

Of course, he knew I would, as I was management oriented. His contract with MK ended the last of August, so I was free again, looking for work and living by my wits.

The pilots at Interior Airways had decided to join the Teamster Union to get more pay. Jim McGoffin, the owner, wouldn't budge, so they called a strike and shut down Interior Airways. Interior Airways had a contract with Federal Electric covering the Alaska DEW Line. McGoffin needed a pilot immediately so I joined him as a scab pilot. Many other pilots did the same. Paul Palmer was named operation officer and I, chief pilot. In a few days, we had the new pilots all trained and checked out and in accordance with CAA and all federal regulations. I am sure it was a better operation than the old one as we brought in many new pilots with experience and expertise.

This was going to be a job for at least one year, so I rented a house along the Chena River (Tumble Turd Creek) in Fairbanks. The family moved to Fairbanks. I even considered buying the house, but I didn't feel that secure even though I liked the location along the river. The Chena River had been known to overflow its banks during spring breakup. When Ruth moved up to Fairbanks with the girls, she rented out our Anchorage home.

One pilot, Bob Rice, was an ace—I had never known him to cancel a trip because of weather. He made Interior Airways a lot of money. He liked the bad weather because he could show the more cautious pilots how to do it—separate the men from the boys, so to speak.

Winter flying into Fairbanks was cold and dark, but despite that, we hardly ever missed an approach. I remember one approach at Barter Island. There was a heavy ice fog that night. Airport personnel had placed barrels in front of the runway. No lights—you just followed the barrels in and they would lead to the runway. Runway lights were turned up as high as they would go. I followed the barrels in while approaching the runway. As I was about ready to land, I said to my co-pilot, "I have lights on the left."

He said, "I don't have any lights on the right." That meant we were landing off the runway.

I advanced the power to do a go-around. This time, we had lights on both sides, but we could only see two lights at a time. We had to make sure the alignment was right before pulling power and landing. It was a hairy situation. I was trying to do all the things Bob Rice was famous for, including completing all his missions. This was one mission that nearly failed.

1957 was an interesting year. Two pilots named Casey and Morgan flew one of our DC-3s into a mountain at night and luckily survived. The airplane was completely destroyed. The only injuries to the pilots were some frostbite around the genitals as the crash had scared the piss out of Casey. We picked them up the next day.

Another young pilot we hired to replace the Teamster pilots was Neil Bergt. He was a low-time co-pilot, so we gave him his three bounces around the airport to check him out. He was a smart young kid, but he had a lot to learn. One day, Bergt decided to take one of Interior Airway's Cessna 180s at Barter Island to go polar bear hunting. He took the mechanic with him and they found a bear about twenty miles out. After landing the plane, they couldn't see the bear. Bergt decided the mechanic, who was also a pilot, should take off, spot the bear again so Bergt would know which way to walk. The wind was quite strong that day and the plane started drifting away. The mechanic was disoriented and lost. He finally got a radio turned on and Barter Island radar tracked him back to the airport. But Bergt was left out on the ice field alone all night. We received word of the situation right away. I was at Point Barrow at the time. Early the next morning, we put together a search operation to get Bergt off the ice.

Fortunately for Bergt, through the darkness he was able to see the rotating beacon on a Barter Island hangar. He had to skirt open leads in the ice as he traveled towards the beacon. He walked into Barter Island about the same time we came in from Point Barrow with the C-47 preparing a search mission to locate him. McGoffin was mad at Bergt and wanted me to take some sanctions against him. I said I thought he's had enough punishment already. That ended it. Bergt stayed with Interior Airways, which eventually became MarkAir with Bergt as its owner. It just goes to show "be kind to your co-pilot, as tomorrow he may own your airline."

One of my new pilots at Point Barrow was having a hard time delivering anything in a Cessna 180 to the smaller sites. So I rode with him to understand the problem. We made the first site, POW-I, okay, but on the take off for POW-II, he lost it. We climbed to about one hundred feet, then the airplane entered a deadman's spiral to the left. I looked over at him and noticed he had broken out in a cold sweat. I recognized his condition as vertigo. I took control of the airplane and completed the mission. When we returned to Barrow, I told him, "I'm going to save your life and put you on the C-46 as a co-pilot, so you can learn instrument flying." Of course, after sending him south for C-46 training, I had to crew his 180 for two weeks until I found a replacement pilot. It was good experience and, believe me, that low level, supposedly VFR flying, is tougher than the big ship IFR flying.

Winter in the Arctic is a gray milk bottle color—you can't tell the horizon from the ground. It is an IFR environment and unless you know how to fly instruments, you are not going to survive. The pilot was grateful for what I had done for him. Many years later, after he had become a Captain on Alaska Airlines 727 jets, he thanked me for saving his life.

The summers in Fairbanks were really great—long, warm days. One summer day, I took the family out to Fox, a mining area just north of town, for a picnic and some gold panning. My daughter dug some material out of the muddy river bank and was working it down to the heavy rocks in her gold pan. Without her seeing me, I dropped a couple of fingernail-sized gold nuggets into her pan. When she discovered them, she let out a scream that could be heard up and down the creek for half a mile. Other panners came running asking, "Where did you find these?" And, of course, she said, "I dug it out of that bank right there." The excitement lasted all day as everyone started digging in that area. I couldn't help but smile while sitting back on the bank and relaxing. No other gold nuggets were found. Much later, I told her that I had salted her pan that day. We had a good laugh over that.

The contract with Federal Electric ended July 1958 and I believe Wien Airlines was the low bidder. Meanwhile, the C-46 airplane, N1244N, the one we had resurrected from Cape Lisburne, was leased to Wien and was flying cargo. I got a chance to keep an eye on it and make sure they kept up maintenance and did not abuse it. After all, I was part owner of this famous airplane.

Interior Airways didn't have any work in Fairbanks for me so McGoffin gave me one of his C-46s to take to Anchorage to see what kind of work I could drum up. I secured a contract with Rabber-Keith to fly construction materials to Sparvon, a military radar site on the west side of the Alaska Range. I had Roger McKenzie as a co-pilot. He was rather timid and quiet in the cockpit. In the noisy cockpit of a C-46, you have to understand communications between the parties. So one day after take off, I reached over and cuffed him on the arm and said, "If you are ever going to be a fearless commander, you have to speak with a ring of authority. When I say 'gear up,' I want to see your thumb come up. When I say 'METO,' I want you to respond." From that day forward, he was a different co-pilot. Many years later, he became a plane commander for Log-Aire.

We moved a lot of freight that summer. We hired off-duty soldiers from Fort Richardson to load us and they did an excellent job. The Teamsters tried to force their high price on me, but I refused. Since we were such a small operator, they moved on to harass other small businessmen trying to make a living. Despite their threats, I refused to be intimidated. After all, I had been a scab pilot in Fairbanks when they tried to get Interior Airways to yield to them. The Teamsters put a lot of struggling companies out of business with their wage demands. Wien Airlines is a classic example.

If you could fly VFR through Merrill Pass to Sparvon, you could save about fifteen minutes of flight time on the other end by not having to make an instrument let down.

This particular day, while I was flying the C-46, it was about thirty-five-hundred-foot overcast, a little marginal, but forward visibility was good until I turned the corner in Merrill Pass. Ahead was a curtain of clouds and fog—my visibility was abruptly terminated. I realized there was not enough space for that one-eighty-degree turn at my thirty-five-hundred-foot altitude. I immediately applied full power and made a max climb up out of the pass to thirteen thousand feet. I was very uneasy until reaching that safe altitude. I had been through the pass many times and knew what headings to maintain. Other pilots have suffered the same fate, though they were not so lucky as the pass is littered with aluminum. After that experience, I decided that if the weather was marginal, I would take the extra fifteen minutes to be safe. It cost more money to run the trip, but safety is number one. We completed the flying contract by December, so I took the airplane back to Fairbanks. McGoffin was very pleased at how well we had done with that C-46.

Al Ghezzi, of Alaska Freight Lines, got the idea he would enter the airfreight business. He was moving a lot of freight by trailer/barge combinations. As far as I know, he may have been the original innovator of this method. He also tried unsuccessfully to drive a big-tire-tractor train to the North Slope. Like Heacock, he was a brain stormer, but needed lieutenants and a big company behind him to function well.

He leased a DC-4 from Flying Tigers and had it equipped with cabin fuel tanks for oil deliveries. I got the job as chief pilot. I hired a couple other pilots and we started flying fuel oil to Sparvon, Cape Yakataga and even freight trips to Shemya. We were a real operation, building business and securing and bidding on other contracts. While flying fuel oil to Cape Yakataga from Yakutat, I saw the future airline I wanted to work for. The CAA's Sabreliner Jet was parked there. Jack Jefford, Lee Burns and Dick Pastro, who worked for the CAA, were moose and bear hunting. They were using loaders and other equipment to skin and load this bounty. I said to myself, "that's the job I want." Here I was flying around the clock, twenty-four hours a day, delivering fuel oil to Cape Yakataga. When I got back to Anchorage, I filled out a Form 57 for employment,[*] but the government does not act quickly. They said, "you may hear from us later."

Meanwhile, I was trying to build business for Alaska Freight Lines, but Ghezzi was in financial trouble. He was not paying the fuel bill. On several flights, I would write a personal check for the fuel and collect later from the company when he had money, which wasn't often. His empire was falling down around him. When Peter and Paul both wanted their money on the same day, he could not pay them. After about three months, he threw in the towel and we returned the airplane to Burbank, California. I think he underestimated the costs of operating a DC-4, as some of the bids he entered were comparable to a surface fuel truck delivery, not air delivery.

---

[*]   Appendix 12.   Howard J. Hunt resume, April 2, 1959.

Chapter 15   Inlet Airlines

Paul Choquette of Homer, Alaska, operated a small air taxi named Cook Inlet Aviation. He had the idea to start a commuter air service to Seldovia with stops in Kenai and Soldotna. I was hired as the operations manager to set up the airline and get it rolling. I hired Slim Walters as chief pilot.

We had one pilot who needed to obtain a twin-engine seaplane rating for the amphibious Widgeon owned by Choquette. Walters acted as his instructor. He was doing pretty fair, so we arranged to bring a CAA inspector aboard for a rating check ride. On the first approach, he must have been nervous as he bounced off the surface of the water. He then applied power and bounced again and ended up in what is called an uncontrolled porpoise. Walters had to take the airplane controls away from him to save himself and the CAA inspector. Needless to say, he did not obtain a twin-engine seaplane rating that day. He was assigned to fly the Super Cub on floats as he could handle it with no problems. A few weeks later our Widgeon met its demise going through the mountain pass heading to Lake Iliamna. When the weather cleared, we found the airplane splattered against the mountainside. It was a total loss.

Choquette was making a deal on some old Lockheed 10s located in South America. I couldn't inspect them before he closed the deal. I plunged into the paperwork hassle that the CAA put us through—writing manuals, figuring out schedules and filing tariffs. While waiting for the Lockheed 10 deal to be finalized, we handled some Bureau of Indian Affairs (BIA) charters. When a Native from a remote village in Alaska needed to be transported to Anchorage for medical care, the BIA would charter our airline to medevac the patient.

We conducted a survey which concluded that if we could put the Lockheed 10s to work, there seemed to be potential business available. Choquette announced that he had the airplanes delivered to Portland, Oregon. Walters and I traveled to Portland to pick them up and fly them back for the Alaska operation. When we arrived in Portland, we found neat and clean airplanes, but the instruments were written in Spanish. There was no time record on any of the engines, components or airframe. Before we could operate these machines in common carriage, they had to meet CAA FAR standards. It was going to cost $25,000 per airplane to meet the standards. We tried to get Choquette to reject the airplanes or at least let us lease a machine that did qualify. Sandy Phillips had a Lockheed 10 in Anchorage that was ready to go. He would either lease it or sell it. Choquette was unable to get out of his bad deal on the South America planes. The creditors were pushing him, so the assets were sold. Choquette was undercapitalized for what he was trying to do.

Cordova Airlines bought the Inlet Airlines certificate and operated the routes with a Twin Beech. Bob Gruber bought the Cook Inlet Aviation shuttle out of Homer and operated the shuttle to Seldovia and Point Graham. Choquette had a good idea and would have succeeded had he learned more about the equipment before committing himself to an unworkable deal.

Just as I was packing up my stuff at Inlet Airlines, the FAA sent a wire, "Would I like to go to work in Fort Worth, Texas, as an air carrier operations inspector?" I was getting a little tired of this moving around all the time and living by my wits. No security, no family life—I was on the razor's edge all the time. I knew one thing—I didn't want to leave Alaska. I answered, "No. I wish to remain in Alaska." At this point, I even stooped so low as to ask Bob Reeve for a job. He reached in his wallet and offered me a twenty-dollar bill. I declined and said that I wasn't that hard up yet.

Chapter 16   CAA/FAA Flight Inspection Pilot

In November 1959, the Civil Aeronautics Administration (CAA)* asked me if I would like to go to work in Anchorage as a flight inspection pilot. I went to the Old Post Office Building to be interviewed by Jack Jefford and Charles Wayer. I accepted the job. They hired Slim Walters, Don Hood and Tom Wardleigh at the same time. It was probably the best job I had ever held. The work was easy and relaxing. I was looking forward to doing some of that hunting and fishing I had seen in Yakutat the year before while hauling fuel oil with Alaska Freight Lines' DC-4.

The CAA had a mission to commission, maintain, and flight check all navaids across the state of Alaska. This was also at a time when the four course ranges were being decommissioned and new VHF Omnidirectional Range/Tactical Aircraft Control (VORTAC) and Instrument Landing System (ILS) were being built. The job involved a lot of flying and since Walters and I had expertise in the industry, our opinions were respected. We had also flown DC-3s, and soon acted as instructor pilots to upgrade other pilots.

My reputation must have preceded me at the CAA. Shortly after I was hired, Regional Administrator, Al Hulen, received a letter from an anonymous person, who said, "Hiring Howard Hunt to work for the CAA is like hiring Jessie James to ride shotgun for Wells Fargo." In spite of this comment, I kept the job. I was always loyal to my employer and gave 110%. My performance was never questioned.

I had only been working for the CAA for a couple of weeks when I was on an administrative flight to Juneau with pilot Bill Hanson along with

---

*   A boom in airplane technology in the 1950s led to an alarming uptick of air traffic collisions due to increased, unregulated, air traffic volume. On May 21, 1958, Congress introduced the Federal Aviation Act, which did away with the Civil Aeronautics Administration (CAA) and established the Federal Aviation Agency (which later became the Federal Aviation Administration) (FAA). In addition, this Act granted full authority to the FAA to set aviation regulations which had been handled by the Civil Aeronautics Board (CAB).

On August 23, 1958, President Dwight D. Eisenhower, signed into law the Federal Aviation Act of 1958. The FAA now had sole responsibility to oversee and regulate safety in the airline industry and the use of American airspace by both civilian and military aircraft. This system of air navigation and air traffic control continues to this day.

Hulen, and his staff. As we climbed out of Anchorage towards Whittier, Hulen sent word to the cockpit asking why the "no smoking" light was still on. I replied, "I don't allow smoking on my airplane." After a few minutes, Hulen reached his arm through the night curtain and turned off the "no smoking" light stating, "This is not your airplane." I had run my bluff as far as I possibly could; he was the head of the CAA in Alaska and my boss.

I had taken up the crusade against smoking. Every chance I got, I would lecture pilots, or for that matter anybody who would listen, about the health hazards of smoking. A few days later, Johnny Johnson, from maintenance, brought me a black box to stand on, with the word "soap" emblazoned on the side of the box. Of course, now years later, it has been proven that smoking is a health hazard. It was difficult trying to sell that message in the 1960s.

During this time frame, I helped one of my daughters plan a school science fair project. The idea was to show that cigarette tar could cause cancer in mice. We procured some white mice for the experiment, a bottle of chloroform, cotton balls, a vacuum cleaner, a special filter, rubber bands, a book of matches and a pack of Lucky Strike cigarettes. We rigged the Filter Queen vacuum cleaner with a special filter rubber banded onto the end of the intake on the vacuum hose. We removed the cigarettes from the wrapper, rubber banded them together, and lit up the entire pack. We turned on the vacuum cleaner, held the cigarettes next to the filter, and within minutes accumulated a quantity of tar and nicotine onto the special filter.

Alaska Sport Fishing

When I first went to Alaska to join the Anchorage Flight Inspection District Office (FIDO) in December 1975, Captain Hunt was one of the first pilots I flew with. Alaska was new to me, and even though I was already type rated in both the Sabreliner and the DC-3, I had no knowledge of Alaska. Mike went out of his way to share his knowledge, expertise, stories, and pitfalls to avoid while flying within the great State of Alaska. Simply stated, Mike made me a better pilot. And I might add, he was one of the best pilots with whom I have ever flown. This is still true today after many years of flying with numerous pilots.

Mike and I flew many, many missions together, both in the DC-3 and the Sabreliner. All pilots have stories, but with Mike, he not only shared stories about flying, he had great stories about fishing in Alaska. I love to fish, so Mike and I immediately hit it off. We fished in Yakutat, King Salmon, and Cold Bay to name a few. It seemed that Mike, John Callahan, and I were a hard crew when the salmon were running.

Memory of Friend and Colleague, Tom Katri

The plan was to shave the backs of the mice so the cigarette tar could be applied directly to the skin. In order to shave their backs, we had to immobilize the mice. We soaked a small cotton ball with liquid chloroform and held it over the heads of the mice for them to breathe in. Putting the mice to sleep would have allowed us to shave their backs and apply the tar. The only trouble was, the mice did not survive the chloroform treatment. One sniff and they never woke up. Consequently, we were not able to spread the tar on the backs of the mice. I don't know what grade she received on the project, but we did prove that mice do not tolerate a large dose of chloroform. My non-smoking crusade continued throughout my lifetime.

The ship, N1244N, that we salvaged from Cape Lisburne, was now on a lease purchase to Arctic Pacific Airways. They were using it for charters and CAM movements. On a foggy night, October 29, 1960, the plane was taking off from Toledo, Ohio, on a charter flight with the Cal Poly Mustang football team onboard. The pilot lost control and crashed shortly after take off after one engine quit. Tragically, of the forty-eight passengers on board, twenty-two were killed when the plane crashed and burned. The Civil Aeronautics Board (CAB) investigation report concluded that the contributing factors to the crash were: overweight aircraft, poor weather conditions and partial loss of power in the left engine.

My name was posted in the cockpit as the registered owner. The lawsuits started piling up in unlawful death claims. I was scared. I said to myself, "I was looking for a job when I found this one, and I guess I'll be looking for another one." The CAA had a strict rule against conflict of interest, like not owning an interest in an aeronautical enterprise while working for the government. In order to meet the rules, I had sold my interest to Fitch for $1.00. Since the airplane was on a lease purchase contract, we had no control of its operations.

The lawsuits were substantial. My name was even mentioned in the national news media. I fully expected to be called on the carpet to explain, but nobody ever asked and I kept a low profile. The insurance company paid us $125,000 for the loss of N1244N which settled all of the lawsuits much to my relief.

Another airplane adventure

It was after this that I again became involved in an airplane trade deal while working for the government. Back in 1953, one of our C-46s, N79995, sustained major damage while landing at Annette Island. The plane had been piloted by Jim Sprick and Roger Grunert. The hydraulic system on the right landing gear failed. The decision was made to barge the airplane to Seattle for repairs, but while unloading it in Seattle, the crane operator dropped it, which did more damage than it sustained on its landing at Annette Island.

The plane languished in Seattle for years and eventually we rebuilt it. About 1960, Bob Reeve of Reeve Aleutian Airways dropped in and said,

"I'll buy it." I think he was feeling sorry for us and wanted to make it up to us somehow—feelings of guilt? I had already gone to work for the CAA, but Fitch and Miller finished the rebuild. As part of the deal, we accepted a Twin Beech as trade along with cash. Since the Twin Beech was located in Anchorage, I tried to sell it. I found no buyers. We decided to fly it to Seattle where the market was better.

I arranged for Bob Sholton to fly it to Seattle. He took off one cold December morning after inadequate ground heat, lost an engine and returned to Anchorage. I then managed to trade the Beech to an Air Force Major for a Howard* on floats and some cash. Then spring came and I sold the Howard to one of the owners of City Bank. It was a beautiful airplane. That transaction got us out of the airplane business. It was a relief to me as I didn't have time for all this moonlighting while working full time for the CAA.

The C-46, N79995, came back to Alaska and flew charters and contracts. It was a real load carrier, as during the rebuild, we had thrown out all the military hardware that had been built into it. Reeve Aleutian Airways operated it for a year or two, but they poked one of its wheels through the ice while landing at Nondalton, Alaska. Reeve finally managed to get it ashore for salvage.

Family Vacation

In the summer of 1961, I decided the family needed a vacation. We loaded into our little compact Ford Falcon and took off down the Alaska Highway. We visited Ruth's relatives in Preston, Maryland. She hadn't seen her mom and dad since leaving in 1945. Now Ruth had three teenage daughters. We made many stops along the way. We took in the Smithsonian, traveled across the southern United States to Disneyland, Knott's Berry Farm, Sea World, and then back to Alaska. We covered the 10,000 miles in thirty days and really had a great time. All during the trip, Ruth complained a little of hip pain, but living and traveling as we did, she just ignored it. We would check into a motel every other night to rest. We would drive all night to get to our next place of interest.

After we arrived home from this vacation in August 1961, I decided we needed a new and bigger house. I had been eyeing a hill to the northeast of our homestead house as a good building site. There were many logistical

---

*   Howard is a single engine, five-place, tail dragger airplane.

Benny Howard started designing and building aircraft in an old factory at Chicago Municipal Airport in 1922. He formed the Howard Aircraft Corporation in 1936. After producing a limited number of airplanes, the company ceased operations in 1944.

Due to the shortage of military aircraft at the beginning of WWII, most of the civilian-owned Howards were commandeered by the military. The Army and the Navy used them as officer transports and as air ambulances.

Howard aircraft are remembered for their roominess and comfort for passengers. They were a very durable, and sought-after plane. According to the FAA, approximately 107 Howards around the world are still airworthy.

Federal Aviation Administration Sabreliner 80, N89, parked at Anchorage International Airport, Anchorage, Alaska, circa 1973. The Sabreliner was equipped with new Automated Flight Inspection System (AFIS) that utilized modern positioning technology with automated flight inspection analysis which was highly efficient for inspecting navaids at airports across Alaska.

problems to overcome, but being the ramrod that I am, I soon had a concrete foundation built, complete with a bomb shelter.

Ruth's Illness

It was during this time frame that Ruth developed a lump on her hip. She went to see Dr. William "Bill" Ivy. He took a biopsy which showed cancer. She then went to Virginia Mason for a second opinion. The diagnosis was deadly bone cancer. It was a terminal disease with no known cure.

Despite Ruth's diagnosis, she and the girls worked with me all winter on the new house until Ruth became bedridden. All my family members are very hard workers. We were drawn closer together by the common desire to finish our new home. I became better acquainted with my daughters, which was a good feeling. I remember one day, I had them mixing cement for sidewalks around the new house. When I came back an hour later, the mixer was not turning and the concrete inside it was setting up. The girls had not emptied the mixer when the concrete was ready to pour into the forms. It took some elbow grease, and quick action to get the concrete into the forms, smoothed out, and the mixer washed out.

Spenard Utilities was installing a water well on top of a nearby hill on land that Vince Huebsch had donated. After hours, I would use their front-end loader and dozer to dig the foundation. I hired a carpenter to help with the framing and to get the house enclosed as winter was upon us and snow was on the ground. By December 1961, we had the house enclosed. I had a place to work all winter. It was tough going as I still worked for the CAA during the day and stayed up until 2 a.m. working on the house.

Of course, I did contract out some of the work, like electrical, plumbing and sheetrock. Ruth helped, but her mobility was getting limited. She never once complained. You would ask her how she felt, and she would say, "Oh, just fine." When I was painting the interior of the house, my mother came up from Iowa to help. She would work along side me until I was ready to quit for the night. She sure had the energy. She stayed about a month and then returned to Iowa to help Dad with the farm. Many CAA pilots and technicians came over and helped out too. They knew I had a dying wife and I wanted to move her into the new home as soon as possible. Around August 1962, the home was livable and we moved Ruth into the new house from the homestead house. We hired a nurse to take care of her needs during the day while I was working and the girls were in school. I would take care of her at night with help from the girls who prepared meals and helped administer her medication. It was a very sad situation to see somebody you love die a little bit every day.

Dr. Ivy's father, also a doctor, lived in Chicago and was experimenting with a drug named "Krebiozen." He agreed to do a clinical trial of the drug on Ruth. At first, the tumors shrank in size, but then grew again. Ruth's decline was rather rapid. She was diagnosed in August, 1961, became bedridden in August 1962, and then on October 4, 1962, two weeks shy of her thirty-eighth birthday, she passed away in our home. This was quite a traumatic event for the girls—especially Barbara and Diane. They were both quite depressed, so I decided the best thing to do was to move them out of their Alaska environment. The CAA had an airplane going to Oklahoma City for maintenance. I flew them as far as Cheyenne, Wyoming, and then put them on a train to my folks' farm in Collins, Iowa. Nancy stayed in Anchorage as she was in her senior year of high school.

Chapter 17   A New Life

Once again, it was a time for reflection. I had been running like a wild man, chasing the almighty dollar. I had three teenage daughters who were growing up and I didn't really know any of them. I'd hardly been home. I decided to change my lifestyle and enjoy life more—stop and smell the flowers, so to speak. My cardiologist said I am a "Type A" personality. I guess back in the fifties he would have called me a "Triple A." Here I was a forty-year-old widower with a family still to be raised.

I knew I didn't want to live as a single parent, so I looked around a bit. One beautiful lady who had recently become available was Carol Pierce. About eight years prior, when I was the project manager at City View Horizon, I had incorrectly hung her drapes. Throughout the years, Carol and Ruth had become friends. Carol's only child, a daughter, Dashelle, was the same age as my daughters. The girls were great friends. After Ruth passed away, as providence would have it, Carol and her husband divorced. I had a hard time dating her though. I think she thought I might be a little obnoxious, especially after a fight I had been in at a CAP party when I knocked a local bully on his ass.

Since she was selling real estate for a living, I decided to list a two-and a-half-acre piece of property I had on Jewel Lake. I listed the property at a very high price (too high to sell). I figured I would have an excuse to call her and maybe make a love connection. The only thing was, she sold the property after only a couple of days. I definitely had not planned on that. I didn't even want to sell the property. I just wanted to get better acquainted

Howard and Carol "Queenie" Hunt in the 1980s.

with her. We dated and had some fun times together. I bought a little Piper J-3 Cub on floats. We took it out on fishing trips. Queenie, my nickname for her, was an expert fisherwoman and she taught me how to catch and dress a trout.

I remember a moose hunting trip when we joined Fred and Pat Klouda on Kenai Lake. I took off with Klouda in the back seat of the little blue bird, the J-3 Cub. Klouda spotted a big bull late in the afternoon. We landed on a small lake and he shot it. By the time we field dressed the moose, it was dark and I had no lights on the Cub. We didn't bring overnight gear, so I decided to fly back to Kenai Lake that night. It was a dark night with some rain showers. It was difficult to navigate. Anyway, I eventually found Kenai Lake and was very happy to see a couple of bonfires on the beach that Carol and Pat had set for us. They knew we would have a problem landing. I set up a shallow approach with some power on, not even looking for the water, as it was impossible to judge height above the water. Klouda was very uneasy. As the J-3 kissed the water, thanks to the light of the bonfires, Klouda wrapped his arms around me from the back seat and gave me a hug. He said, "Good man, Mike." We thanked the ladies for their alertness. As we sat around the campfire that night, the northern lights came out with a display that I have never witnessed the likes of before. It was like Roman candles bursting overhead in a brilliant display of color. I will always remember that scene.

The next day we flew back looking for the moose. I had a hard time finding the exact spot where the moose was shot as we had taken off at night. I never got a look at the lake in reference to other terrain features. We finally located the moose. It took several trips to get that big moose out. I don't know whether Klouda ever shot a moose that big again.

The little J-3 Cub provided us with many fun trips—camping, hunting and fishing. Once I remember loading a moose that had been shot by my friend, F.O. Smith. The Cub was so overloaded, I was afraid it would set down backwards in the water as I pulled away from the shore. The lake was about six miles long, so I decided I would see if she could lift the load. We used about five miles of the lake before getting airborne. The really scary part of it was I ran out of forward stick. The stick was all the way to the firewall and I was leaning forward to move the center of gravity forward as we took off. We were on the verge of a tail stall all the way back to Kenai Lake. A tail stall would have been fatal. I made a power-on approach at Kenai Lake to avoid it. I had also just learned the load limit of the Cub.

One Cub fishing trip that I remember was to Judd Lake in early spring. Carol and I set up our fishing poles. We were fishing when another Cub landed and taxied over. It was the Alaska Department of Fish and Game. He wanted to see my fishing license which I displayed. He then asked to see Carol's license. What do you know, she had neglected to renew hers. It cost Carol her fishing pole and new left-handed reel as well as a $25 fine. That ruined the whole day. She never forgot the trooper's name—Schultz.

If you ever wanted to get Carol's attention, just say, "Do you know a guy named Schultz?"

By the winter of 1963, I decided she was the one for me. We made some secret plans to get married. After the office Christmas party, we invited F.O. Smith and his wife Millie to go to dinner with us. I announced that we had made a little business deal and wanted to celebrate by taking them to dinner at the Rabbit Hutch Restaurant. I drove by it and passed several other restaurants along the Seward Highway. I finally announced we were taking them to Seward for dinner. Several hours later we arrived in Seward. I stopped in front of a seafood joint and said, "Wait in the car. I'll see if they can handle us." Actually, I was calling to get directions to the magistrate's house. I came back to the car and said, "I'm sorry, but there's a private party going on in there and they can't handle us. There is another eating place on the other side of town."

I drove to the magistrate's house. F.O. demanded to know why I was stopping there. He was hungry and wanted to eat. I responded by saying a friend, Wyman Owens, lived there and I wanted to take him to dinner with us. I went into the magistrate's house and made the final arrangements to get married. I then went back to the car and said, "Wyman's not quite ready. He's in the shower, but come on in, we'll have a drink while he's getting ready."

F.O. and Millie were getting angry now at my ineptness in this whole situation. They had no choice but to go into the house. As we stepped into the magistrate's home, I asked them, would they please be the best man and woman at our wedding? F.O. made so much noise, I was afraid the magistrate would arrest him for disturbing the peace. He finally settled down and we were married. It was now too late to eat, so we drove back to Sunrise Motel on the Kenai for a snack and lodging. That probably was the biggest finesse you could pull on two people. Queenie was part of the plot from the start.

The next day, December 24, 1963, we drove back to Anchorage. The highway was glassy ice so we let half the air out of the tires to stay on the road. We also had a slight bump with a moose on the roadway, but it was nothing serious. The only disappointed people were daughters, Dashelle and Nancy, who would have wanted to be included in the wedding party. I still smile when I think about how we pulled it off.

1964 Alaska Earthquake

The Big Alaska earthquake occurred March 27, 1964, at 5:30 p.m. I had just landed and refueled the J-3 Cub at Lake Hood and was starting to drive away when all at once I could hardly keep the car on the road. The trees around the lake were whipping forty-five degrees every which way, back and forth. Mud and water were spurting up through cracks in the ice and the ice was wavering up and down. I noticed part of the control tower on top of the terminal building had collapsed. Emergency crews started working to get the tower employees out.

I drove home to check on Carol. She was busy picking up things from the cupboards that had shaken out onto the floor. Of course, all electricity and telephone services were out and emergency broadcasting was not yet established. Nobody knew the extent of damage or the welfare of friends and relatives. Our home was well built. Outside of some cracks around the fireplace, it survived unscathed. Later on, with our portable radio, we started getting reports from around Alaska. The damage was extensive with loss of life. A large section of Fourth Avenue in downtown Anchorage had collapsed as well as other major buildings. J.C. Penney's front wall had completely collapsed.

Anticipating an emergency role for the FAA, the next day I went in early to FAA headquarters to do what I could to help with the civil emergency. The FAA had that function, but our leaders were afraid to act. They simply wanted us to stand by. We flew out and restored a few navaids and communications, but with our fleet of airplanes, we could have done a whole lot more. We had the responsibility, but did not act, in my opinion. Most work was accomplished by individual effort and not organized through the FAA.

We had friends who lived in the Turnagain area of Anchorage which was completely destroyed. The next afternoon, we helped Tom Wardleigh, Dusty Sloan, Dave Evanson and families dig for their personal belongings from their destroyed homes. We hauled Evanson's personal belongings to our garage. Clara and Dave Evanson and family shared our home for several months until they got a new home built.

Later we bought the remains of Wardleigh's home and another house for $500. We moved them and joined the two together, erecting a duplex on the corner of Turpin Road and East Eighth Avenue. The walls and doors were no longer true, they were pushed out of shape when they fell into the earthquake slide area. It was a good investment of about $15,000, which paid for itself annually in rental income.

Reuniting the Family

During late spring of 1964, the FAA sent me to a refresher course in Oklahoma City. While there, I bought a new Chevrolet Chevelle car and drove it to Iowa to pick up Barbara and Diane from my folk's farm. Barbara and Diane were very ready to return to Alaska. School was out for the girls in Iowa. We then drove to Seattle where I had prearranged to meet Carol and Dashelle at a friends' home in Gig Harbor, Washington. We visited with our friends, and then departed for Prince Rupert to catch the ferry back to Alaska. It was a beautiful, panoramic trip along the Alaska coast which was awesome that time of the year.

The girls spent their time on deck watching boys. It was nice to be putting the family back together and try living together again. Nancy was away at college and was not along on this trip. We debarked the ferry at Haines and drove into Anchorage. It was a very memorable trip and one that I will always remember. I was happy and things were going our way.

Hunt taking a break while assembling a boat dock for the Big Lake cabin, circa 1970s.

I had a good job with security and time to enjoy life. In fact, I started playing as hard as I had worked. We enjoyed many good times at our Big Lake cabin—water skiing, fishing, swimming, and roasting hot dogs around the camp fire.

On March 22, 1965, Carol went into labor. I took her to Providence Hospital. I had planned on being in the delivery room, but her labor was extensive, so she asked me to go to Spenard to check the mail. That's when the drama happened—and I missed it. A very alert, professional nurse by the name of Phyllis Holliday noticed that the baby's heartbeat was very weak. She called the doctor and he immediately performed a Cesarean section. The baby was jammed in the birth canal with the umbilical cord wrapped around his neck. Our baby was under stress and unable to move through the canal. Fortunately, the doctor was able to deliver our son with no mishaps. I saw him in the nursery shortly after he was cleaned up. As I stared at him, one of the nuns came by and said, "Don't worry, he'll look different in a few days." His skin was totally red, his head came to a point, and I'm thinking—yeah, they told you not to have kids after forty. Well, the nun was right. In a few days, his head was round and he was a beautiful baby boy. Carol had given me a son—there is something special about a son after being a father to four daughters. We named him Howard Michael Hunt with the nickname of Mike.

The little blue bird, the J-3, was no longer big enough to carry all the equipment necessary for a small baby. We sold the blue bird and bought a

Cessna 180 on floats. We couldn't really afford it, but reasoned if we waited until we could, we would be too old to enjoy it—so we bought it. Other than that, we lived very frugally and saved our money and accumulated real estate whenever possible.

In the fall of 1965, Mike was six months old when we took him on a moose hunt. From the air, Carol had seen a big bull next to a lake. I landed and shot the moose. By the time I dressed out the moose, it was dark. We put up our tent and stayed the night. Early the next morning, the weather was down and Carol and Mike were still sleeping, so I decided I would run that load of moose meat to town and then come back and pick them up.

The ceiling and fog were low. In about twenty miles, I was forced to land on another lake for about four hours. After the weather lifted a bit, I made it into Anchorage. I then flew back to pick up Carol and Mike, but I couldn't find them. There are thousands of lakes out there, and they are all round in shape. Since I had left in bad weather, I didn't have a good picture of the lake in my mind. I was getting worried. Finally, late afternoon, after a two-and-a-half-hour search, I located them. Carol had used all her baby formula and was worried what she would do next. As we flew back to town, I thought of the flaws of my actions. Suppose I had crashed with that load of moose meat going into town, nobody would have known where they were. It was a dumb move and I never did that again. Many a person has been stranded when the pilot crashed en route back to base and no one knew where he left his passenger.

Chapter 18   Mother Goose Lake

Bill Stivers was one of my good friends, with whom I have shared many a campfire, ski trail, fishing hole and moose hunt. One of these trips was to Mother Goose Lake on the Alaska Peninsula, southwest of King Salmon. It was to be a moose and bear hunt.

We had been planning our hunt all year. After registering our bear hunting camp, we set out early on the morning of September 14 from Anchorage to Mother Goose Lake. Flying down the west shore of Cook Inlet, we crossed over to Iliamna Lake and on to King Salmon for refueling. We arrived at Mother Goose Lake about noon. We set up camp and decided to look for a moose. After a short walk along the south shore of Mother Goose Lake, we spotted a nice bull moose. Stivers decided to shoot the moose.

The next day we spent packing some of the moose to our camp. We were able to finish by dark and just as a storm was moving in. Before going to bed, we dragged the airplane up on the beach and secured it to the scrubby willows and cottonwood along the shore. About midnight, we were awakened by the howling wind with horizontal rain beating against our cabin. Our Cessna 180 was crunching and dancing a jig on the beach and was in imminent danger of pulling the ropes and being blown away. We decided the only way to hold the airplane against the gale force winds and ocean-like waves was to fill the floats with water. We used the float pump to fill the airplane floats. That maneuver securely anchored the plane to the shallow, sandy bottom of the lake. All night long the wind howled and horizontal rain seeped into the cabin through unexpected leaks in the roof and necessitated frequent dodging around inside the cabin to keep dry.

At the first light of day, Stivers was up making breakfast. The first words out of his mouth were, "Mike, the water is about six inches above the floats." Since the wind was still howling and large waves were crashing in, we figured that as we were anchored in a small cove, it was only the wind that had pushed the water up and that as soon as the storm passed, the lake would return to normal. We discovered how wrong we were later!

Since brown bear hunting was our mission, we decided to check our moose kill for bear signs. Carefully stalking up the mountain, we found the tracks of a giant bear who had eaten about half of the carcass. The bear was nowhere around. We decided to check again just before dark to try and catch him feeding on the carcass.

We went back to the lake and found the wind and lake still rising. Again, we reasoned that it was caused by the pushing effect of the wind. Later that evening, we returned to the moose carcass. During our absence, the bear had been there and cleaned up everything but the rack and hide—such luck! We walked back to our camp contemplating how to catch that bear.

During the night, the storm subsided. Instead of Stivers awakening me with the fresh smell of bacon and hotcakes, he said, "Mike, the water is only six inches below the fuselage." Shocked awake by his statement, I hit the floor. What kind of crazy place was this Mother Goose Lake, I wondered? Water was three feet above the floats and still rising like an ocean tide. Bear hunting no longer entered my thoughts—but how to save the airplane from destruction weighed heavy on my mind.

Since there was another party camped at the exit end of the lake, we decided to hike over and see if they had contact with the outside world. As we were now overdue on our hunt, we knew our wives would be pushing the panic button unless we could get word to them. The Flynn hunting party was not much better off than we were. They had flown in on wheels and, since the lake had risen, their beach landing strip was inundated with water. While there, we observed the King Salmon River running into Mother Goose Lake instead of out as the map indicated.

Flynn then filled us in on the fact that Painter Creek, which empties into the King Salmon River, was also running into Mother Goose Lake. So that was the answer to the rising lake—a big flood crest was moving down Painter Creek, causing the King Salmon River to flow backwards—a weird phenomenon that mother nature had directed against us.

The next morning, Monday, September 18, the lake was still rising and now was three inches above the airplane's cabin floor. In order to save the battery and other equipment, we waded chest deep into the cold lake water, salvaging all important equipment. By late afternoon, it appeared that we had reached the flood crest. The water level was just a few inches from getting the engine wet.

Necessity being the mother of invention, our attention turned to saving the airplane. We came up with lots of ideas—everything from Archimedes Principle to a hollow tree standpipe. Since the plan had to work with equipment we had on hand, it finally boiled down to a modified float pump. Most of the night we worked on the pump, which basically was a little plastic pump, the kind normally carried aboard aircraft, with a suction extension vent and cover to seal the float compartment hole. Parts were taken from the aircraft engine, my web belt and down cloth. We finally finished modifying the pump that night. The question was, would it work under water? In the morning, we would find out. The urgency of refloating the airplane before another storm came in was paramount as the giant waves would crush the airplane like so much tinfoil.

We nearly sank the Cessna in Mother Goose Lake. To save it, we jerry-rigged parts together to pump lake water from airplane floats.

Early the next morning, we went out to try our new pump invention. Several bugs were discovered in its workings and modifications were made to correct these deficiencies. We were working in three-and-a-half feet of water above the floats. As a float compartment was pumped out, it was necessary to quickly jerk the pump out and put the float cap on the hole before the float could again fill with water. This meant submerging up to your shoulders in the icy lake water. After about five hours of this cold work, we finally had to quit. We were so cold that the only thing that would move was our rattling teeth. We suffered mild shock from our long exposure in the frigid lake water.

Meanwhile, back in Anchorage, our wives had pushed the panic button. Since we were two days overdue on our hunt, they had contacted the FAA to check on us. The next morning, MacDonald and crew were flight checking in the King Salmon area. They diverted to Mother Goose Lake to check on our whereabouts. As soon as we saw the friendly DC-3 on emergency frequency of 121.5, we exchanged information. We asked them to contact our wives to let them know that we were okay. Meanwhile, we made some more modifications to our little pump and the next day would again try to refloat the plane.

The next morning, another storm struck and miraculously, the submerged aircraft rode out the storm. As the giant waves crashed against the fuselage, it sounded like a drum beating and vibrating. Every time we heard the noise, we felt a little pain as the next big wave might twist the airplane loose from its floats.

By Saturday morning, the storm had subsided and the lake water went down about six inches. We went to work once again on pumping out the compartments and refloating the airplane. First, we pumped one side and then the other. When a compartment was emptied, we would clamp the float cap on. The little homemade plastic pump was doing a tremendous job. After about three hours of hard pumping and swimming around in the icy lake water, the right float bobbed ever so slowly to the top. Then after some more pumping, up came the left float. The battle with nature and Mother Goose Lake was now won.

We soon readied the airplane for the flight home and broke camp. What was left of our moose, we loaded aboard and took off for King Salmon. After refueling, we headed for Anchorage, winding our way along Pile Bay through fog and rain, too low to turn around—the only way was straight ahead. I know Stivers was worried as we twisted our way through the Pile Bay Canyon, wing tips only a few hundred feet from the canyon walls. Visibility was down to one-eighth mile in rain and fog. Not knowing whether we could maintain visual, we had passed the point of no return. We had to continue.

Finally, we started breaking out into better weather. We knew we were just about home. Our families were very glad to see us since they had heard all kinds of conflicting stories about us. We, of course, were happy to be home in one piece and with the Cessna 180 float plane none the worse for wear. We were already plotting how we could overcome the obstacles of our next brown bear hunt at Mother Goose Lake.

Chapter 19   Reflections on Good Times

Sheep Hunting

A few years later, approximately 1969, I took Bill Stivers on a sheep hunt in the Alaska Range. We landed on Smith Lake which is a small lake about one hundred and eighty air miles northwest of Anchorage. The weather was rainy, typical for fall sheep hunting. The next day we took a full curl ram and packed it back to our camp. The following morning we took off in the rain and into strong downslope winds. This is one of those lakes you have to have a little altitude before starting out of the canyon. We didn't have enough altitude after takeoff, so I had to make a 180-degree downwind turn over rising terrain. We were just about to run out of altitude, airspeed and ideas all at the same time. The floats were just about to make contact with a rocky ridge as I traded a little airspeed for altitude. It was very close and I believe Stivers felt he would never make his FAA retirement if he kept flying with me. That probably was the last hunt I took him on.

Preparing to Climb Mt. McKinley

Also in 1969, I had started overnight cross-country skiing with Barney Seiler as a guide. I made a four-day trip from Girdwood onto Whiteout and Eagle Glacier and came back down on the Eklutna Glacier. Seiler was gathering a group together to climb Mt. McKinley, so I trained with these guys. As a practice climb, we took on Mt. Bona, 16,500 feet high, to get some experience before taking on Mt. McKinley at 20,360 feet. I enjoyed the activity. Some guys got mad at the mountain, some at one another, but I was just a team player and did whatever was necessary to complete the mission. At forty-seven years of age, I held up better at altitude than some of the younger men. It's how you manage your physical resources that count.

As we neared the summit of Mt. Bona, the guys wanted to unrope and streak to the summit for picture taking and retrieving the Japanese flag buried there. Seiler said, "No, let's probe the route first for a crevasse." Sure enough, just a few feet ahead was a large crevasse several hundred feet deep, hidden by a thin bridge of snow. The first guy to step there would have fallen to his death. Once we knew where it was located, we could jump it before proceeding to the summit. I was experiencing a lot of things in my playtime activities and enjoying them immensely.

Part of mountaineering training was rock climbing on the Seward Highway. As I hung out over the Seward Highway with a piton driven in a rock, I looked down and saw those little cars moving along on the highway. It dawned on me I was putting a lot of trust in that piton and rope. Queenie finally put her foot down and said, "Mike needs a father a lot more than you need to climb Mt. McKinley." I thought about that for a while and concluded that I had waited a long time to have a son, and everyone needs a father. It was good advice. One family had already grown up and left home. I didn't really get to know my daughters very well because I was always gone on some adventure trying to make a buck. Now I had a second chance to reform and enjoy my son. Mike was born to a mother and father who both had a second chance to enjoy the thrill

---

Hanagita Lake Mining Claim

Hunt had some gold mining claims in the Hanagita Lake/Copper River area. He usually flew up to the lake and climbed to his claims. This time, we planned to land on a sand bar in the river below his claims.

We landed on a river sandbar and started the steep climb to a large cabin on one of his claims. It was a hard climb. We saw many signs of bear scat. It was getting late and we were not sure if we would make it before dark. Hunt finally spotted a flag that was on the roof of the big cabin and we pressed on and made it.

On the way up, we had marked the trail by breaking small brush to guide us back down to the sandbar and plane.

We were there to do the annual assessment work required to retain ownership. I posed with a lifted shovel at a mine entrance. We moved some more material, and assessment work was completed. There were tunnel entrances to some of his claims. They were very dangerous to enter due to the old dynamite in some. Old dynamite is very unstable and almost anything can set it off.

Hunt wanted to check some more of his claims that were located up over a steep climb of loose shale. I stayed at the cabin and watched with glasses until he disappeared over the top of the hill. If he did not make it back, I was to go back to the plane and fly in for help. The marked trail would guide me back down.

He made it back okay. We stayed overnight and hiked back down to the plane the next day. We flew off of the sandbar with no problem.

I have some good reminders of the trip: a small, leather, nugget pouch and some small cups used to powder samples for testing.

Memory of Friend and Colleague, Z.W. "Ski" Kowalewski

of parenthood and the child development that follows. I retired to more sedate sports like cross-country skiing, downhill skiing, hunting, fishing and prospecting.

Silver Mining Claims on Nelson Mountain

Jack O'Neill, one of the partners in Air Transport Associates, had gold mining claims on Dan Creek and, at one time, owned the general store at McCarthy, Alaska. Every spring he would grubstake a man by the name of Jack Ohara. Years ago, Ohara staked some silver claims on Nelson Mountain.* Ohara died suddenly in Cordova about 1939.

The claims lay idle until about 1967 when I took a look at them. I had studied the geology of the area and had O'Neill's old correspondence with Ohara. So along with a friend, Bill Fike, I planned an expedition to Nelson Mountain. The nearest I could get was to land a float plane on Hanagita Lake† and walk eleven miles in, up one mountain, cross a valley floor, then up and over Nelson Mountain to the north side—a very rough trip. We hadn't progressed but a couple of miles when Fike wanted to call it off. He said, "Mike, let's turn around and go back."

I replied, "Bill, I have been planning this trip for years, and I'm not going to give up until our ten-day supply of food is gone, which we are carrying on our backs. I'll divide the food with you and you can go sit in the airplane for ten days. But I'm going on, with or without you."

Fike came along, but he was scared and overly cautious all the time. After beating our way through brush and sleeping under trees, we reached our destination. It was just like O'Neill had described—an old log cabin that bears had torn up. There were some mountainside diggings. We rehabilitated the cabin enough to stay in. Then I explored the old tunnels. Fike was afraid to rock climb, so he worked around the cabin. I liked what I saw and staked six claims before we started back to Hanagita Lake.

On the hike back to the plane, we ran into ground clouds and couldn't move because we couldn't see. Fike was worried sick and asked, "What are you going to do now, Mike? Are we lost?"

I replied, "Nothing, Bill. I'm going to sit and rest until the clouds lift so I can see again." We made it back to the airplane just fine and flew home. Frankly, I was surprised at the lack of courage that Fike displayed. Perhaps it was for the best as he certainly slowed me down.

The next year we went back and landed on the shores of the Chitna River. We built an airstrip and cut a trail to the Nelson Mountain cabin and the silver mining claims. We continued to add claims each year and finally ended up with twenty-eight claims. Some of the claims were ruled invalid by the Bureau of Land Management (BLM) because of Alaska Native Claims Settlement Act, referred to as the D-2, but ten claims were valid. I

---

*   Nelson Mountain is a 5,300-foot mountain located due east of Anchorage, north of Cordova between Chitina and McCarthy.

†   Hanagita Lake is located approximately eleven miles due south of Nelson Mountain.

did geophysical work on the claims and had a good showing of zinc and lead. I arranged for a Canadian mining engineer to look at them.

Fike died of a heart attack in 1978. In order to help settle his estate, I managed to sell the claims to Conoco Oil Co. for $25,000. Conoco did some drilling for the Natives, but nothing developed. The land is now owned by the Natives and has been designated with a historical marker and gravesite area. The old cabin remained there intact after we fixed it up and stocked it with supplies. I never had a chance to return and pick up my personal gear still in the cabin. My son, Mike, who was about thirteen years old also helped with the assessment work. He was a good rock climber and was a big help.

The Super Cub was the way we transported and airdropped gear and supplies to the cabin. I would slow down to about forty-five miles per hour and Mike would toss the stuff out the open door into the willows and alders that surrounded the old cabin. The boughs would break the impact of the fall; we lost very little gear.

One night the ground squirrels kept coming up through the holes in the floor keeping us awake. Mike decided to kill one and skin him out. He did, but he didn't enjoy it. It was best to enjoy their chirping. After all, we were only there two weeks out of the year. It was their home the rest of the time.

I enjoyed my trips to Nelson Mountain and trying to retrace the thoughts that must have gone through Ohara's mind fifty years earlier. He had packed in a complete assay lab to analyze the ore. He relied on horses and dogs as there were no airplanes or helicopters for airlifting back then. He had to have been one tough man to survive. One of his tunnels had eleven cases of dynamite stored in it.

Later I investigated some prospecting Ohara did on Standard Creek and Golconda Creek in the Wrangell-St. Elias National Reserve. I knew I had found his old quartz vein when I located a rusty pick, shovel and crow bar. The description matched a letter he had sent O'Neill at the store in McCarthy. I didn't find much gold, but it didn't matter as the area is part of the St. Elias Park and the land has been withdrawn from mineral locations, like so much other land.

Flight Inspection District Office House Party

Leroy MacDonald gave a Flight Inspection District Office (FIDO) party and invited all personnel. There was a little drinking going on. Everyone was having a good time. Stivers and I were testing our strength against each other by trying to pin one another to the floor. Stivers was getting the best of me as he had me bent over the hors d'oeuvres table. As he did so, one end of the table collapsed, dumping all the hors d'oeuvres on the floor. Stivers still had his death grip on me and proceeded to use me as a mop on the floor. The hostess, JoAnne, was pounding on his back yelling, "Go home, you son-of-bitches, go home!" It was a horrible mess and the last thing I remember was MacDonald burning some of his furniture in the fireplace as we left.

The next day, JoAnne called everybody but me and apologized for using such abusive language. It was a long time before we ever were invited back to MacDonald's house. Stivers reformed, but back in the 1970s, we managed to get into all kinds of mischief.

We also had some good Christmas parties together. While leaning over my secretary's desk, Stivers spilled a drink into her typewriter. Of course, it was against the rules to have a drink on government property. As far as I was concerned, there were two exceptions—Christmas and New Years.

Moose Hunting—One Too Many

One day I took off with Gene Stoltz for a little moose hunting on the Kenai. We flew around and spotted three bull moose standing together close to a lake. They were not visible after landing, so we climbed a little knoll to observe. After standing there for a while, Stoltz said, "I'll go down and see if I can find them." I told him I would stay on the little knoll so I could observe the action. Stoltz no sooner entered the brush at the bottom of the knoll when a shot rang out. Then he yelled, "There is one coming your way."

Sure enough, I stood up and shot a bull that was trotting towards me. Just after my shot, Stoltz shot again thinking his first moose was getting away. I shot because I thought Stoltz had missed his moose. He then yelled, "Don't shoot anymore, I've just killed another one."

I replied, "So have I." When we got through counting moose, we had three bulls, all within two hundred feet of one another and only two moose tags. We dressed them out and hurried to town with a load and promptly brought Carol's moose tag back for the third moose. This same thing has happened to more than one hunter. They shoot a moose, it goes down; immediately another one stands up in approximately the same place. The hunter, thinking the first moose is getting away because they missed the shot, takes a second shot and, of course, when the smoke clears, there are too many dead moose.

Pranks—Many Pranks

Carol smoked and one of her habits was to light up before driving away in her car. During the Cuban Missile Crisis, the FAA had asked us to place twenty gallons of gas in the trunk of the family car so we could quickly drive to Gulkana, approximately one hundred and ninety miles east-northeast of Anchorage, in case the Russians retaliated with a missile. After a few months, one of the cans developed a leak. You could smell gas fumes in the car. "Queenie," I said, "You're going to blow yourself up if you don't stop lighting up."

She didn't listen, so I went to a novelty store and bought a car bomb and wired it to her ignition. The next day, she lit up, started her car and the bomb went off. She bailed out and ran through deep snow, across the driveway before looking back to see what had happened to her car. I was watching from the dining room window. I almost fell on the floor laughing. When she came stomping back into the house, my mood quickly changed.

I pulled another prank on a flight inspection trip to Dawson, Yukon Territory, Canada. The crew and I went into a bar after dinner. The owner of the establishment, a beautiful woman, sat down at our table to visit with us. She then pulled out a mini cigar and started to smoke it. She was called away from the table for a few minutes. While she was gone, I loaded her cigar with an exploding probe. After a short while, she came back to the table and lit up again. This time her cigar blew, showering tobacco all over the room. She bolted from her chair and headed to the back room. I said to my crew, "Let's leave quickly. People have been killed in the Yukon for less than this."

The next day returned to Anchorage. Well, this little episode beat me back to town. FIDO Chief Husky wanted to know what had gone on in Dawson. I explained we were just having a little fun. She had complained to the DOT, and they, in turn, sent a wire to the FAA in Anchorage.

Another prank involved Dorothy Revel, the FIDO administrative assistant. Dorothy received a promotion and was relocated from the Anchorage International Airport hangar office to the Hill Building in downtown Anchorage. To celebrate the occasion, she put out a box of fine 1886 cigars and delicious treats for everyone to enjoy. I happened to be working in the Hill Building that day running mission control. The cigars were left unattended during the lunch hour so I loaded up a bunch of them with exploding charges. That afternoon, as the congratulators lit up, the cigars started exploding. Dorothy was very embarrassed as well as furious with me. She wanted me to apologize to everyone and buy a new

---

Trinity Lakes Cabin

I had a PA-12. Mike and I decided to fly to the Trinity Lakes area to overnight in a cabin. I was the pilot and Mike was in the back seat. We flew over the snow-covered lake. The snow looked like it was very deep. I made a pass on the surface without landing to test the snow conditions.

I was undecided to land and thought I would ask the old Alaskan what he thought. I yelled to Mike, "What do you think?"

He said, "Go ahead."

I pulled back the throttle. We settled into about one foot of light snow. We were stuck. We got out of the plane and talked over what to do. If I flew back to Campbell Lake and unloaded all of our gear, I could come back and make a takeoff with only Mike on board. We snowshoed a flat area for my takeoff. I got off okay and returned with a lightened plane to get Mike.

Memory of Friend and Colleague, Z.W. "Ski" Kowalewski

box of cigars. When I denied her request, she threw the remaining cigars away. Pranks of this nature would never work in today's world, but back in the 1970s, it was funny and marginally acceptable.

Kids Growing Up

By this time, the family was pretty well on its own. The girls had grown up and left home, and I hadn't really bonded with any of them. In the beginning, I was absent and now they were absent. Nancy had gone off to college in Oregon. Barbara put in one year at the University of Alaska, Fairbanks and then joined the Navy, taking Dashelle with her. Dashelle didn't stay long as she missed her mother terribly. The Navy sent her back home after a few months. Diane rebelled against all of the family and threatened to become a vagabond for a while, but she came back into the fold later on. Losing their mother at a critical time of their lives had a negative effect on my daughters. Carol was the best stepmother they could have had. My son, Mike, was an active five-year-old who kept Queenie and me busy.

Good Friends—Great Times

Reliable Fred Goff was one of my favorite technicians, always ready to work and do the job. Goff also shared my interest in fishing and hunting. The only time reliable Goff ever let me down was one day when we flew all the way to Juneau to flight check the Landing Distance Available (LDA). The only thing Goff remembered to bring along was his lunch, no navaid flight checking gear.

Ski Kowalewski, the Polish aviator, shared some hunting adventures with me. I remember taking Ski out on his very first moose hunt after he was transferred to Alaska from Oakland, California. He killed a moose on the backside of Mt. Susitna and needed some help. I received a message from the FAA that Ski needed some spark plugs delivered to a certain lake. The next morning, I took off in the rain and fog and a few hours later, I picked up Ski and his moose. The weather was so bad, Ski didn't think I would be able to find him, but I did.

My friend Emitt Soldin was always helping me to maintain and keep the Cessna 180 airworthy. Soldin was everyone's friend and was well known throughout Alaska. I made so many good friends while in the FAA, I could write a book about just that phase of my life—Tom Wardleigh, Slim Walters, Dick Pastro, Jack Wright, Dave Carr, Don Christenson, Jack Jefford, Charles Wayer, just to name a few.

The constant noise from airplane engines destroyed my hearing to the point that I could no longer pass the first class physical. So in 1980, at the age of fifty-eight, I accepted a medical retirement, thus ending twenty years of government service. I enjoyed every minute of it. I feel sorry for people who go through life not being able to do what they love. I was able to do what I wanted to do, and was paid while I did it. The cockpit of an airplane was my office. I really enjoyed flying. Working for the CAA/FAA was like a paid vacation.

The Spark Plug Hunt

I had flown to the Trinity Lakes area and decided to camp in my tent until I got my moose. I selected a good camping site and flew each day looking for a moose. You could fly and hunt the same day in those early Alaska times. I did not see any animals for three days.

I decided to hunt for one more day and if not successful, pack up and fly home. I lifted off for my last day hunting. At about two hundred feet on my left, I spotted a big bull moose. I did not dare to turn left at him, afraid he would notice and dash into the woods. I slowly retarded the throttle and made a gentle landing straight ahead. I very slowly taxied back to a suitable tie-down spot. I was careful to securely tie down the plane. You want it there when you come back.

I hiked to the area where the moose was. He was between me and a high brush patch. I slowly worked around the brush and there he was. He made a small step to a large brush area but made one big mistake. He took one last look at me. That was his last look. I fired and had me a fine bull moose.

He fell beyond a small stream that I could not cross. I shot him again to be sure he would be there when I got back by way of more solid ground. I hiked back to my plane and taxied to a more accessible route. Then it started to rain. I gutted him and propped the rib cage open with small branches. I was soaking wet and cold as I flew back to my tent.

In the morning, I decided what to do. My good friend and old-time Alaskan had a Cessna 180 float plane. We had made arrangements that if I called needing some SPARK PLUGS, it meant that I had a moose and he would come and help me get it back home.

I called the Flight Service Station and asked if they would call his number and advise him that I needed some spark plugs.

Flight Service Station asked, "Do you need any help?"

"No, the plugs are all I need."

The weather was foggy, raining, very poor visibility. Surely Mike will not make it today, I thought. Later I heard this 180 engine drone. Here came Mike out of the mist. We harvested the moose, loaded it all into his big 180. We both ended up with a nice one-half a moose.

Memory of Friend and Colleague, Z.W. "Ski" Kowalewski

PART II

The Winter of my Life

Chapter 20 Prospecting, Hunting, and Fishing

After my retirement from the FAA in 1980, I was still full of energy and enthusiasm to get on with life and strike it rich—live my dreams. The Cessna 180, N9141C, and the Super Cub PA-18, N7524K, were going somewhere all the time. I was interested in prospecting, finding a valuable mineral deposit that could be marketed to a miner. Flying over this great state, you visualize what kind of rocks you are flying over, sedimentary, igneous, metamorphic, greywacke rock. I had taken all of Leo Mark Anthony's prospecting classes, including geology and chemistry, so I had a basic knowledge of how minerals are formed and where to look for them.

It was during one of these classes that I met Glenn Heatherly, my future prospecting partner. He was fourteen years older than I, but still full of enthusiasm to strike it rich. A radioactive anomaly had been reported by BLM northeast of Fairbanks, which triggered an immediate reaction amongst prospectors, myself included.

For this adventure, I started out on a snow machine that soon broke down and we had to abort the mission. Meanwhile, Heatherly had hauled his Nodwell up to the site and headed out on his own. He also ran into trouble and had to abort. We didn't know each other very well then, but in talking to Anthony about the event, he put me in touch with Heatherly who was skeptical of me at first. He wasn't sure he could trust me. At the time, he was using his Nodwell to haul steel into Collinsville Mine for a guy named "Shorty." The mining claims belonged to an

Short Note About N9141C

We always looked forward to receiving a Christmas card from Mike because it contained a picture of an airplane he was familiar with and included a short note about N9141C, the airplane he flew when he took us on fishing trips while we were visiting him in Anchorage in 1968. The trip to Alaska will remain in our minds forever, and we find ourselves talking about it with friends who have been to Alaska on vacations.

Memory of Friends, Alvin and Esther Shaw

Hunt panning for gold on mining claims at Collinsville in 1979.

aunt of Charlotte Bradley who later became the owner of the claim after her aunt's death.

It was March 1979. I flew the Cub as support to help get the Nodwell to Collinsville Mine. It's a long route over land with eight feet of snow that starts building up at the Forks Road House at the end of Petersville Road. Then through Petersville Hills, down Pickle Creek, across Kahiltna Glacier, up Summit Creek, across Lake Creek and from there you can see the Fairview Mountains where two-hundred-plus claims are located. It is a forty-five-mile trip off the road system. This is an old mining area that was first worked in the early 1900s with a dry land dredge. After getting Shorty into the mining area, and setting up the mine, Heatherly drove his Otter into the area. I think that after this trip, Heatherly had no more skepticism about my ability to fly an airplane.

Before I met Heatherly, he had purchased an airplane with a partner, Lindy Loudermilk. He didn't want Heatherly to fly the airplane for fear he would crash it. So what did Loudermilk do—he went out and crashed it himself. He totaled the plane and almost killed himself. He was a little goofy after the crash. I think something scrambled in his head. I was flying for the FAA when that crash happened near Eureka. Loudermilk was an FAA mechanic at the time.

In the fall of 1979, Heatherly and I chartered a helicopter from Alyeska Helicopters and staked eight claims on Slate Creek, five claims on Idaho Creek, three on Sunflower Creek, six on California Creek. We had twenty-two claims in total.

We had trouble with a nearby owner who had patented numerous five-acre sites on Sunflower Creek. He used the sites for hunting charters and

Cabin at Big Boulder Creek, Alaska in the 1980s.

didn't want any company from miners who would use his airstrip. In fact, he once swore out an arrest for me to the Alaska State Troopers after he found our Super Cub parked above his strip off in the boonies. Weather was down, so he couldn't find us as we were up in the hills in the clouds digging test holes for gold. He left a note on the Cub. The trooper actually showed up at our home. Queenie, being the charmer that she was, talked him out of pursuing the complaint.

After I returned home from that trip, I flew up to Rabbit Creek with my son Mike where Heatherly had previously dug some test holes with the Nodwell. Mike panned up to nine colors from the deepest hole. The colors came from the old flood plain. There was no gold in the creek. We then scrounged up an old sluice box from Mill Creek and drug it over to the site. We never did mine anything, maybe because we didn't know how or it was too late in the season to start. A few days later, I loaded Mike and Heatherly into the 180 and headed for Meadow Lake, which is located near Iliamna. Heatherly had a large number of silver and copper claims at Meadow Lake. We dug holes for assessment work and then flew home. It rained most of the time we were there.

Over the years, I accumulated and prospected twelve state-owned forty-acre claims on Big Boulder Creek. The creek had been hand worked before by old timers in the early 1900s. It panned out pretty well, so I decided I would try mining it. Since it was a test run, I received special permission from BLM to sidestep most environmental regulations for a hundred-yard test.

I engaged the help of a good friend, Jess Hanson, as a partner. He was an experienced miner. We drug a sluice box to the site, built a dam up river to bring water into the sluice. We borrowed a Komatsu loader from Charlotte Bradley as my old John Deere had thrown a bearing on the final drive to the mine. We moved a hundred yards of material in about four days and

Silver salmon fishing on Kustatan River, Kenai, Alaska.

did a cleanup. Out of that hundred yards, we recovered about 4.5 oz. of mostly fine gold. At today's price of $1,400 per ounce, that would be a day's wages, but in my assessment, if you complied with all the EPA requirements, it would not pay wages. The claims are in a steep valley and by the time you put in five settling ponds, you would have to build a road up on the ridge top to access your mining area. The best use of the Big Boulder claims was for recreational mining. We had a nice cabin on the claims for shelter while working there.

Over on Mill Creek, we had five claims on Fergy Gulch that had the potential for machine mining. During 2011, I intended to spend some time there to identify pay ground. Around the same time, Jack Cross was working at the mouth of Fergy Gulch where it empties into Mill Creek. He found gold. I made a deal with him to move up to Fergy to my claims for a percentage of the gold. It was too late in the season for him to continue as it was freezing over. That winter, Cross became ill and died. His gold plant still sits unattended at the Collinsville Mine. His widow had no interest in the plant as it slowly rusted away. I don't think he had any heirs. He was in his late eighties when I met him. Several people have tried to appropriate his Caterpiller bulldozer, but it won't start as it has been left to sit for too long. An old man's dream of striking it rich is now a memory.

In 2018, I sold various claims and let other claims go back to the State of Alaska as assessment work was getting to be too much—too expensive and too time consuming.

Chapter 21　Helicopter

I had always been interested in helicopters as they were the ultimate off-airport vehicle. While running ATA, we would occasionally haul a Bell 47 from Seattle to Anchorage in our C-46s and again haul them back in the fall when Rick Helicopter, based in San Francisco, California, was through with their Alaska work. On one occasion, while ferrying a helicopter from Merrill Field to Anchorage International Airport for loading, the pilot asked if I would like to fly it. Of course I said "Yes." Things went pretty well until we arrived at International Airport and the pilot said, "land it." The helicopter then became a different animal. I overcontrolled it and the pilot had to take control away from me as I was sashaying all over the ramp. I knew what I was doing—only thing was my control inputs were too great and too late. The feeling was like a floatplane porpoising when trying to land on water.

Owning a helicopter became my goal especially after the 1955 Hudson Bay escapade. After staking about seventy mining claims on foot, up and down mountains, I understood how valuable a helicopter could be in the mining business. In 1983, I had accumulated a little money from developing some of the Anchorage homestead, so I went shopping.

One day while flying the Cub, I noticed a helicopter working on some of my Nelson Mountain claims, which I had sold to Conoco Phillips. Flying over their mining camp, I dropped a note out the window of the Cub stating that I was landing on a sandbar in the Chitna River and wanted to be picked up. A few minutes later, a pretty blue Enstrom F-28C, N51727, landed to pick me up. The pilot and owner of the helicopter, John Spencer, a local boy, ferried me up the mountain to about 2,500 feet where the camp was located. The miners were drilling for lead, zinc and silver. I asked the foreman why they were drilling on my claims without tendering the $25,000. He was a little embarrassed and said he would contact the head office immediately. He did, and in a few days, I received a $25,000 check. I was impressed by how easily the helicopter could climb up the mountain. By foot, it would have taken six hours to climb up from the sandbar.

After Spencer finished the job on Nelson Mountain, he put the helicopter up for sale. I bought it for $49,000. Now, I had to learn to fly it. Ken Triplett of Alyeska Flight Service was an excellent pilot. He gave me some training, but I needed to get some formal training, so I found a school in Bakersfield, California, where I received my private pilot's license in rotary wing. On my return to Anchorage, Triplett gave me a lot of valuable instruction. He was a Vietnam helicopter pilot and wore that machine like a shirt. He would do things that I would never dream of as I thought they were too dangerous. For example, he would run up against a tree and start picking leaves off with the rear rotor. He was a cowboy and pushed things a little too far. One time Queenie said I tickled some leaves with my tail rotor when I left our cul-de-sac in front of the house.

I loved using my new skills. I flew almost every day. I was staking more claims, doing assessment work, finding great fishing holes and hauling friends to these great places. I had so much confidence and time built up that in 1984 I went to Oakland, California, to a helicopter school and earned my commercial rating in rotary wing. By now, I was a five-hundred-hour helicopter pilot.

A helicopter is expensive to operate because of all the moving parts and time life of certain components. For instance, the lamiflex bearings must be changed every five years regardless of the time or condition. Three changes at $1,300 each is equal to $3,900. I did most of my own maintenance, overhauled the engine twice, the transmission once, and tail rotor once. There was always something to work on. Just bending a blade tip a bit, or

---

Digging a Trench in 1985

Dad ALWAYS had a project. This particular project involved digging a trench for an electric line at the Merrill Field hangar where he housed his helicopter. The line had to be buried before asphalt was poured the next morning.

Working alone, Dad started digging the trench mid-morning, figuring he could finish the job that evening. After about eight hours, he realized he would not be able to finish, as it was a more difficult project than he had anticipated. The ground was solid gravel, which required swinging a pick ax to break through rocks to make a trench. He called me about eight o'clock in the evening and asked if I could come help him.

Since I would do anything for my Dad, I immediately dropped everything and headed over to help him. I was in the prime of my life at age thirty-nine and figured digging the trench with a pick ax and a shovel was doable. Dad was so relieved to have help, and since I wanted to impress him, I started swinging the pick ax like Paul Bunyan. It took several hours of backbreaking work, but between the two of us, we got the trench dug, the electric line buried and the trench filled in.

It was a good feeling to know Dad needed me. He was a man of power and strength, and rarely needed or asked for help.

Memory of Daughter, Nancy Verlinde

Helicopter fishing at Alexander Creek, Alaska in the 1980s.

pumping too much grease in one blade grip could put a "hop, skip, and a jump on it."

The helicopter could take you places you could not walk home from. For instance, say you flew across several major rivers, set down on top of a mountain and shut the engine down. Later you try to start your engine; but your battery might be dead, your vibrator might not fire, or your starter is dead—you are stuck. No way can you spin a prop and start your engine. These things have all happened to me, so I made up a spare parts kit, plus tools to change components, and carried them in the baggage compartment which had a maximum forty pounds.

One nice sunny day, I took Queenie on a fishing trip to the Theodore River located about thirty miles west of Anchorage across Cook Inlet. After catching our limit of king salmon, we prepared to leave. The engine would crank over but would not fire up. It was getting late in the day and I was having visions of spending the night in the helicopter. We had a very small emergency kit, but no sleeping bags. We were up a narrow canyon with no radio contact. The vibrator was not firing. Just as I was about to give up, my hand came off the starter switch and there was enough cranking momentum for one cylinder to fire. The engine mags came to life. That was a close call, so now you can see the need to carry a fly-away kit with all the spare parts and tools necessary to do repairs.

Hunt Helo Backyard Landing

My wife and I lived on Bailey Drive south of the Anchorage airport. We had a small lake in our back yard big enough for a small helicopter to land.

One winter, Mike landed there on the frozen surface and asked if I would like to take a helo ride. I had ridden in a helicopter before and asked if my wife could go instead. Patricia decided to go. Mike made the take off from on the lake which was surrounded with small trees. It was a tight squeeze and took a skilled pilot to pull off the maneuver. They went on a tour of Campbell Lake. I recorded a good video of the return landing.

Later I heard that he frequently landed his Enstrom helicopter in the street in front of his house.

Memory of Friend and Colleague,
Z.W. "Ski" Kowalewski

One day I received a call to fly out and rescue Jerry Harmon who was in his Enstrom helicopter. He was stuck on the Alexander River with a broken starter. Ken Triplett and I landed as close to him as possible, spread a blanket under his engine to catch all dropped hardware and tools and proceeded to change his starter. It's a good three-hour job for two men, as the starter is buried behind the cooling fan. The tail rotor driveshaft and other parts have to come off to get to the starter. A poor setup but that's the way Enstrom built the machine. Harmon was lucky that he could call us for help and we had everything aboard to rescue him. He was very grateful.

I leased thirty-five mining claims to Marmot Mining Co. They asked me to fly support for them as they moved their equipment from Eureka to Gold Creek. This was their first attempt at mining and their lack of experience soon showed. They were always breaking down and I was forever flying parts to them.

One breakdown was on the Little Oshetna River on a hillside about 4,000-feet elevation. It was brushy and I was looking for a landing spot so as not to strike my blades. At about a hundred feet, I lost my translational blade lift and I was settling fast with full power. Somehow, I plunked into the brush without striking anything. After that, I had them tie wands on their equipment so I could tell where the wind was coming from. I needed to land into the wind. I had ended up landing downwind and lost my lift as I slowed for landing. It was a close call and could have put me out of business.

The miners lack of experience soon caused them to go broke and pull out of the mine. They brought a lawsuit against me claiming I misrepresented the claims. My defense was that they didn't know how to mine for gold. You can't pick up gold by using a clawed backhoe digging in water. Gold has a specific gravity of eighteen and gravel about three to five. Anytime you rolled that rock, the gold went to the rocks below. They enriched the bottom, but did not recover much gold. The court finally dismissed the case but it cost us about $20,000 in attorney fees. Marmot Mining probably lost $500,000 of their investors' money.

I had staked five gold claims up on Colorado Creek via helicopter and continued to do assessment work with the helicopter as access was difficult. I had also staked and brushed out a possible landing strip for the Super Cub, but never tried it as the risk was too great.

On one of my assessment work trips, I took along Jess Hanson. After working all day digging test holes, we cooked dinner outside in front of an old-timer's log cabin. We then bedded down for the night in the cabin. About 2 a.m., there was a noisy ruckus outside the cabin amongst my cooking utensils. We figured it was a grizzly bear. Not wanting to confront a grizzly in the dark of night, we blew a whistle and yelled loudly. The ruckus stopped, but about thirty minutes later, it started again near where the helicopter was parked. This time we bailed out of our bed rolls with weapons drawn. It was too dark to see so we made loud noises and that seemed to scare the bear away. As soon as daylight came, we ventured out to see what had been damaged. One of my cooking pots had teeth marks

---

Hunting and Fishing

In my mind, Mike was a bold, fearless individual who lived on the edge. When it came to hunting, fishing and prospecting in the wilderness, he was in his element.

Bears are plentiful in Alaska but Mike had his surefire bear repellent, the mighty "whistle," which he assured me would scare any bears away. While on a hunting trip with him at a remote fly-in location where he had staked mining claims and set up a small utilitarian trailer, signs of bear were everywhere. We spotted a grizzly on a nearby hill, but Mike was not concerned because he had his whistle hanging on a lanyard around his neck. A grizzly bear had recently damaged his small travel trailer by ripping his claws across the aluminum siding trying to access it. Every year Mike had to repair the travel trailer cabin due to heavy snowfalls and bear intrusions.

While fishing one year at a remote fly-in location, a grizzly was watching us from the river's edge when Mike hooked a salmon. Immediately the bear charged into the river heading for the thrashing salmon on the end of Mike's line. Mike pulled out his whistle and blew it, expecting the bear to turn and run. But no, the bear just cocked his head and grabbed the salmon. Mike was not about to let that bear have the fish and pulled back on his fishing line. A tug-of-war ensued. No amount of noise created by the blowing whistle bothered the bear. Mike finally realized he had to cut the line before the angry bear turned on him—so much for his bear repellent.

Memory of Son-in-law, Jim Verlinde

all the way through it and gear was scattered everywhere. At the helicopter we found the left door plexiglass window had been ripped off as the bear went for a sack of Werther's candy that I had left on the seat.

The damage could have been much worse if our noise hadn't driven the grizzly bear off. Had he bitten or clawed into a tail rotor blade or broken out the front windshield, we would have been stranded for a very long time. Fortunately, all good bush pilots carry a roll of Duct Tape. We picked up all the pieces and Duct Taped the side window together. We made the decision to pack up and leave after that incident as we seemed to be parked on a grizzly bear trail. That bear or another one would return looking for something to eat. I strongly considered contacting Werthers Candy Co. and relating the story. They might have used it in an advertising campaign.

Mark Miller's son had fuselage and tail fabric ripped from his Super Cub when he was bear hunting on the Aleutian Chain. He had Duct Tape, but had to get more before he could fly the Cub out. Bears have twice destroyed my cabin on Gold Creek. When a grizzly gets hungry, he can break into almost anything. The bears go around looking for a soft spot and when they find it, they go for it. They can drag a thousand pound moose a long way. Grizzly bears are amazingly strong—the top of the food chain.

Another helicopter mission was for Chugach Electric. Chugach needed a big grader tire hauled to Beluga, approximately thirty-five miles west of Anchorage on the shores of Cook Inlet. Ken Triplett figured that would be good experience for some of my sling training. We picked up a big tire with our sling off of a truck in the Anchorage Harbor. As soon as we lifted the tire off the truck, we encountered rotor decay and started sinking. We temporarily set the helicopter down on the tidal flat to regain rotor RPM by bouncing the tire along the tidal flats a few times. We finally achieved translational lift and the helicopter started flying. We were obviously overloaded, full of fuel, and probably had eight hundred pounds of swing on the hook. Good training in what not to do: don't overload.

First Flight

In 2012, when I was seven, Great-Grandpa took me flying for the first time. We were flying in his Cessna 180. I was riding in the front right seat. My mom was sitting behind me in a low-slung, canvas seat. Mom was freaking out because Great-Grandpa kept putting his hands up in the air, letting me fly the plane. I was so short I couldn't even see over the instrument panel, but I was having a great time flying the plane all by myself. We flew around for about thirty minutes all the while Mom was petrified. We landed safely, of course.

After that flight, I decided I wanted to be a pilot. Great-Grandpa was my hero.

Memory of Great-Granddaughter, Tenley Hollman

Skydiving, Vacaville, California, 2007, age 85.

After that, I would practice picking up a barrel filled with water and carry it from Merrill Field to Campbell Airstrip. Things went pretty well until one day I was coming in downwind so I decided to abort. As I advanced the power and adjusted the cyclic trim, my thumb brushed the hook pickle switch, which dumped my barrel and sling down through the canopy of trees. It embarrassed me, but I did not inquire about the incident as that is one thing you are not to do with a helicopter—endanger people and property on the ground. That's about the only CAB law that applies to rotary wing aircraft. Lots of joggers use the Campbell Airstrip and I could have hit or frightened one of them.

In 1980, Queenie and I bought two lots at Point McKenzie, sight unseen. Point McKenzie is a large area of land located north of Anchorage, across the waters of Cook Inlet. The two lots were part of a large paper subdivision being developed. One of the ways Anchorage will grow in the future is toward Point McKenzie once the Knik River Bridge is built. Point McKenzie has a deepwater port suitable for large container ships to load and unload. A railroad line is being built to the port leading to a new transportation hub for south central Alaska. I was a visionary, putting myself in the path of progress.

After five years, it finally dawned on me that I'd better do something with those two lots. I flew Queenie over in the helicopter and landed in a swamp. We poked around, but were not sure of our exact location as we could not find any property line markers.

Later, on a different trip, I met a local man, Bill Frasier, who pointed me even closer to the lots. Since I was planning to build a cabin, I wanted to build it on our land. Ken Lang was a land surveyor. I contacted him and flew him via helicopter to the McKenzie property. We finally found a monument one-half mile south. From there, we measured to our corner monument. Somebody had run over the monument with a bulldozer and bent it over. We had to use a metal detector to find it. We then staked out the corners. Access to the property is difficult as the area is surrounded by swamp. A helicopter or snow machine is the best form of transportation to get to the area.

The helicopter was used to haul in all the material to build the cabin. I made at least a dozen trips. I constructed the 12' by 14' cabin single handedly—floor, walls, rafters and roof. A wood stove was used for heating the cabin and a Coleman stove was used for cooking. The cabin had two bunk beds, a table, a number of shelves, three windows and a door—all hauled in by helicopter.

Chapter 22   Change of Pace

Heart Bypass

In 1982, I had been noticing that when I exerted myself too much, I was getting a little tightness in my chest, which was diagnosed as angina. I had been very active: running, skiing, climbing mountains, hunting, and fishing. Even my eating lifestyle was considered healthy. I tried alternative methods of cleaning out my arteries such as chelation therapy, which is a method of scrubbing plaque from arteries with an IV drip of a mild acid. Over a period of two years, I did forty-seven treatments at $100 a treatment. At first, it seemed to work; but once while chelating, I stated to the doctor that I had trouble just walking across the parking lot in front of the clinic. He said to see my cardiologist right away, which I did.

Dr. Sonnerborn performed an angiogram and said I had 90% blockage of four arteries. I needed by-pass surgery to survive. I didn't want surgery because I knew it would ground me from flying and thereby curtail my active lifestyle. So I searched for an alternate treatment. I was not going to give up and submit to surgery. While I was lying in the hospital bed contemplating my options, Queenie called me. She was angry and stated that if I died on her, she was going to sell all my property, find a young man and travel the world. Those were very strong words and she meant them. After thinking about it some more, I called Dr. Sonneborn and said I was ready to have surgery. A day later, Dr. Arndt Von Hipple performed four by-pass grafts onto my heart. My recovery was quick and about six

---

Plenty of Dreams

Thinking about my visits to see my great-grandfather in action, I saved this snippet of one of his weekly clanograms to family and friends.

"I've got at least another ten years to live and I don't plan on spending it in a rocking chair. So many things yet to do and I do have plenty of dreams yet to live."

I re-read it whenever I feel down or lost.

Memory of Great-Granddaughter, Sydney Braun

---

months later I asked Dr. Sonneborn if I could run the 5K Mended Heart Run. He said, "Yes, go ahead." I came in number one in my age group and continued to run races for more than twenty years.

I accumulated a wall of awards. I stopped running at age eighty-nine, but continued to "wog." Most of my running competitors have "flown west to the big hangar in the sky." Many members of my family joined in my running program. We competed in many Frostbite Footraces during the Anchorage Fur Rendezvous, winning awards for costumes and oldest competitor.

Traveling

Queenie had always wanted to travel so we started cruising in our spare time. If I had died in 1982, she would have been cruising with some young man. Usually our cruises were in the winter months to escape from Alaska's cold. The first couple of cruises, the Caribbean and the Panama Canal, I enjoyed. Later, cruising became boring. To me, it was a big floating hotel, surrounded by water—too much fattening food and too many old people who sat around and drank too much. The cruise companies also try to extract as much money as they can from you for souvenirs and photos. Queenie was a good mixer and mingled well with everyone. We met a lot of nice people. However, one couple we met wanted a free fly-in fishing trip to my favorite fishing hole—no deal.

During the Panama Canal cruise, I was on deck most of the time as the big locks opened and closed to allow ship passage from the Atlantic to the

Howard Hunt, standing, and Duncan Miller, sitting in cockpit of BT-13, shaking hands. Nut Tree Airport, Vacaville, California, circa 2009.

ATCF reunion in 2009 at Travis AFB, California. Left, Howard Hunt; right, Duncan Miller.

Pacific. It was a wonderful engineering job by U.S. engineers. I also spent a lot of time jogging around the deck in the early morning hours to stay in shape and burn off that rich food. We cruised off and on for about ten years, but the adventures soon became boredom for both of us.

Nut Tree Hangar Purchase

In the late 1990s, we visited my old pals from ATA days, Duncan Miller and Wilbur Fitch. Miller and Fitch both lived in northern California and owned several hangars at the Nut Tree Airport in Vacaville, California. One day, while visiting, we heard about a guy who was trying to sell his hangar. The intended buyer had no money. Queenie said to the seller, "If you don't sell it to him, we'll buy it." She gave him a $500 earnest money deposit. A week later, he called and said, "You bought yourself a hangar. Pay up." We did.

Now we had a hangar and needed something to put in it. Roger Grunert had a Harvard MK-IV for sale. He was working for FAA at the time as an air carrier operations inspector. He was a friend of Fitch and Miller and flew the Harvard at air shows. It was a Royal Canadian Air Force (RCAF) warbird and was part of the Goldilocks Acrobatic Team. It was a beautifully maintained warbird—just what we were looking for, so we bought it.

Air Transport Reunions

During World War II, there were thousands of Air Transport Command ferry pilots whose job it was to ferry various aircraft around the world. It wasn't unusual to fly bombers, such as the B-17, B-25, B-26, B-29; transport planes such as the C-46, C-47 and the C-54, and even smaller planes like the A-26.

Thousands of us attended the annual reunions, which started in 1981. These annual reunions were a way to get together and share our stories. As I mentioned earlier in this book, we had named ourselves the "Wilmington Warriors." As the years rolled by and the pilots flew west to that "big hangar in the sky," the attendance started to drop. Queenie and I enjoyed these annual reunions—she was the life of the party and made new friends at every reunion. We attended these reunions together until 2005 when Queenie passed away. As so many of the Wilmington Warriors were "flying west," the Wilmington Warriors gathered for the last time in 2007.

After 2007, it was decided to combine all the Air Transport Command Ferry (ATCF) reunions into one. At one of the reunions, an ambitious director wanted to increase the membership. I replied that was a good idea, but there was no way to retrieve those old pilots out of that big hangar out west. The last ATCF reunion I attended was 2009. I attended that reunion with my good friend and business partner of sixty-five years, Duncan Miller. Only twenty-four ATCF pilots attended the reunion in San Diego.

At the 2009 ATCF reunion, Miller and I wore our original uniforms and gave oral histories that were recorded. We had a great time. We shared a lot of memories with our small group. As I was driving back to the Nut Tree from San Diego, I announced to Miller that I did not feel well.

We made it to Nut Tree, I stayed overnight, but then asked Miller to take me to the emergency room. It was discovered that I had a bowel obstruction. The doctors went right to work on me and warned me that I might lose some of my upper and lower intestines. They made a twelve-inch incision and started squeezing everything back into my stomach where it was pumped out. During this grueling procedure, I had another heart attack. I was moved to another hospital close by for a heart operation. Interestingly, the heart surgeon, rather than do another bypass, was able to ream out the original arteries that had been bypassed in 1982. Heart operations had advanced dramatically.

In military fashion, my son mobilized the whole family to help out. First to the hospital in California was Barbara who flew in from Spokane, then, Dashelle, Nancy, Jim and Denise showed up to take charge. We kept a journal that shows I was in the hospital for eleven days. In my mind, I had only been there for three days. On the eleventh day, Jim, Nancy, and Dashelle drove me to Seattle where Dashelle and I flew home to Alaska.

My recovery was rapid and I was once again airworthy. I managed to revive my third class medical and was able to continue flying. I missed the 2010 ATCF reunion. Not too sure how many more reunions there will be as we are all dying off at the rate of a thousand per day. I'm one of the lucky ones. I'm so hard of hearing that if the Dear Lord says, "You're cleared to land," I might not hear my clearance and keep right on flying.

Chapter 23 Accolades and Achievements

Over the years, I have told my World War II stories to my family and friends. My son, Mike, was always interested in my military life. He followed up on his interest by attending and graduating from the Citadel and being commissioned as an officer in the U.S. Army. He subsequently retired from the military after twenty years reaching the rank of Lt. Col.

In 1990, I received the China War Memorial Medal by the government of the Republic of China.[*] Known as the "lost" decoration of World War II, this medal commemorates service in China with our Chinese allies in the defeat of the Empire of Japan.[†]

---

[*] Appendix 14. Chinese Air Force Award, August 21, 1990.

[†] Appendix 13. CBI Hump Pilots Association, Inc., Press Release, 1989.

Captain Howard John Hunt with his son Lt. Colonel Howard Michael Hunt in 2005.

In 1995, the Russians celebrated the fiftieth anniversary of the end of World War II. The Russians planned to gather a group of American veterans for a trip to Magadan, Russia. The Alaska Airmen's Association sponsored the trip from Anchorage to Magadan on a chartered Russian jet. For three days we were wined and dined by our Russian counterparts. They really appreciated our World War II help in supplying warplanes and other necessary supplies. Without our help, they would have lost the war.

At the various veteran parades in Russia, everyone turned out to thank the veterans for saving their country from the Germans. In an American veterans' parade, you would never get that kind of response. They had tears in their eyes. Their reaction touched me. Never in my military career have I felt so honored.

We stayed with a Russian host family and were escorted around by young Russian military cadets who spoke very good English. I further honored them by giving memorabilia from my uniform. That was a real treasure to them. Now, many years later, it would be nice to know what happened to these fine young men. They are probably Russian military officers now. On a side note, a statue was erected along the Chena River in Fairbanks honoring the lend-lease pilots and the Russian pilots who flew the planes. I was honored to be part of this effort flying P-39s, A-20s, B-25s and C-47s.[*]

Another glory day was in 2007 when the FAA awarded me "The Wright Brothers Master Pilot Award" for fifty years of safe flying.[†] My son, Mike, was the Master of Ceremonies for that presentation. We were dressed in our military uniforms. The event was held at Alaska Aviation Museum on Lake Hood with about two hundred in attendance. A slide show of my aviation career was presented to an enthusiastic crowd. I have talked to CAP cadets and appeared on KAKM Public Broadcast to tell war stories. Tom Wardleigh of Aviation Safety Foundation started the program years ago. The program was called "Hangar Flying." After Wardleigh's death, the popular program ended. I probably appeared on the show a dozen times to talk about aviation safety. I have given oral history presentations to the Alaska Veterans Museum and the Air Transport Command.

As I mentioned earlier in this book, during my military career, I ferried warbirds from Great Falls, Montana to Ladd Field in Fairbanks, Alaska. In 2012, the army was looking to celebrate the seventieth anniversary of Fort Wainwright. They were looking for memorabilia of that era. My son was in on the planning of this celebration even though at the time he was on active duty in Iraq. He knew of a real live icon of that era, who still proudly wore his original World War II uniform. The next thing you know, I was one of the focal points of the anniversary celebration. Apparently, I was one of the last surviving pilots of the 1942 Lend-Lease Program.

---

[*]   Appendix 18.   Happy Victory Day letter from the Russian ambassador, 2019.

[†]   Appendix 16.   Department of Transportation, Federal Aviation Administration, The Wright Brothers "Master Pilot" Award, July 13, 2007.

The Commemorative Air Force (CAF) flew the Harvard MK-IV to Ladd Field and parked it in the old Russian lend-lease hangar. The banquet tables were set up around the warbird. I sat nearby with a packet of original, moldy, navigation maps that were given to me in 1942. Actual photographs of an A-20 warbird were on display with photos of the ferry pilots, including myself. I entertained interested people by telling them of some of the lend-lease trips in 1942. Major General Raymond Palumbo and other officers congratulated me for making their seventieth anniversary such a success. It made me happy to be honored in such a way.

In telling my war stories to family members, my son said, "Dad, your glory days are over." Well, he was wrong. As long as I can share my WWII experiences with interested people, the memories will continue to be passed on to future generations. Whenever I wear my World War II flying jacket and uniform, people have asked me, "Why don't you put new cuffs on that flight jacket?" I say, "It would not be authentic." After all, I was eighty-nine years old, relatively healthy, and still airworthy. I'm lucky as most of my peers have flown west.

In 2013, I was honored by the Alaska Aviation Museum when I received recognition as one of the Living Legends of Alaska Aviation. To be recognized in the Alaska aviation community as a legend was rewarding as well as humbling. Also, in 2013, I was privileged to attend the Alaska Veteran's Honor Flight to visit Washington, D.C.

Memphis Belle logbook.

Two World War II veterans, Z.W. "Ski" Kowalewski and Howard Mike Hunt salute each other at the March 2018 Alaska Aviation Museum Life Achievement Award Banquet held at the Hotel Captain Cook, Anchorage, Alaska. Photograph courtesy of Rob Stapleton, Alaskafoto

Another memorable accolade in my aviation career was attending the Seventy-Fifth Anniversary of the B-17 Memphis Belle. The celebration was held in May 2018 at Wright Patterson Air Force Base, Dayton, Ohio, after a restoration of the Belle that took over fifteen years. After diligent research, it was determined that I was the last living pilot to have flown the Memphis Belle.

The Memphis Belle saw combat in World War II. After completing twenty-five missions in Europe, the plane returned to the United States and was then used to sell war bonds across the country in an effort to help fund the war effort. It was at the end of her War Bond tour in late December 1943 that I was assigned to the task of piloting the Memphis Belle from Spokane, Washington, to Tampa, Florida, where she would spend the remainder of the war being used as a training aircraft at MacDill Air Force Base, Tampa, Florida.

My last, but by no means least, award came on March 24, 2018, when I was inducted into the Alaska Aviation Museum "Hall of Fame" as one of 2018 recipients of the Lifetime Achievement Award. The annual Hall of Fame event celebrates pilots and entrepreneurs who have shaped Alaska's aviation history. I was honored to be a recipient of this award.[*]

---

[*]   Appendix 17.   Alaska Legislature, honoring Howard Hunt, Aviation Hall of Fame, 2018.

Chapter 24 Commemorative Air Force

The national Commemorative Air Force (CAF) began with the purchase of a single airplane in 1957. Lloyd Nolen and a small group of ex-service pilots pooled their money to purchase a P-51 Mustang. By 1960, the group had expanded their search for more World War II aircraft.

The mission of the CAF is to keep warbirds flying. The CAF, chartered as a non-profit in 1961, is a national organization headquartered in Dallas with hangar facilities in Midland, Texas. The CAF has wing chapters around the country including one in Anchorage. Air shows are staged all around the United States featuring B-17s, B-24s, and a variety of other warbirds. A wing can be established when a group of approximately twenty-five interested people garner enough financial support to proceed

Hunt flying over Anchorage in his Cessna 180.

with procuring a warbird. Donations are the main source of revenue for the CAF. Donations can be cash, time, or equipment, and in my case, the donation of warbirds.

I first learned of the CAF when I was attending an Alaska Airmen's Association meeting in 2003. CAF headquarters sent a salesman up to Alaska to try to convince us to accept a C-46 named "Tinkerbell." Cliff Everts owned a hangar in Fairbanks and offered to hangar *Tinkerbell*. This was not a good solution as traveling to Fairbanks to work on the plane was inconvenient since the Alaska wing would be based in Anchorage. Also, the two 2,000 HP engines burned one hundred gallons of aviation fuel per hour. There was no money for fuel.

Another problem was how to keep pilots current. It was a totally unworkable situation. At the meeting, I piped up and said, "You can't afford that. The airplane has to be hangared. It can't sit outside." Terry Holliday, one of our CAF members, offered up a hangar. Unfortunately, soon afterward, he sold the hangar. We were back to square one. In the end, we could not accept *Tinkerbell*.

Harvard MK-IV flying over Sacramento, California, circa 2012.

Harvard MK-IV

I talked it over with Queenie and we decided to donate the Harvard MK-IV (American equivalent is an AT-6.) to the CAF to establish an Alaska Wing. Because the Harvard was built in Canada, we were unable to license it for passenger carrier. Passengers could be hauled, but you could not advertise "common carrier." Passengers could leave a donation in the seat, however. The CAF flew passengers under these restrictions.

I was willing to donate the Harvard, but it had to be hangared. That is when I purchased the Birchwood hangar. Donations were vital to get the wing off the ground. I knew I could not take the planes with me when I passed away. I wanted other pilots to enjoy flying the warbirds, so I donated the Harvard to the CAF. I was a large financial supporter of the

Alaska wing. It was important to me to launch the effort. At a certain point, the Alaska wing had to be self-supporting. In 2007, my donations had given birth to the wing.

Since I planned to donate the Harvard to the CAF, the plane needed to be ferried to Alaska from the Nut Tree Airport in Vacaville, California. Carter Teeters was a CAF certified pilot. He was offered, and accepted, the opportunity to ferry the Harvard to Alaska. He thought this would be a good chance to see Alaska and figured the trip would be a lot of fun. On July 28, 2007, Teeters flew into Sacramento. He was picked up by my partner, Miller, and driven to the Nut Tree Airport. That afternoon Teeters loaded his survival gear, maps and other equipment into the back seat of the plane. Since the plane had only a ferry certificate, he was not allowed to fly with anyone on board.

He flew to the Tacoma Narrows Airport in Tacoma, Washington, that evening by following Interstate 5 north from Sacramento. The next morning he flew the Harvard to Boeing Field where he parked it for a couple days. On August 1, he once again headed north following the Alaska Highway. Although there was plenty of daylight, the stops for aviation fuel were few and far between. He flew into Vancouver, Prince George, Fort St. John, Fort Nelson and then overnighted in Watson Lake—the "mosquito capital" of Canada. From Watson Lake, he flew to Whitehorse and then to Northway where he had to check in with U.S. Customs. Weather was moving in so it was important to get through customs before the weather deteriorated. Being stuck in Northway could end up lasting many days.

The customs inspector detected a radioactive reading emanating from the plane and was on high alert asking a series of questions. It was finally determined that the dials on the instrument panel were made of radium because all the instruments on the plane were original. Once the source of the radioactivity was determined, the customs inspector waved him on through so he could get into Anchorage before inclement weather moved in. Teeters was able to land in Anchorage just as the weather deteriorated.

The next step was to have more pilots checked out to fly the Harvard. Although I had owned the Harvard for twenty years, I was not a certified CAF pilot. Teeters had the job of certifying me. On September 2, Teeters gave me the required check ride. We flew out to Birchwood Airport to practice touch and go landings and did some acrobatics. The check ride went just fine until we returned to Anchorage International to land. The transponder was set accidentally to an emergency setting (7700). We were cleared to land, but had some explaining to do later on.

That same day, Teeters checked out and certified Robert "Cricket" Renner. His check ride involved taking off and landing at Elmendorf Air Force Base. Everything went smoothly. In 2008, John Hartke and Alex Roesch were checked out and all three became sponsor pilots for the new wing in Alaska. In due time, more pilots were checked out and became qualified to fly the Harvard. They included Jeff Severs, Ed Kornfield, Tom Sharkey,

Gordon Bartel, Fred Amicangioli, and Richard Pulley. By now the wing had enough qualified check pilots within the organization who could then handle certifying new pilots for the wing.

BT-13 in flight over Alaska, Ed Kornfield piloting, Col. Hunt in the back seat, circa 2011.

BT-13

The BT-13 was reconstructed from airplane parts that were discovered in Sheldon, California by my long-time friend, Duncan Miller. We hauled five truckloads of BT-13 parts from Sheldon to the Vaca-Dixon (VD) Airport in Vacaville, California. From VD Airport, we moved the parts to a couple of hangars at the Nut Tree Airport. It's a good thing we moved most of the parts to the Nut Tree as a fire raced through the old VD Airport destroying our hangar. The fire was so intense that it melted all the aluminum parts stored there.

A group of five formed a partnership to work on the project. We hired two mechanics for the rebuild. Most of the expense for the restoration consisted of labor costs. It took five years and $50,000 to complete the rebuild of the BT-13. We stripped her down completely—inside and out. In order to achieve the correct color scheme, we went to Travis AFB about five miles away to study the paint job on an original BT-13. At the time, one was on display in the museum at Travis. When completed, our BT-13 was a beauty. We took it to airshows around California where it won many first place ribbons.

One of the partners said he was getting too old to fly and wanted to sell. The partnership voted four to one to put the BT-13 up for sale. An airplane collector from Australia heard about the sale and put in a bid. I said, "This airplane isn't going to Australia. It needs to stay in the USA." I proceeded to outbid the Australian and became the sole owner of the BT-13. My partners growled about my getting the airplane that way, so I kicked in another $10,000 for a total sale price of $83,000. That quieted everybody down and we continued to be friends.

I was able to house the BT-13 in Duncan Miller's Nut Tree hangar as I had the Harvard in my own hangar. Twice a year, for about two weeks, I went to my Nut Tree "toy box" to play with the airplanes. This twice a year visit went on for years until I decided to bring the planes to Alaska. Because I had planned to donate the Harvard to the CAF, I brought it to Alaska first.

A few years later in 2013, I decided to donate the BT-13 to the CAF. The plane was capable of being flown to Anchorage—we just needed a pilot to make that happen. Ed Kornfield, a CAF pilot, volunteered to fly the BT-13 for us. On May 27, 2013, Kornfield showed up at the Nut Tree Airport in Vacaville to pick up the plane. He expected someone to give him a briefing on any particulars about the plane that he should know before flying north. One of my partners, Lloyd Tischner, was supposed to check Kornfield out in the BT-13. However, on that particular day, it was raining. Everyone was relaxing in the hangar, talking, and drinking coffee. No one was interested in flying that day. However, Kornfield wanted to be on his way despite the light drizzle. He went out to the tarmac, fueled up, started the engine and took off.

Kornfield planned to take in the Reno Air Races on his way to Anchorage. The weather deteriorated even more as he flew on to Reno. About halfway there, he decided to abort the Reno stop and instead headed north to Alaska. Six days later, June 2, he showed up at Merrill Field in Anchorage with no major problems along the way. If he had had any problems, he was capable of fixing them as he was an excellent mechanic, pilot, and instructor.

Now that the CAF had two airplanes—we needed another hangar. I was able to purchase a hangar on Merrill Field for the BT-13.

Col. Hunt at the Alaska Aviation Museum.
Photograph courtesy of Rob Stapleton, Alaskafoto.

Restored L-2M

L-2M

A few years went by. Rusty Mays discovered an L-2M warbird stored in a barn in California. An L-2M is a Taylorcraft, which was used for artillery spotting during World War II. It was referred to as the "grasshopper." Mays brought the L-2M over to me in pieces at the Nut Tree. I liked what I saw so I bought it. Now I had another project to complete. It took about two years to restore. We put in all new wood, new fabric, interior, and instruments. When completely restored, it was authentic, even down to the color scheme.

The L-2M was unable to be flown to Alaska. It did not have enough long-range fuel capabilities. With the right-sized trailer, and the wings removed, the airplane could be hauled up the Alaska Highway from California. As luck would have it, my son had just been discharged from the Army, and was interested in a road trip. He bought a camper and a haul trailer, loaded up the L-2M, and headed north.

In May 2018, I donated the L-2M to the CAF. Now we had three airplanes to hangar so I purchased another hangar at Merrill Field. The Harvard MK-IV, the BT-13 and the L-2M were now housed in three different hangars at Merrill Field.

Naming the Wing

On September 12, 2015, the CAF surprised me during a special member appreciation event. Due to my airplane donations and monetary support, the Alaska Wing of the CAF presented me with a plaque stating that the Alaska Wing was officially being renamed the "Col. Hunt Alaska Wing." I was quite humbled and honored.

Col. Robert Renner, Col. Howard Hunt, and Col. Ed Kornfield at the ceremony naming the Alaska Wing after Col. Hunt.

The Alaska Wing is slowly growing. It is self-funded by selling BT-13 rides, tee shirts, miscellaneous memorabilia, and performing at air shows around Alaska. It continues to be an ongoing presence in Alaska aviation. It is a successful organization due to good pilots who are a dedicated band of brothers keeping the warbirds flying. I'm leaving a legacy—a footprint in Alaska aviation. The Alaska Wing will be successful far into the future with the passion these pilots have for flying—and especially flying these warbirds.[*]

---

[*]   Appendix 15.   2006 Commemorative Air Force Award, February 17, 2007.

Photographic Journey with Col. Hunt

Memories of Col. Hunt date back to an Alaska Airmen's Association's trade show and convention where I first photographed him. In his original U.S. Army Air Corp. uniform, he sat and watched with glee as young children climbed in and out of the small peddle plane made to the likeness of his canary-yellow Harvard MK-IV. He explained that he was helping start a squadron or wing of the Commemorative Air Force in Anchorage. He held up a box and asked if I wanted to donate to the cause. It's pretty hard to deny an eighty-something-year-old former World War II pilot a donation, so I popped in a bill or two.

Later I began to know Col. Hunt in different ways as he attended many of the events at the Alaska Aviation Museum at Lake Hood in Anchorage. In my stint as an Aviation Museum volunteer and, later a board member, Mike could be seen at every aviation event being held either at the FedEx hangar, Aviation Museum, Merrill Field, or over at Peggy's Café on Fifth Avenue in Anchorage.

I knew that he was a World War II pilot, but it was not until I heard him telling stories during a liar's poker game at the home of Emitt Soldin that I heard details of his flying career. A gathering of Alaskan aviators, including Ruth Jefford, Ski Kowalewski, George Pappas, and others, played liar's poker every Thursday. The weekly Thursday Liar's Poker gathering continues although many aviators have "flown west."

Some years later, the Alaska Air Carriers Association and the Alaska Aviation Museum jointly agreed to do a living legends type of acknowledgment, which honored Col. Hunt and other legendary Alaskan pilots who were still living. It was hard to get Mike to sit down and tell a story about himself until his family started encouraging him. In the meantime, he had donated several of his WWII training aircraft to the Commemorative Air Force Wing at Merrill Field. At a gathering at the Wings of Freedom Hangar, the CAF recognized his donation by naming the Alaska Wing the "Colonel Mike Hunt Wing." This was a surprise to Col. Hunt as he thought the party was to celebrate his birthday. He was delighted and accepted the honor graciously.

He was a well-accomplished man, who loved flying, a pioneer Alaskan aviator, and a true legend with the stories to back it up. Many times I photographed him at events held in his honor. With a sparkle in his eye, he was always polite, smiling, and making humorous comments. The best images were when Mike was sitting in an airplane or getting out of the cockpit after a flight. He loved flying with a passion and always said, "I am lucky. Flying is not work, it's what I love to do."

It was an honor to photograph the exploits and accomplishments of a true Alaskan aviation legend. Col. Hunt, you will be missed.

Rob Stapleton, Alaskafoto

Epilogue

The last few chapters of this book, *Saga of an Aviation Survivor*, were dictated to me by my father the week before his passing in August 2019. He gave instructions to transcribe, edit and publish. His goal was to have the book published with the sale proceeds going to the Alaska Aviation Museum at Lake Hood and the Alaska Wing of the Commemorative Air Force, Anchorage, Alaska.

He penned an earlier version of this book in 1992 when he was seventy. That book was distributed to family members with a few copies given out to friends. My father felt that the last twenty-seven years of his long aviation career weren't nearly as interesting as the first seventy years of his life, but I am sure you all will agree, he was an interesting and vibrant man with many stories to tell right up to drawing his last breath. His mind was sharp. He always had a mission for the day, whether it was going to lunch with his fellow FAA retirees every Thursday at K's Restaurant, or "chowder at noon" on Fridays at Peggy's Airport Café with the pilots from the CAF.

My father checked on his warbirds every chance he could, which generally was several times a week. He was always giving encouragement to his children, grandchildren and great-grandchildren to follow their dreams, work hard, and do the very best they can no matter what the job entailed. To say he was bigger than life is a true statement.

Blue skies and tail winds, Dad.

Nancy Hunt Verlinde

August 2021

Left to right, Howard, Carol, Barbara, Baby Mike, Dashelle, Diane, Nancy and Paladin, the black lab, 1965.

Hunt family, Dashelle, Diane, Howard Michael, Howard John, Barbara, and Nancy, 2005.

Answers from Grandpa

Dear Aiden,

Below is the letter Grandpa wrote to answer your questions.*

When Japanese attacked Pearl Harbor I was in my third year at Iowa State College. I was planning to get my requirements to become an Army Air Corp pilot, which at that time was a two years of college or pass an exam of its equivalent. Our President, Roosevelt sensed that, and had started a program. I had just finished that program with over eighty hours of pilot training including aerobatic flying.

I was really mad from the attack and wanted to fight right now and with the training air corp was happy to sign me up for flight training. Two weeks later, I boarded a train for Bakersfield, California for formal training, primary, basic and advanced flight training. Army training was easy for me as I had already experienced eighty hours of flight training. I was already a hot pilot and it showed.

Everybody was mad at the Japanese for the attack, there was known dissent. Everybody was ready to do something for this attack. The Japanese had to be defeated and everybody did whatever they could to make this happen, man, woman, and kids. All at once I was an energized kid and I was a fighter pilot going out to kill the enemy. I had to grow up fast and become a fighting man. The command pilot of a four engine at age nineteen/twenty is a big jump forward, but youth has no fear. Show me the enemy and I will take him out. Everybody came together—kill the enemy. We are the strongest nation in the world when we all come together and we were all at the event.

Now as I have aged to ninety-five, I know that I'm not indestructible like I was as a young man of twenty. I have seen a lot of destruction in my lifetime, but I was never afraid. I acted with the best judgment I had at the time. Most of my peers have gone to that big hangar out west. I will continue to leave my foot print and when I do go, this world will be a better place to live.

Letter Written by Great-Grandpa Hunt
to Great-Grandson, Aiden Pearcy

---

* This letter was found among Hunt's keepsakes. Aiden is a great-grandson of Howard Hunt. The letter was perhaps a school assignment for Aiden. Although the letter is not dated, it was written in 2017 when Hunt was ninety-five years old. The essence of the message is quite moving and personal and reflects the true personality of the author, Howard Hunt.

Howard John "Mike" Hunt Obituary

Howard John "Mike" Hunt, age 97, passed away peacefully at home on August 31, surrounded by his family. Howard was born on January 16, 1922 in Polk City, Iowa. He was an Alaskan pioneer who came to Alaska in 1949 to establish a new airline—Air Transport Associates (ATA). Howard and his wife, Ruth, along with their three young daughters, homesteaded forty acres in the Anchorage bowl area. Ruth passed away in 1962. Howard then married Carol Pierce, who had a daughter and, later, Howard and Carol had a son.

Throughout his life, Howard's love of flying took him all around the world. He was a ferry pilot in World War II with the Army Air Corps, flying every type of plane the army had in its inventory including the B-17, "Memphis Belle." In 2018, Howard was honored at the seventy-fifth anniversary ceremony celebrating the restoration of the Memphis Belle. He was the last known surviving pilot to have flown the Belle on a ten-day bond drive from Spokane, Washington, to Tampa, Florida, at the end of World War II.

Airplanes, especially warbirds, were his passion. He helped finance the restoration of three warbirds and eventually donated them to the Alaska Wing of the Commemorative Air Force (CAF). These warbirds are hangared in Anchorage and are proudly flown at airshows around Alaska. On many Saturdays during the summer months in Anchorage, one warbird, the BT-13, is available for paid rides. These rides support the upkeep and maintenance of the warbirds.

Howard is survived by his sister, Virginia Silver; daughters, Nancy (Jim), Barbara, Diane (Tony), Dashelle, and son, Howard; grandchildren, Terry, Tracee, Gary, Carlie, Karilynn, John, Kelly, Jack, Denise, Elizabeth, Caroline and Trinity; and fifteen great-grandchildren; nieces, Maxine (Don), Kathy, and Jan (Roger).

A memorial service was held at the Alaska Aviation Museum at Lake Hood, on October 12 from noon to 4:00 p.m. At noon, the CAF warbirds performed a flyover in the missing man formation.

In lieu of flowers, memorial donations may be made to the Alaska Aviation Museum or the Commemorative Air Force.

"Let's keep those warbirds flying."

Howard "Mike" Hunt would be pleased.

Howard Hunt in cockpit of BT-13, circa 2018.
Photograph courtesy of Rob Stapleton, Alaskafoto.

Appendix List

Appendix 1.
Reproduction of Veterans of Foreign Wars of U.S. Press Release,
October 1951

VETERANS OF FOREIGN WARS OF U.S.
Publicity and Press Service
610 Wire Building, Washington 5, D.C.

The Veterans of Foreign Wars of the U.S. has taken up the cudgel on behalf of the nation's operators of non-scheduled airlines, most of whom are war veterans, by appealing to the Civil Aeronautics Board to modify or rescind some recent restrictions on such independent operations.

In a brief, filed with the CAB by the Veterans of Foreign Wars, through John C. Williamson, of Washington, special counsel, the V.F.W. has contended to the CAB that the government is needlessly if not capriciously forcing out of business many independent airlines just now becoming well established after it had urged veterans and others, through the Veterans Administration, the War Assets Administration and other agencies, to start their own enterprises.

The current V.F.W. effort to protect such fly-when-asked enterprises, which operate usually in remote areas not sufficiently profitable for regular commercial airline service, has a focal point in the revocation by the CAB of its letter of registration issued to Air Transport Associates, Inc., operating between Seattle, Washington, and Anchorage, Alaska. This airline was established chiefly by former veteran pilots of the Ninth Air Transport Command, and the V.F.W. emphasizes that most other similar free-lance aviation companies not only provide fast passenger and freight service in sections ignored by the major airlines, but has an important potential function in current defense preparations, with their personnel, planes, airport facilities and area familiarity being available instantly and fruitfully in a major defense effort.

The V.F.W. intercession in support of the Seattle-to-Anchorage line is the first such step undertaken as a result of a resolution, adopted by the V.F.W. at its national encampment in New York in August, protesting increasingly restrictive interpretations by the Civil Aeronautics Board of its own basic regulations.

Such recent curbs, which the V.F.W. calls arbitrary and not adding to operational safety, have so increased operating costs and handicapped service to passengers and shippers that many such independent lines are having to go out of business, the V.F.W. points out.

In its plea to the Board, which has granted a temporary stay on its registration revocation of the Air Transport Associates, Inc., pending appeal, the Veterans of Foreign Wars has cited the report of the U.S. Senate Small Business Committee which favored a minimum of unnecessary restrictions and a maximum of encouragement by the government for individuals, including war veterans, contemplating independent business ventures of general public benefit. The V.F.W. brief also reminded that sixty per cent of service performed during the September, 1950 Korean air lift, and fifty per cent performed during the Berlin air lift by commercial aircraft, was provided by non-scheduled airlines.

The V.F.W. also supports claims by the independent lines that, because they get no government subsidy, as for carrying mail, they by their increasingly successful operations and extended service are providing a yardstick demonstration of efficiency as well as private enterprise which the government should encourage instead of hampering.

Appendix 2.
Air Transport Associates, Inc., Whale Meat Recipes

WHALE MEAT WITH ONION

2 pounds pounded whale meat
2 onions, sliced
Pepper and salt
1 bouillon cube
Water

Fry the onions in a little fat until lightly browned and then remove from pan and keep warm. Cut slices of meat until about ⅓ inch thick and put them in the pan. Sprinkle with salt and pepper. Brown well on one side, then turn and brown on the other side. Brown well but do not cook dry. Put onions on top. Dissolve the bouillon cube in a little hot water and pour over the browned meat. Cover frying pan and simmer gently for 10 minutes, then remove cover and simmer until all the liquid has nearly evaporated. Serve the meat and onions. Mushrooms may also be used instead of the onions.

CURRIED WHALE MEAT

2 tablespoons fat
1 large onion, chopped
2 tablespoons flour
1 tablespoon curry powder
½ teaspoon salt
¼ teaspoon pepper
1 bouillon cube
1 cup water
½ lb. whale meat

Fry the onion in the fat, add the flour, curry and seasonings and cook for a few minutes stirring constantly. Dissolve the bouillon cube in the water and add to the flour and fat mixture. Stir and cook until you have a smooth sauce. Cut the meat into small cubes and add to the curry sauce. Cover the pot lightly and simmer slowly for 40 minutes. Add a little more water if necessary during the cooking.

Whale Meat Recipes

Edith Adams' Recipes
From The Vancouver Sun

"Boneless and gristleless, whale meat is all meat. Pan-broiling the thin steaks is a popular way of serving them if the steaks have been tenderized first by pounding with a meat cleaver. Covering them with water and simmering in order to tenderize them also insures a more tender steak. Whale meat is excellent, too, for soup stocks, stews, roasts and curries. Whale meat looks very similar to beef when cooked and tastes like baby beef."

AERO-FRESH WHALE MEAT
AIRBORNE PERISHABLES, INC.
426 SMITH TOWER   •   SEATTLE 4, WASHINGTON

Whale for Dinner? ...
... How To Cook It
By EDITH ADAMS

"Here are tested recipes to help you in your use of this new meat."

WHALE BURGERS

½ pound minced whale meat
1 onion, chopped
½ cup bread crumbs, dry
1 egg
1 teaspoon Worcestershire sauce
1 teaspoon chopped parsley
Salt and pepper

Mix all the ingredients together and form into balls or patties. Toss in flour and fry in fat very slowly, turning so that all sides are browned. Serve hot with tomato sauce. If desired also a half can of tomatoes may be poured over the balls after they are browned and allowed to cook down. Serve the balls with the tomatoes poured over them.

WHALE MEAT PIE

1 pound whale meat
2 tablespoons seasoned flour
2 tablespoons drippings
3 onions, sliced
½ can tomatoes
1 cup stock
Seasoning
Pastry

Cut whale meat into cubes and toss in the seasoned flour. Slice the onions and brown the onions and the meat in the drippings. Turn the meat and vegetables into a casserole dish. Some chopped celery is nice added, too. Add the stock and seasonings, marjoram, thyme, garlic salt or celery salt, as desired. Cover with pastry. (To prevent the pastry from sinking into the pie, put an egg cup in the centre to hold it up). Bake in a hot oven, 400 deg. F., for 40 minutes.

FILLET OF WHALE WITH MUSHROOMS

2 pounds of whale meat
3 tablespoons butter or fat
Salt and pepper

Cut the whale meat into small steaks. Melt fat in the frying pan, add steaks and sprinkle with salt and pepper and let it stand in the frying pan (without cooking) for 1 hour, turning the steaks over once. Pour the fat off into a saucepan and make a sauce as directed below. Then brown the whale steaks, cover with water and simmer, covered for 30 minutes or until tender. Cook away all the water at the end of this time.

SAUCE

1 tablespoon flour   ½ pound mushrooms
1 cup water   2 tablespoons lemon juice

Make the sauce by adding the flour to the melted fat. When well blended, add the water and mushrooms which have been peeled, washed and cut up and lastly add the meat. Cook until the mushrooms are done, add the lemon juice and serve. Serve the whale in the centre of a platter with the sauce over and around it.

WHALE MEAT CASSEROLE

1 pound minced whale meat
2 tablespoons fat
2 onions, sliced
4 carrots, cubed
1 cup water
1 bouillon cube
2 stalks celery, diced
4 to 6 potatoes, sliced
1 teaspoon chopped parsley
Salt and pepper
½ teaspoon thyme

Fry the meat in the fat until browned. Arrange the meat in a greased casserole and add all the vegetables and seasonings. The potatoes may be sliced and laid on top of the casserole for variety. Dissolve the bouillon cube in the hot water (add more water if necessary). Then pour this over the meat and vegetables. Cover and cook in a slow oven, 325 deg. F., for 1½ to 2 hours. Thicken gravy with flour if desired.

Appendix 3.
Air Transport Associates, Inc., Letter to Under State Secretary for Aviation
Affairs, December 10, 1951

P. O. Box 55
BOEING FIELD
SEATTLE 8, WASH.
RAINIER 1035

Air Transport Associates, Inc.

10 Dec. 1951

Under State Sect. for Aviation Affairs
Ministry of War and Marine

Dear Sir:

Air Transport Associates an American company wishes to
purchase ten of your C-46 Commando aircraft located at
Farouk Airport. These Airplanes would be used only in the
United States for domestic hauling.

A.T.A. herebye offers to purchase for fifty thousand U. S.
Dollars, ten Commando aircraft. Condition of sale must include
export permit to the U.S.A.

A.T.A. would also be interested in overhauling Commandos
for the Egyptian Gov. on a one for one basis providing missing
radio's, instruments and compoent parts were made available
by Egyptian Gov. A.T.A. has considerable knowledge of the
commando do to its operations, overhaul and mainteance of this
type aircraft for the past five years.

Sincerely

H. J. Hunt Sec/Treas.

ANCHORAGE OFFICE
217 - 4TH AVE.
PHONE 4-5555   4-0401

SEATTLE OFFICE
GEORGIAN HOTEL
1420½ - 4TH AVE.
SENECA 0436

FAIRBANKS OFFICE
GREIMAN
BUS DEPOT
PHONE EAST 501

ALASKA'S LEADING NON-SCHEDULED AIR LINE

Appendix 4.
Air Transport Associates, Inc., Letter to Amos Heacock,
September 17, 1952

P. O. BOX 55
BOEING FIELD
SEATTLE 8, WASH.
RAINIER 1035

Anchorage, Alaska
September 17, 1952

Amos Heacock
1012 Barr Building
910 17th Street N. W.
Washington 6, D. C.

Dear Amos:

As per our telephone conversation of the past week, I give you the following information. On September 8th, 9th and 10th we conducted a poll in Anchorage to determine
the strength of various political candidates, particularly of the delegate to Congress
whom, as you know, being eith Bob Bartlett or Bob Reeves. Reeves, in the Anchorage
area, had a show of about three to two over Bartlett, however, this poll was conducted
only in Anchorage and it is felt that Bartlett has more strength in Fairbanks, Juneau
and some of the outlying areas. However, it is enough of a warning for us to get to
work and help put Bartlett back in office. We have mapped out various radio programs,
speeches and cartoons to run. I have discussed this with Bartlett and he would be
glad to have you make certain talks for him, however, he would want to approve of everything you had to say beforehand, in other words, no liable. It was also felt that the
best time for you to enter this would be the first of October. At that time you would
make various speeches throughout the territory supporting Bartlett in the October 14th
election. In return for this help, he has agreed to testify for us as a witness in
the irregular air carriers investigation, which I think would be of much value. We
have tried to hold expenses down in this campaign for Bartlett but radio and newspaper
costs so much and it looks like we will spend in the neighborhood of $1500.00.

In regard to your voting in the Territory this year, Amos, I don't think it is possible. I have talked with several people about it and they say you can't do it legally.
The requirements are a one year residence in the Territory and thirty days residence in
the precinct in which you vote. In your case it would be difficult to establish your
residence in the Territory for a year. In your discussion with me you told me how it
could be worked out but after thinking about it awhile I don't believe it practical
since you would certainly be challenged to that claim.

Amos, please let me know if you can make this October 1st speaking engagement. If we
can't get started on the 1st perhaps we could start on the 6th. Speeches could be made
the week of October 6th and Monday the 13th, the day before election. We should spend
a day with Bartlett to discussthe text of your speeches.

Sincerely yours,

AIR TRANSPORT ASSOCIATES

HJH:vr
Howard J. Hunt, Alaska Mgr.

ANCHORAGE OFFICE
217 - 4TH AVE.
PHONE 4-5555   4-0401

SEATTLE OFFICE
GEORGIAN HOTEL
1420½ - 4TH AVE.
SENECA 0436

FAIRBANKS OFFICE
GREIMAN
BUS DEPOT
PHONE EAST 501

ALASKA'S LEADING NON-SCHEDULED AIR LINE

Appendix 5.
Howard J. Hunt Statement before a Subcommittee of the Select Committee Small Business, United States Senate, May 4, 1953

Statement of Howard J. Hunt , Secretary-Treasurer, Air Transport Associates, Inc., Before the Select Committee on Small Business, United States Senate, May 4, 1953.

Mr. Chairman and gentlemen:

My name is Howard J. Hunt. I'm just a simple Iowa farm boy, whom Uncle Sam taught to fly during World War II. In fact, I liked it so much as did a lot of other Veterans that we, instead of returning to our plows, organized veteran airlines. We were young, ambitious, and happy because we had just won a War preserving freedom and equality for all.

However, now, after working five years to build a legitimate business in Alaska that was encouraged by the same government I fought for, I find I am stopped from continuing in business because an agency of the Federal Government says it is a crime for me to compete with its pet carriers. Gentlemen, if the boys in Korea felt the shock of this injustice as I do, they would believe as I do, that I was fighting for Bureaucracy and not the free United States.

Alaska was chosen as our operation because it was the last Frontier of the United States and stood on the threshold of a large development. I went to the Territory five years ago just to organize the Alaska operation and I've been there ever since. I never did get the job done to my satisfaction. I have been Alaska Manager of Air Transport Associates, the last of several independent air carriers to be put out of business by the Civil Aeronautics Board.

We were put out of business this month, not for any reason involving safety – we have flown over 125,000,000 passenger miles without injury to any of the 75,000 passengers we have transported – but we were put out of business because we filled the demand of Alaskans for low cost cargo and passenger transportation – put out of business by the regulation of the Civil Aeronautics Board restricting the number of flights we could make – the same regulation this Committee said in its report to be "a regulation that seems clearly unreasonable."[1]

I've gone sour and I have no dough so I guess I'm a true sourdough. I live in Alaska and have lived there for the past 5 years. I know their problems. Air Transport Associates' complete operation was built upon the demands and needs of the Territory. Whatever service Alaskans have asked us for we have supplied. Ours has been a personalized one. People have come to me and said "Mike, how can I move this or that." I've given them an honest answer. We've developed special techniques for handling perishables, specially insulated and heated trucks for delivery of perishables in 40 below weather.

Our schedules are planned for early morning arrivals so the produce may be sold that day. We pay off any damage claims immediately so as not to cause undue hardship on small business men. Our service has become the standard of the industry and as our competitors have found out, one of the chief complaints they hear is "Why don't you do it like ATA does?" 75% of the people of Alaska, if they had their choice today, would say "Please ship ATA".

Alaskans are very fearful of what will happen to air freight rates and passenger fares once the competition has been throttled by the Civil Aeronautics Board. The rate trend is already up and I'm very surprised that Mr. Fitzgerald, who heads the Civil Aeronautics Board in Alaska, whom you had here a few weeks back did not tell you about it. The truth is, gentlemen, most Alaskans do not even know this gentleman. In fact, the first time they saw him was last year when Joe Adams of the Civil Aeronautics Board was out looking for facts accompanied by Fitzgerald and I'll tell you that the local people sure burned him. I never saw a red neon go on and off so many times so fast.

---

1   Report No. 540 of the Select Committee on Small Business of the United States Senate (82nd Cong. 1st Sess.) entitled "Report on Role of Irregular Airlines in the United States Air Transportation Industry" states that the record of the Civil Aeronautics Board with respect to Irregular Air Carriers has been "confused and devious". This Committee stated it found itself "in strong disagreement with the Board's admitted policy of banishing all large irregular carriers on the grounds that they are 'wilful violators of a regulation that seems clearly unreasonable.'"

Appendix 5, continued.
Howard J. Hunt Statement before a Subcommittee of the Select
Committee Small Business, United States Senate, May 4, 1953

Mr. Fitzgerald did not give you the facts on freight rates nor did he give you the true picture of Ocean Van Lines service to Alaska and Fairbanks.

Alaskan Airlines and Pan American Airways to Fairbanks has a .19 perishable; .17 meat and eggs, .15 mile and .19 dry rate.

Northwestern Airlines to Anchorage has a .18 perishable, .17 dry rate.

Pacific Northern Airlines to Anchorage has a .17 perishable, .15 mile and dry rate.

Air Transport Associates to Anchorage and Fairbanks has a .17 perishable, .16 meat and eggs, .15 dry rate.

Ocean Van Lines which recently went bankrupt, had an 8½¢ rate to Anchorage for controlled refrigeration of perishables.

Gentlemen, can you imagine an ocean-going truck competing with an airplane? It does not and it never will. Speed is the airplane's stock in trade and I doubt very seriously that trucks shall ever have that speed. It is ridiculous to think that surface transportation, however efficient, will ever replace low-cost air cargo service to Alaska. It is only a smoke screen put out by Fitzgerald to conceal the facts concerning the termination of Air Transport Associates' cargo service ordered by the Civil Aeronautics Board.

Air Transport Associates has not carried air freight since March 15th and for that reason the scheduled airlines increased their service. Also, the increase in air cargo transportation is a seasonal increase that comes every year at this time and not because Ocean Van Line goes belly up.

You can see from the rate structure that Alaskans are already paying more for air produce and other fresh foods whether they like it or not. Without non-scheduled competition it will go higher. Air Transport Associates has been pressured right along by scheduled airlines to raise rates but would have no part of a scheme to gorge (sic) Alaskans for higher rates.

The Civil Aeronautics Board is being very near-sighted when they say Alaska has enough air service. What Alaskans are saying is "At what price"? There was plenty of air transportation at 68¢ a pound as early as 1946!

Gentlemen, the Civil Aeronautics Board in carrying out the execution of Air Transport Associates on April 24th as completed a transportation monopoly. Alaskans can use scheduled airlines or else. Gentlemen, the Bureaucracy that Congress has created has become stronger than the elected body that created them. If left unchallenged, this bureaucracy in joint conspiracy with the scheduled airlines will destroy completely the irregular airline industry. As proof, the last surviving air transportation service to Alaska that operates in free enterprise without subsidy has just been destroyed. The Civil Aeronautics Board takes the position that the law passed in 1938 with respect to the revocation of licenses to operate in air transportation relates only to the certified air carriers and does not relate to the nonscheduled carriers, although the law does not state it is inapplicable to the nonscheduled carriers who were not in existence when Congress passed this legislation in 1938. The Civil Aeronautics Act requires[2] the issuance of a cease and desist order before that agency is authorized to revoke an air carrier's operating authority. The Civil Aeronautics Board did not follow this procedure in our case but proceeded to summarily stop us from flying in the same Order they decided that our operations were contrary to their vague and non-understandable regulations which this Committee stated seems "clearly unreasonable."

---

2   Section 401(h) of the Civil Aeronautics Act provides that the Board may revoke a certificate (license) for intentional failure to comply with any order or regulation issued and further provides
"That no such certificate shall be revoked unless the holder thereof fails to comply within a reasonable time to be fixed by the Authority, with an order of the Authority commanding obedience to the provision, or to the order (other than an order issued in accordance with this proviso), rule, regulation, term, condition, or limitation found by the Authority to have been violated."

Appendix 5, continued.
Howard J. Hunt Statement before a Subcommittee of the Select
Committee Small Business, United States Senate, May 4, 1953

In other words, the Board took a short circuit to revoke our operating authority without going through the procedure required by law to first accord us the opportunity to adjust our operations so as to achieve compliance with the Board's orders and thus enable us to keep our property and personnel. Instead, they revoked our authority in the same order and at the same time that they told us that what we were doing did not comply with their interpretation of their regulations although there was an honest difference of opinion as to their legality and interpretation. In other cases the Board issued cease-and-desist orders and in the case of Alaska Airlines, Inc., it issued two cease-and-desist orders and this carrier was later awarded a certificate of public convenience and necessity to fly from the States to Alaska. Member Adams of the Civil Aeronautics Board filed a strong dissent to the decision of the Board to revoke our letter of registration and summarily stopping our operations without first issuing an order to us to "cease and desist" from doing what the Board felt was contrary to the regulations. He said

"I find no justification for taking a short cut in this case"

and

"The more orderly procedure of issuing a cease and desist order, prior to considering revocation of a Letter of Registration, has been followed in a majority of the cases handled by this Board in dealing with the problem of irregular carriers."

I would like to give you at this time the Alaska Development Board's Biennial Report. Also an excerpt by Ralph Browne of the Alaska Development Board concerning non-scheduled airlines. Also my letter to our attorney advising him why Alaska needs more air service. This may be just cumulative evidence because this committee, in its Report No. 540, 82d Cong., 1st Sess., made the following recommendation:

"The Board should act promptly to relieve the hardships it is imposing on Alaska through its restrictions of flights from the United States. The Board should recognize the special need for cargo transportation to Alaska and the lack of alternative forms of low-cost passenger service."

However, the Board did not comply with the Committee's request by relieving the hardships it imposed through its restrictions of flights from the United States, although they had almost two years in which to do this. We feel it is time that the American people find out whether they can look to the Members of Congress they elect to represent them or whether this country is being run by Bureaucracy. I don't know what we can do about it and must leave it to you gentlemen to figure out. I am told that thousands of letters have been received by this Committee and the Civil Aeronautics Board from persons in Alaska making their individual complaints and to make this hearing complete I believe it should be shown how many such letters have been received, if this information is available.

After a study of these exhibits that I have referred to, you become aware that Alaska is about to make a big industrial development that is evidenced everywhere in the territory. Compare Alaska to the Scandinavian countries that support 15 million people on the same latitudes. Alaska now has only 160,000 but is growing so fast it is busting its britches all over. Alaska will support many more airlines just as it will support 15 million people.

Non-scheduled airlines really came into Alaska after World War II during 1946 when the first long maritime strike hit the territory. It was then that the nonskeds really started to fly. They were about 20 in number. Rate reductions were immediately made and the whole air transportation industry began to grow.

These rate reductions brought air transportation direct into Anchorage homes since it became economically possible for local merchants to bring in by plane a large volume of fresh produce, meat, and other essential commodities. It is a matter of record that low-cost fares and freight rates offered by non-sked airlines resulted in subsequent rate reductions by the scheduled lines

Appendix 5, continued.

Howard J. Hunt Statement before a Subcommittee of the Select Committee Small Business, United States Senate, May 4, 1953

as well as improved service on U.S.-Alaska routes. Prices as a result of this competition have dropped from 68¢ a pound to 15¢ on freight and passenger fares from $185 to $60.

Of the original 20 nonscheduled airlines who flew States—Alaska, the last one that still gave service has been ordered out of business. The Civil Aeronautics Board through enforcement of its regulation prescribing such limited frequency and regularity has eliminated the most of them. Others, particularly the DC-3 operators, were swallowed up by competition, but it was not competition that eliminated the large efficient carriers using C-46s—it was the death edicts of the Civil Aeronautics Board.

Everybody in the Territory of Alaska has supported irregular airlines. The Veterans of Foreign Wars on a territorial and on a national basis and the Legislature at Juneau have passed memorial after memorial supporting irregular airlines. Civil organizations, laborers, businessmen, in fact, Alaskans from every walk of life have sent thousands of letters to your committee. Your committee heard voluminous testimony in 1951 including the Governor of Alaska, supporting irregular airlines serving Alaska.

However, the Civil Aeronautics Board, despite your recommendations for Alaska, has gone right ahead with their calculated plan to eliminate irregular airlines just as the Board has followed the Goodkind Plan since 1948. Gentlemen, the only people that don't like the irregular airlines in Alaska are the Civil Aeronautics Board and the scheduled airlines. If this decision were left to the Alaskan people, the decision would be unanimous for the independent airlines.

As one editorial read,

> "The closure of ATA will be a decided loss to this community. It appears there might be some merit to revamping of CAB regulations so that rules of safety will be maintained but which will not discourage and kill good American free enterprise."

Alaska needs more air transportation on all economic levels, and it is morally wrong for an agency of the Federal Government to decree that all Alaskans shall be forced to pay the same price for their air transportation, regardless of their income or their personal desires. The Senate Armed Services Committee appointed a Preparedness Subcommittee which had a task force make a study of Alaska and made a comprehensive report of its findings to Congress in 1951.[3] I believe the contents of the report of that committee, of which Senator Hunt was a member, would be valuable to this Committee. This report shows how Alaska's inaccessibility to the mainland of the United States has been a primary reason for its lag in development, and transportation is one of its greatest problems. This report states—

> "Vast distances and rugged terrain have made the airplane the accepted medium of transportation in Alaska. The percentage of freight and passengers transported by air is 30 times higher in Alaska than in the United States. In addition, air travel has done much to promote the growing Alaskan tourist industry."

Although it was recommended that the report be referred to the departments and committees of Congress interested in the Committee's recommendations, which pointed out that regulations designed to meet the requirements of commercial flying in interstate commerce in the United States should not be applied within Alaska unless local conditions indicate that they are desirable, the Civil Aeronautics Board has continued to apply its regulations applicable to interstate commerce in the United States to flights from the States to Alaska. As Senator Lyndon B. Johnson, Chairman of the Preparedness Subcommittee, recommended to the Chairman of the Senate Armed Services Committee in his letter transmitting this report dated February 13, 1951:

> "At the outset of the Preparedness Subcommittee's work, we agreed that no outpost of America's defenses was of greater strategic importance than Alaska. To ascertain

---

3   Seventh Report of the Preparedness Subcommittee of the Committee on Armed Services, U.S. Senate, under authority of S. Res. 18 (82d Cong.).

Appendix 5, continued.

Howard J. Hunt Statement before a Subcommittee of the Select
Committee Small Business, United States Senate, May 4, 1953

the state of our defenses in Alaska, a three-member task force—Senator Hunt,
Chairman; Senators Morse and Saltonstall undertook an on-the-site investigation.
The investigation has been supplemented by extensive studies and inquiries here
in Washington. The result of their painstaking, diligent, and vigorous labors is the
attached report.

"A strong Alaska is essential to our security. Our continental defenses can be no
stronger than our Alaskan defenses. The security of every American home begins in
the snows of Alaska."

Gentlemen, look at your map. Alaska is an island surrounded by oceans of wilderness. In
case of enemy attack, shipping by truck and water is easily knocked out and your only supply
line is by air. I'm sure that if Uncle Joe were alive today he would be very happy to know that
the Civil Aeronautics Board had killed another non-sked airline operating to Alaska.

The recent action of the Civil Aeronautics Board in putting my company out of business is
only another step in the campaign to put Alaska on ice for another decade or two. Pioneering
and the reward of the frontier certainly are dead. The spoils now go to the boys with the best
pipeline into the Federal Treasury.

Yes, ATA the paradox—last week we paid for our crime against society by death. Our crime
was giving Alaskans too much service too well—a service they voluntarily demanded and we
provided. Since 1948, it amounted to 55,000 passengers and 12 million pounds of freight.

Today as a result of the Civil Aeronautics Board revoking my company's operating authority,
many war veteran employees are out of jobs. Many thousands of dollars worth of airport
equipment must be sold. The Territory of Alaska has lost another pioneer that has done what it
could to settle the new frontier.

On May 9, 1949, my company asked the Board for a certificate of public convenience
and necessity to operate to Alaska and later urged that this application be considered by the
Board, but the Board refused to act although the law says[4] that the Board "shall dispose of such
application as speedily as possible."

The Board held that certain non-certificated freight operators were in violation of the Board's
Regulations but permitted them to operate pending the conclusion of the Air Freight Case then
under consideration by the Board."[5]

In the field of foreign air transportation, the Board found that Trans-Ocean and Seaboard &
Western willfully and knowingly violated the act and the regulations[6] but only cease and desist
orders were issued, pending the determination of their certificate proceedings.

This policy has been established in the field of irregular air transportation. The Board had
ordered the cancellation of the Letters of Modern Air Transport prior to the institution of the
investigation (Docket No. 5132). This order was based upon willful and knowing violation of
the Act and Regulations.

The precise grounds for revoking the Letters of Registration of Air Transport and Modern
are identical. The Letters of Registration of both carriers were revoked upon the finding that
they knowingly and willfully violated the same regulations promulgated by the Board which
limited the frequency and regularity of their flights.

On the same day that the Board revoked our operating authority the Board granted Modern
permission to operate until the conclusion of its investigation of the large irregular carriers,
designed for the purpose of determining their place in the air transportation field. As a result,

---

4   Section 401 (c) of the Civil Aeronautics Act provides:
    "Such application shall be set for public hearing, and the Authority shall dispose of such
    application as speedily as possible."

5   Investigation of Nonscheduled Air Services, 6 C.A.B. 1049; Regulation 295.

6   Trans-Ocean Air Lines, Enforcement Proceeding, Docket No. 3244, decided June 5, 1950; Investigation of
Seaboard & Western Air, Docket No. 3346, decided June 5, 1950.

Appendix 5, continued.
Howard J. Hunt Statement before a Subcommittee of the Select
Committee Small Business, United States Senate, May 4, 1953

Modern is still flying and will continue to do so until this investigation is over. However, our company's license has been revoked.

Through the efforts of the Veterans of Foreign Wars of the Department of Alaska, the Veterans of Foreign Wars of the United States formally intervened in the court case of *Air Transport Associates, Inc. versus Civil Aeronautics Board*[7] and stated in their brief:

"The following is a list of irregular air carriers operating in Alaska which were organized by war veterans:

"Arctic-Pacific Airlines, General Airways, Inc., Trans-Alaska, Pacific-Alaska Air Express, Arnold Air Service, Mt. McKinley Air Service, Inc., Rainier Airlines, Northern Airlines, Inc., Golden North Airlines, Inc., Oswald Airlines, Yakima Sky Chief, Associated Airlines, Seattle Air Charter, Pearson-Alaska, Totem Airlines.

"Of the foregoing, Mt. McKinley Air Service, Inc., and Golden North Airlines, Inc., have had their Letters of Registration revoked by the Civil Aeronautics Board and were thus put out of business. In addition, Arctic-Pacific Airlines was reduced to eight trips on a consent cease-and-desist order which was a settlement of a revocation proceeding. Arnold Air Service received a similar cease and desist order and went into bankruptcy. Of the balance, only General Airways, Inc., is still in business in Alaska, with Trans-Alaska, Pacific-Alaska Air Express, Rainier Airlines, Northern Airlines, Seattle Air Charter, and Totem Airlines having gone out of business for various reasons. However, most of these carriers operating DC-3 equipment, it is understood on information and belief, were unable to survive after certificated airlines reduced cargo rates to 15¢ per lb. and established 'tourist' and other low passenger rates below their costs, supported by mail subsidy.

"Although many of these were forced to discontinue operations because of their failure to meet the vigorous competition of other lines, it must be apparent to any beholder, as it is to the Veterans of Foreign Wars of the United States, that something more than competition has caused this drastic decline in the number of such carriers operating between Seattle and Alaska. * * *

"The case of Air Transport Associates, Inc., has been under study by the Veterans of Foreign Wars of the United States for more than a year; and while the past success of its young veteran pilots is a source of pride, the series of orders which led to its present 'death sentence' is a source of considerable alarm and dismay to this veterans' organization."

Let us examine how all of these air carriers came to go out of business. When the Civil Aeronautics ordered the Alaska Cargo Investigation on March of 1948 they were inquiring into a strange new phenomenon. Non-subsidized independent airlines were providing a huge amount of cargo service to Alaska. Twenty to thirty-five times the cargo transported by the regularly certificated carriers, Northwest Airlines and Pan American Airways was being transported by the independents. Such a volume of non-subsidized transportation threatened the very foundations of the subsidy system.

Why did not the certificated lines provide this cargo service? To any unbiased observer, the reason for this tremendous increase in cargo transportation was obvious. It had cost 68¢ a lb. to transport cargo to Alaska by the certificated lines. It had cost up to $185 each person to go to Alaska on the certificated lines. The independent lines, however, reduced rates to 32¢ to 20¢ to 18¢ per lb. and finally even to 15¢ per lb.

Air cargo transportation to Alaska had come into its own! Fresh fruits, vegetables, eggs, and milk, almost unknown in Alaska, were being transported to this northern territory by the ton.

---

7   Air Transport Associates, Inc. v. CAB, No. 11260 in the U. S. Court of Appeals for the District of Columbia.

Appendix 5, continued.

Howard J. Hunt Statement before a Subcommittee of the Select Committee Small Business, United States Senate, May 4, 1953

Passenger fares quoted by the independents went down to $100 to $80 to $75 to $70 to $69 to $60. A new air coach industry was born out of constructive competition.

The reaction of the Civil Aeronautics Board, however, was not to consider this a good or desirable development. I quote the following excerpts from the report of an examiner[8] to the Board when considering the Alaska situation:

"* * * The City Manager of Anchorage who appeared as a witness submitted estimates of the operations conducted out of the Municipal Airport (Merrill Field) by the nonscheduled carriers between January 1, 1948, and October 27, 1948. These estimates revealed that the non-certificated carriers operated during this period a total of 1,317 trips between Anchorage and the United States or an average of about 132 trips per month for the 10-month period. It was also estimated that these carriers hauled 16,516 passengers and 6,151,000 lbs. of cargo on these trips. An examination of the reports filed with the Board by the large irregular carriers for the fiscal year 1949 lends support to the above estimates in that they show that for the third quarter of 1948, 408 such flights were operated. The total of the flights so conducted for the first and second quarters of 1949 are 220 and 413, respectively, or a total of 1,531 flights for the fiscal year 1949.

"* * * A fair estimate of the total passengers carried by the irregular operators and Alaska Airlines between Anchorage and Seattle (including Everett) would indicate that in the 10 months immediately preceding the hearing in this case there was a pool of at least 19,000 passengers and approximately 9,000,000 lbs. of freight upon which the certificated carriers realized nothing."

The reaction of the Board, therefore, was to view this tremendous advantage to the economy and the people of Alaska as only undesirable competition with the privileged and subsidized certificated carriers. The Board refused to believe that these independent air carriers had the tremendous and overwhelming support of the people of Alaska. Letters to the Board and to your Committee by Chambers of Commerce, housewives, businessmen, labor organizations and even memorials by the Legislature of Alaska were considered only so much "inspired propaganda." Your committee has a file of hundreds of these communications!

The following is a verbatim quotation from Examiner Cusick's report in the Alaska Service Case:

"The fact that a number of city intervenors were of the opinion that the nonscheduled carriers are performing a very essential service and requested that the Board refrain from any action which might jeopardize their existence has not been overlooked * * *. The traffic hauled by the irregular and nonscheduled operators must be viewed as traffic which should be available to the certificated carriers if the public interest would be thereby served. 'Public interest' as used here is an all-inclusive term and encompasses the financial well-being of those carriers supported in whole or in part by funds in the Federal Treasury. * * *"

Certainly a more damaging admission would be hard to find. The policy of the Board is to interpret "public interest," not as the interests of the public to be served, as their interests were expressed by the City intervenors in this case and the popularly-elected legislature, but as the interest of the Civil Aeronautics Board in the "financial well-being" of the subsidized carriers!

When Jack Scavenius, President of Mt. McKinley Airlines, was put out of business by the Civil Aeronautics Board, he was promptly elected to the Anchorage City Council and to the Legislature of Alaska. Apparently the people of Alaska that elected Jack Scavenius didn't believe

8   Report of William F. Cusick, examiner, CAB, Docket No. 3286, U.S.-Alaska Service Case. The CAB had changed the name of the proceedings from the Alaska Cargo Investigation to the U.S.-Alaska Service Case after it was underway.

Appendix 5, continued.

Howard J. Hunt Statement before a Subcommittee of the Select
Committee Small Business, United States Senate, May 4, 1953

that he was a "flagrant and willful" lawbreaker as the Board had implied by the revocation action. A candidate for Mayor of Anchorage attributes his defeat to campaign information linking him to the elimination of the "non-skeds." He was head of the Civil Aeronautics Board in Alaska; he is now working for a scheduled airline. Alaskans have crossed party lines to vote against candidates opposed to the independent airlines. The legislature of the Territory of Alaska has consistently passed memorials urging the Civil Aeronautics Board to preserve the non-scheduled lines, regardless of which party was in control of the legislature.

When Golden North Airlines, operating to Seattle a single aircraft based in Fairbanks was declared a "flagrant and willful" violator of the Board's frequency and regularly regulation and unmercifully put out of business, Chuck Evans, President of Golden North, a former B-17 bomber pilot, appealed his case, but shortly ran out of money in the expensive litigation in the Ninth Circuit Court of Appeals at San Francisco, California.

The residents of Fairbanks were furious. The Civil Aeronautics Board was called Public Enemy No. 1. The residents of Fairbanks hadn't forgotten that in the big freeze of the winter of 1946–47 when for 3 weeks they had suffered temperatures of 50 to 60 degrees below zero, the only carrier that continued to bring them food was Golden North. Both Pan-American and the Army were grounded by the terrific cold, but Golden North kept bringing in vital supplies. Golden North, based at Fairbanks and surrounded by Siberia, Canada, and the Arctic and Pacific Oceans, could find traffic only on the route to Seattle, the U.S. gateway city to Alaska. Although Golden North operated only one C-46 aircraft and interrupted its irregular service for maintenance, the Board found its operations sufficiently "frequent and regular" to put it out of business!!

Examiner Cusick recognized this public support for the non-scheduled air carriers but dismissed it as unimportant when compared to the vital public interest in those carriers supported by the Federal treasury.

Congress, however, had given the Civil Aeronautics Board another definition of "public interest" for their guidance—a definition which was clearly stated in Section 2 entitled "Declaration of Policy" of the Civil Aeronautics Act of 1938. This orders that the Civil Aeronautics Board

> "* * * shall consider the following, among other things, as being in the public interest and in accordance with the public convenience and necessity. * * *

> "The promotion of adequate, economical, and efficient service by air carriers at reasonable charges, without unjust discriminations, undue preferences or advantages, or unfair or destructive competitive practices.

> "Competition to the extent necessary to secure the sound development of an air-transportation system properly adapted to the needs of the foreign and domestic commerce of the United States, of the postal service, and of the national defense."

The 13 carriers operating between the U.S. and Alaska at the time hearings were held in the U.S.-Alaska Service Case had indeed promoted "adequate, economical, and efficient service by air carriers at reasonable charges" but the Board itself had adopted unjust discriminations against these carriers and had permitted undue preferences and advantages for, and has allowed unfair and destructive competitive practices by, the certificated carriers.

The unfair and destructive competitive practices permitted and in fact encouraged by the Board were for the most part in the nature of permitting certificated air carriers to quote cargo rates at ½ to ⅓ of the certificated carriers' costs of providing the cargo service, with the result that many of the non-subsidized operators were driven from business. These rates were resorted to at tremendous expense to the taxpayer to eliminate the non-subsidized competitors.

Appendix 5, continued.
Howard J. Hunt Statement before a Subcommittee of the Select
Committee Small Business, United States Senate, May 4, 1953

It was aptly stated in the brief filed on behalf of the Postmaster General in the Alaska Service Case (Docket #4826):

> "Most of the nonscheduled services listed in exhibit PNA 811–R are entirely unknown except to people who live in Alaska and the Northwest section of the U.S., yet the fact that Pacific Northern characterizes their competition as one of the "intolerable conditions" under which it must operate makes it clear that they are active in seeking, developing, and getting business. In meeting this competition practically all of the certificated carriers have run special flights at fares and rates considerably under those published. In other words, the competition of the type which must have been in the congressional mind is producing the adequate, economical, and efficient service which that congressional mind envisioned. The energetic independents in winning traffic are really bringing about the encouragement and development of Civil Aeronautics."

The above statement makes it clear that the mail subsidy as presently administered is the greatest deterrent to the development of civil aeronautics. That is why the Civil Aeronautics Board is the most formidable obstacle in the way of mass air transportation and a really adequate civil airlift reserve for national defense. Let's take the matter of mail pay away from the Civil Aeronautics Board and place it in the Post Office Department, now headed by a man who it is believed is anxious to save the taxpayers' money where this can be done without adversely affecting service to the public!

The charts of Costs, Rates, and Fares between Seattle and Anchorage and Fairbanks as presented in the Pacific-Northwest Alaska Tariff Investigation (C.A.B. Docket No. 5067) shows how the Board ignores costs in permitting certificated air carriers to quote the same rates as the more efficient demand-type independent carriers. Such below-cost operations which took away this traffic, rapidly drove the operators of DC-3's out of business.

Golden North, Arnold Air Service, Arctic-Pacific and Air Transport Associates, however, operated more efficient C–46 aircraft. All of these air carriers, therefore, were necessarily eliminated by the Board's enforcement activities directed at revocation of their Letters or Registration. Golden North and Air Transport Associates had their Letters of Registration actually revoked, but Arnold Air Service and Arctic Pacific, to avoid litigation, accepted consent "cease and desist" orders to settle the revocation cases entered against them. They went out of business trying to exist on only eight trips a month! To date, no air carrier that has accepted the suicidal eight-trip consent order has survived in common carriage air transportation!

You have heard the views of the Post Office Department. Similar views have been expressed in at least three memorials of the Alaska Legislature. The last one of these, passed by the House March 26, 1953, I present herewith.

Here are the views of the Department of Justice, another government department that is convinced that it is the purpose of the Civil Aeronautics Board to eliminate the independent air carriers and turn their traffic over to the certificated carriers: I quote from "Views of the Department of Justice" concerning the "Amendment and Partial Repeal of the Irregular Air Carriers Exemption, Section 292.1 of the Board's Economic Regulations."

> "The certificated carriers, finding that the business developed by the irregular carriers has become profitable and substantial, are now endeavoring to divert this business to themselves and exclude the irregular carriers from the traffic thus developed.

> "One of the most important questions confronting the Board is whether or not non-scheduled, non-subsidized carriers should be admitted to the air transportation field. The Board has frequently stated their objective is to reduce subsidy in the direction of ultimately eliminating all subsidy.

Appendix 5, continued.
Howard J. Hunt Statement before a Subcommittee of the Select
Committee Small Business, United States Senate, May 4, 1953

"One of the best ways of eliminating subsidy is to permit the non-subsidy carriers to develop in air transportation so that operating statistics showing actual cost of operation would be readily obtainable. The non-subsidized irregular carriers would thus furnish the Board a yardstick for determining the extent to which air carriers can furnish service without subsidy.

"* * * Certainly the Board should have complete up-to-date factual information covering this entire subject matter before adopting a program so drastic as to eliminate the irregular carriers as competitors of the certificated airlines in this important field of transportation.

"The narrowing of the exemption provision in Section 292.1 of the Economic Regulations embodied in the pending proposal will facilitate the elimination of the competition provided by the irregular carriers.

"The purpose of the proposed revisions to Section 292.1 is to effect a tightening of 'restrictions' upon irregular carriers. In the light of interpretation Number 1 to Section 292.1, the definition of 'irregular' air transportation which is proposed would require such infrequency of service as to render the continuance of service by the irregular carriers economically impossible. The scope of irregular operation would be so narrowed as to prohibit the handling of a substantial volume of traffic and to prevent the performance of the amount of service for which there is a demonstrated public demand. The definition is so stringent as to be tantamount to a prohibition against effective irregular carrier operations."

The deadly purpose of the Civil Aeronautics Board to eliminate rather than regulate the independent air carriers, therefore, has been apparent not only to the independent air carriers themselves, but also to the Post Office Department and the Department of Justice. Yet none of these groups were aware of the Goodkind and Wanner Reports which confirms their allegations! In the face of the incontrovertible facts that the Board has now destroyed the right of every self-supporting air carrier operating to Alaska to carry passengers, my company, Air Transport Associates, was ordered out of business and was not permitted to continue its operations beyond the 24th of last month. The Civil Aeronautics Board now has enforcement actions under way directed at eliminating the operating authority of many of the remaining common carrier operations of independent airlines within the continental United States; nevertheless, the Civil Aeronautics Board expects you to believe their totally insincere argument that it is merely enforcing the law against a small group of flagrant and willful violators of its own regulations which were designed to eliminate these Independent Air Carriers from the air transportation business.

In taking this position the Civil Aeronautics Board contends that everybody is out of step except the Board. The Board is saying in effect that not only are the irregular air carriers wrong, but the Post Office Department that pays the bill is wrong, the Department of Justice that enforces the antitrust policy of the United States is wrong, and finally they would have you believe your own investigation Senate Select Committee on Small Business is wrong. I quote from your Committee's official recommendations which were rendered in its report filed July 11, 1951 after several days investigation of the Role of the Large Irregular Airlines in United States Air Transportation:

"In selecting carriers, the Board should not consider the matter of past violations of Section 292.1 which resulted from greater regularity or frequency than may have been considered allowable at that time. Your committee believes that the record of the Board in this matter has been confused and devious. Your committee does not want to imply any approval of violations of regulations, but it finds itself in strong disagreement with

Appendix 5, continued.
Howard J. Hunt Statement before a Subcommittee of the Select
Committee Small Business, United States Senate, May 4, 1953

the Board's admitted policy of banishing all large irregulars on the grounds that they are 'willful violators' of a regulation that seems clearly unreasonable.

"2. ALASKA

"The Board should act promptly to relieve the hardships it is imposing on Alaska through its restriction of flights from the United States. The Board should recognize the special need for cargo transportation to Alaska and the lack of alternative forms of low-cost passenger service."

The only action of any importance taken by the Civil Aeronautics Board as a result of the Senate Small Business Committee recommendations was the delaying action of ordering the Large Irregular Air Carrier Investigation on September 21, 1951. However, the Board on the very same date ordered the revocation of my Company's Letter of Registration.

It is Air Transport Associates' belief that the Board and the scheduled airlines are of the opinion that to break Air Transport Associates, Inc. is to break the back of the resistance to the Board's policy of eliminating these lines. Indeed, as if to place sole emphasis upon the importance of the revocation of Air Transport Associates, Inc., Letter of Registration, the Board on the same day, September 21, 1951, ordered the reinstatement of Modern Air Transport, a carrier previously branded as a "flagrant and willful violator" for whom they had previously denied an exemption to continue operations. Dozens of other carriers have had their exemptions denied also, but the Board's order on September 21, 1951, as a result of the Senate Small Business Committee investigation, reinstated them until the conclusion of the Large Irregular Air Carrier Investigation. My Company, the last survivor of the Board's campaign to eliminate independent airlines operating to Alaska, and the first independent air carrier to be put out of business in defiance of the Senate Small Business Committee's report and recommendations, has operated its last flight to Alaska by the defiance of this Committee's recommendations unless this Committee will do something that will require the Board to reinstate its operating authority. Observers on both sides of this controversy see in the elimination of my Company the beginning of the end of all common-carrier operations of the independents.

The best proof of the Board's insincerity in ordering the Large Irregular Air Carrier Investigation, however, was their action in placing Lewis W. Goodkind, the author of the secret master plan of 1948, in charge of the Board's prosecution of the Investigation so there would be no question about the plan which he authored. This was a most unusual procedure, in that ordinarily a member of the Board's legal staff would have been assigned these duties.

The Large Irregular Air Carrier Investigation was the only major action taken by the Civil Aeronautics Board to eliminate the independent air carriers that was not planned in 1948 by Lewis W. Goodkind and John H. Wanner of the Board's staff. (Incidentally, Mr. Wanner, as Assistant General Counsel of the Civil Aeronautics Board, handled the Board's end of the court proceedings that resulted in the confirmation of the revocation of Air Transport Associates, Inc.'s, operating authority.) The reason for the only major deviation from the master plan is clear. The Senate Small Business Committee stepped in and forced the suspension of the planned procedure of wholesale denials of individual exemptions after the blanket exemption applying to all large irregular carriers had been repealed in accordance with the master plan. This committee can again step in and save the industry. It can also save my Company if it will.

The denial of exemption applications is only one of four distinct methods employed by the Civil Aeronautics Board in its efforts to reduce and eliminate non-scheduled air carriers. The first is the method of increasingly restricting interpretations of Regulation 291 to the point where no non-scheduled air carrier dependent upon revenues from common carrier air transportation can survive under them. The second method is to encourage the quotation of tariffs below the costs of operations of the scheduled air carriers to drive the independents from the field by economic means through authorizing mail pay reimbursements to cover the losses sustained therefrom. The third method is to conduct enforcement proceedings under Regulation 291 to secure cease

Appendix 5, continued.
Howard J. Hunt Statement before a Subcommittee of the Select
Committee Small Business, United States Senate, May 4, 1953

and desist orders and orders to revoke the Letters of Registration of these carriers. The fourth method is accomplished by means of denials of individual exemption applications, after the blanket exemption was terminated. The Board, therefore, did not suspend its plan of elimination of the independent air carriers, but merely modified the fourth method of putting these air carriers out of business in response to pressure from the Senate Small Business Committee.

It substituted "death by delay" through expediting enforcement actions while delaying certificate and exemption proceedings. This was true in the case of Air Transport Associates, Inc. The Civil Aeronautics Board has apparently finally succeeded in putting Air Transport Associates out of business a bare couple of months before it would have to consider Air Transport Associates' four year old certificate application, filed in May, 1949.

How has this affected the transportation between the Pacific Northwest and Alaska? In the words of Examiner William F. Cusick in his opinion on the U.S.-Alaska Service case—

"There was a pool of at least 19,000 passengers and approximately 9,000,000 pounds of freight upon which the certificated carriers realized nothing."

On an annual basis the freight carried, therefore, was greater than the less than 10,000,000 pounds of cargo transported by both Northwest Airlines and Pan American Airlines to Anchorage and Fairbanks in the year 1951. The costs of these carriers for this service are covered by the chart of Costs, Rates, and Fares which I will submit as a part of this record.

Based upon this chart's cost information which was established in the Northwest-Alaska Tariff Investigation, the loss on cargo operations by Northwest Airlines and Pan American Airways for the year 1951 was over one and three quarters millions of dollars—a loss which was made up in mail pay at the expense of the taxpayers. The result has been, therefore, that the Civil Aeronautics Board has been able to drive out an entire non-subsidized air carrier industry operating to Alaska and replace it with subsidized carriers at the expense of the tax payers.

The two new carriers, Pacific Northern Airlines and Alaska Airlines, are awarded over three quarters of a million dollars in mail pay per year without any increase in mail service over that provided originally by Northwest Airlines and Pan American Airways to Anchorage and Fairbanks. There is no doubt, therefore, that the elimination of independent non-subsidized air carriers between Seattle and Alaska is costing the government approximately four million dollars per year! The Board and the scheduled airlines contend that the Civil Aeronautics Act was a mandate to establish a regulated monopoly. However, a careful reading of the Act makes clear that this is not true. The Congress provided for a regulated competition—not a regulated monopoly!

What is Air Transport Associates, Inc. able to do for the people of Alaska and for the shippers of the Pacific Northwest? Air Transport Associates has clearly demonstrated that it is within striking range of providing a non-subsidized cargo service to Alaska in connection with its low cost passenger service. The cost of 16.64¢ per pound (see Cost Chart) that Air Transport Associates, Inc. established in 1951 between Seattle and Anchorage as against prices of 15¢ to 17¢ a pound is hardly an indication of what the limit of its capabilities could be under a Certificate of Public Convenience and Necessity providing for non-subsidized service to Alaska.

The certificated and subsidized carriers' costs as shown on the chart are almost 29¢ a pound. A reduction of subsidy applied to these four carriers will force increased cargo rates or reduction of cargo service if non-subsidized cargo carriers are eliminated. The authorization of unlimited non-subsidized cargo service, however, would confine the presently certificated carriers to the profitable passenger and mail service, eliminating this need for subsidy! The obvious solution for the benefit of Alaskans, the taxpayers, the four certified mail and passenger airlines, and Air Transport Associates, Inc. is to grant Air Transport Associates, Inc. a non-subsidized cargo certificate.

Appendix 5, continued.
Howard J. Hunt Statement before a Subcommittee of the Select
Committee Small Business, United States Senate, May 4, 1953

Air Transport Associates, Inc. has been negotiating with the Chase Aircraft Company, manufacturers of the Chase C-123, a military assault transport. If difficulties of delivery involved in a large backlog of military orders can be overcome, and the commercial version of this aircraft known as the Chase Super Avitruck with R-3350 engines instead of R-2800 engines can be produced for Air Transport Associates, Air Transport Associates would then be able to provide much more adequate service to meet the needs of the development of Alaska. In addition to reequipping with these more efficient aircraft capable of transporting over 25,000 pounds non-stop from Seattle to Anchorage, Air Transport Associates would also invest in the development of a southbound freight haul so that Alaskans need not pay round trip costs to get their cargo to Alaska.

The management of Air Transport Associates contemplates rates in the region of 10 cents a pound northbound and 8 cents per pound southbound to provide a profit on the round-trip. 17 to 19 cents per pound northbound, with little southbound cargo is the prevailing situation now. The substantial reduction in rates, we are convinced, will greatly increase the market for northbound air freight and stimulate the fishing industry, which is Alaska's largest industry to expand and develop the fresh seafoods industry. At present the $100,000,000 a year industry in Alaska is engaged almost exclusively in the production of canned and frozen fish and seafoods with most of the production occurring during a very limited season. Alaska has developed my business. My Company hopes to reciprocate by investing in the development of Alaska, if given the opportunity.

I have thoroughly investigated the fishing industry in Alaska, having hauled in nets and pewed salmon in Cook Inlet, dug, transported and marketed razor clams from Polly Creek Beach, investigated shrimp and Dungeness crab at Homer and Seldovia, discussed dragging operations for king crab with fishermen of Kodiak and Prince William Sound, and have transported hundreds of thousands of pounds of fish, crab, and clams to the United States from Cook Inlet area, from Kodiak, from Prince William Sound, and from the Yakutat area.

Within the continental United States what is ordinarily termed air freight is in reality air express because air shipment is usually a method of specially expediting the shipment of commodities that ordinarily are transported by surface means. In Alaska, however, a true air-freight industry has been established in the northbound direction, because air shipment is the ordinary method of transporting fresh fruit, vegetables, eggs, fresh meats, and other perishable foods to Alaska. When markets are developed in the midwest United States for fresh fish fillets, clams, Dungeness, and king crab, shrimp, scallops, and other fresh seafoods on a volume basis, and when these seafoods are transported from Alaska to the midwest by new and large economical transport aircraft, then we will truly have a new industry in Alaska, made possible by lower rates and better methods of air transportation.

The independent airline industry has pioneered and developed every new air transportation market since World War II and has later seen these markets taken from them by bureaucratic edicts. This includes the aircoach market, the air freight market, the agricultural labor transportation market, and the combination passenger-cargo market from the United States to Alaska. New frontiers remain to be developed. When they are developed, the initiative will again come only from the free enterprise segment of the air transportation industry that the Civil Aeronautics Board has been determined to wipe out. Air Transport Associates, Inc., wants only Civil Aeronautics Board permission to develop the new frontiers of all-cargo service between the United States and Alaska.

The great airlift that would be made available by encouraging non-subsidized air carriers operating to Alaska instead of stamping them out of existence would be a tremendous aid to the defense of Alaska and the United States on our northern frontiers. The Chase Super-Avitrucks which Air Transport Associates, Inc., hopes to use, are capable of landing men, vehicles, and guns up to 155 mm. howitzers on any level beach or bush airfield in Alaska—or in Siberia, for that matter!

Appendix 6.
History of Air Transport Associates, Inc.

WORLD-WIDE CHARTERS

Air Transport Associates, Inc.

BOX 55, BOEING FIELD TERMINAL
SEATTLE 8, WASHINGTON
RAinier 1035

● 7½ hours non-stop
Anchorage-Seattle

● Lowest Passenger and
Cargo Rates on non-
scheduled flights
Seattle-Chicago-New
York-San Francisco

● Seattle Passenger Office:
1420 - 4th Ave.
Phone: Se. 0436

● Anchorage Office:
Trade Winds,
237 4th Avenue
Phone: Main 406

● Fairbanks Office:
c/o Model Cafe
P.O. Box 501
Phone: EAst 501

HISTORY OF AIR TRANSPORT ASSOCIATES, INC.

The idea of Air Transport Associates was born in the
summer of 1946. Flying officers of the Air Transport Command
led by Amos E. Heacock worked out a practical plan for
transition from war to peace-time service. Ten veterans and
one non-veteran formed a partnership known as the Northern
Pacific Aero Trading and Transportation Company.

This partnership, the forerunner of Air Transport
Associates, established its place of business on John Rodgers
Airport, Honolulu, Hawaii. From this base of operations, three
C-46-F Curtiss Commandos were obtained in Guam, Marianas Islands.
Two C-46's were constructed from three salvage aircraft and
flown to Honolulu. Three PBY-5A Catalina Amphibians were purchased from war surplus near Honolulu. The very successful
operations, including an apartment housing project, were
liquidated by March, 1948.

With capital more than doubled by the successful operations of Northern Pacific Aero Trading and Transportation
Company, five of the partners formed Air Transport Associates,
Inc., which was incorporated in May of 1948 under the laws of
the State of Washington. Arrangements were made to lease three
C-46-F Curtiss Commandos from the United States Army Air Forces.
The first of these aircraft left the Air Base at Pyote, Texas
on June 18, 1948. On July 23, 1948, ATA's trip was made
to Anchorage and Kenai, Alaska.

Throughout the summer of 1948 operations were strictly
cargo. In the first three months of operation, ATA transported
more fish, crab, and other sea foods south to Seattle than all
other Seattle-Alaska carriers combined. Late in October, and
in November and December, with considerable operational experience under its belt, ATA developed its famous "Sleep to Seattle"

ALASKA AIR FREIGHT
AND PASSENGER SERVICE

★

THREE HUGE C-46
CURTISS COMMANDOS
TO SERVE YOU!

Appendix 6.
History of Air Transport Associates, Inc., Continued

WORLD-WIDE CHARTERS

Air Transport Associates, Inc.

BOX 55, BOEING FIELD TERMINAL
SEATTLE 8, WASHINGTON
RAinier 1035

7½ hours non-stop
Anchorage-Seattle

Lowest Passenger and
Cargo Rates on non-
scheduled flights
Seattle-Chicago-New
York-San Francisco

Seattle Passenger Office:
1420 - 4th Ave.
Phone: Se. 0436

Anchorage Office:
Trade Winds,
237 4th Avenue
Phone: Main 406

Fairbanks Office:
c/o Model Cafe
P.O. Box 501
Phone: EAst 501

History of Air Transport Associates, Inc. - 2

service which for the first time offered the public southbound
sleeper service from Anchorage to Seattle. Within two weeks
of the opening of its campaign for passengers, ATA became the
leading non-scheduled carrier of passengers from Anchorage to
Seattle.

By the end of December, 1948, ATA had become the leading
non-scheduled carrier to Alaska. Its service had by that time
been extended to Fairbanks. In addition, ATA transported two
capacity loads of soldiers on Christmas and New Year's leave
from Fort Lewis, Washington, to Chicago and New York, and return.

By this time ATA had equipped one of its airplanes,
N1301N, the "City of Cordova" with a fifty-two seat installation
of Gugler seats on aluminum hat sections riveted to the floor.
This space and weight saving cargo-passenger installation soon
became the standard for the C-46's operating to Alaska and even
in other parts of the country. A good deal of the installation's
efficiency lay in the ability to fold the Gugler seats completely
for efficient cargo handling.

In February, 1949, ATA was one of the first C-46 operators
to convert its engines and accessory installations to complete
fire-proofing forward of the fire-wall. The latest of CAA fire
prevention requirements were complied with at that time.

ATA northbound passenger operations did not get under way
until after the first of the year. Revolutionary low fares
southbound for passengers in January and February had proved
that there was an untapped market even in these poor winter
months. By March and April ATA had conclusively demonstrated
that it was possible to conduct profitable operations at the
lowest fares that Alaska ever had known.

ALASKA AIR FREIGHT
AND PASSENGER SERVICE

THREE HUGE C-46
CURTISS COMMANDOS
TO SERVE YOU!

Appendix 6.
History of Air Transport Associates, Inc., Continued

WORLD-WIDE CHARTERS

Air Transport Associates, Inc.

BOX 55, BOEING FIELD TERMINAL
SEATTLE 8, WASHINGTON
RAinier 1035

7½ hours non-stop
Anchorage-Seattle

Lowest Passenger and
Cargo Rates on non-
scheduled flights
Seattle-Chicago-New
York-San Francisco

Seattle Passenger Office:
1420 - 4th Ave.
Phone: Se. 0436

Anchorage Office:
Trade Winds,
237 4th Avenue
Phone: Main 406

Fairbanks Office:
c/o Model Cafe
P.O. Box 501
Phone: EAst 501

History of Air Transport Associates, Inc. - 3

At the same time, quoting the same freight tariffs as
the scheduled airlines, ATA, by superior service, had attracted
most of the larger freight accounts. It had become the leading
air service for the U. S. Government, serving the Alaska
Railroad, the Alaska Road Commission and the Post Quartermaster
at Ford Richardson.

April, May and June of 1949 were months of very rapid
expansion of ATA. The public demand for its services had
doubled and tripled. In June over $67,000.00 gross revenue
was recorded by the company at the lowest passenger and freight
rates Alaska ever had known.

An idea of the volume of traffic handled by ATA is
indicated by the following figures for the last three months,
comprising the second quarter of 1949 :

425 Operational Landings and Takeoffs

201,000 Ton Miles of Cargo Transportation

3,300,000 Passenger Miles of Transportation

ALASKA AIR FREIGHT
AND PASSENGER SERVICE

THREE HUGE C-46
CURTISS COMMANDOS
TO SERVE YOU !

Appendix 6.
History of Air Transport Associates, Inc., Continued

WORLD-WIDE CHARTERS

Air Transport Associates, Inc.

BOX 55, BOEING FIELD TERMINAL
SEATTLE 8, WASHINGTON
RAinier 1035

● 7½ hours non-stop
Anchorage-Seattle

● Lowest Passenger and
Cargo Rates on non-
scheduled flights
Seattle-Chicago-New
York-San Francisco

● Seattle Passenger Office:
1420 - 4th Ave.
Phone: Se. 0436

● Anchorage Office:
Trade Winds,
237 4th Avenue
Phone: Main 406

● Fairbanks Office:
c/o Model Cafe
P.O. Box 501
Phone: EAst 501

History of Air Transport Associates, Inc. - 4

On May 26, 1949, Amos E. Heacock as president of the
National Independent Air Carriers expounded his views before
the Senate Committee on Foreign and Interstate Commerce. His
central theme - that the public was demanding more and better
low cost air transportation - was acted upon by ATA. Stopping
at Wright Field on his way back from Washington, Mr. Heacock
located two additional aircraft in Tulsa, Oklahoma. By taking
over the lease of the two aircraft, Air Transport Associates
obtained the means for offering additional service. Although
licensed by the CAA in Oklahoma, the aircraft were below the
company standard for fire protection. For this reason, extensive
modifications were completed on them before being put into service.
N5075N with low time engines was put into service after the maintenance and modification work was completed and test flights
indicated the fine condition of the aircraft. This aircraft was
in operational service for approximately 100 hours before the
accident at Boeing Field. Although the engines on N5076N had not
reached their full allotment of time, President Amos. E. Heacock
ordered both engines changed because of lack of knowledge of
exact condition and previous maintenance.

In his presentation before the Senate Committee, Heacock
pointed out that at 22¢ a ton mile ATA's costs were a fraction
of those of its scheduled airline competitors. ATA's most
efficient scheduled competitor to Alaska had a cost of 77¢ a ton
mile. As freight service is offered by scheduled and non-scheduled
carriers at from 20 to 22¢ a ton mile, it is apparent that only
the ATA operation is economically justified. It is apparent that,
without subsidy, no scheduled carrier can maintain the service to
shippers and to Alaskan consumers.

Mr. Heacock also pointed out to the Senate Committee that
ATA had made its savings in unnecessary general and indirect
expense. Thus, ATA Direct Aircraft Operating Expense is 76½%

ALASKA AIR FREIGHT
AND PASSENGER SERVICE

THREE HUGE C-46
CURTISS COMMANDOS
TO SERVE YOU!

Appendix 6.
History of Air Transport Associates, Inc., Continued

WORLD-WIDE CHARTERS

Air Transport Associates, Inc.

BOX 55, BOEING FIELD TERMINAL
SEATTLE 8, WASHINGTON
RAinier 1035

7½ hours non-stop
Anchorage-Seattle

Lowest Passenger and
Cargo Rates on non-
scheduled flights
Seattle-Chicago-New
York-San Francisco

Seattle Passenger Office:
1420 - 4th Ave.
Phone: Se. 0436

Anchorage Office:

Trade Winds,
237 4th Avenue
Phone: Main 406

Fairbanks Office:

c/o Model Cafe
P.O. Box 501
Phone: EAst 501

History of Air Transport Associates, Inc. - 5

of its total expenses, whereas its scheduled competitors'
Direct Aircraft Operating Expense is from 46 to 47% of their
entire cost, while their General and Indirect (overhead)
Expenses ran from 52 to 54%. Thus it can be seen that ATA has
made cost reductions without reducing emphasis on any factor
that may affect safety.

Recently, during the month of July, ATA has engaged in
large scale fish operations, the largest ever attempted by any
air carrier. Fish are purchased and flown to Seattle for canning.
This is extremely significant in terms of potential service to
Alaska because the ATA report which was presented to the Senate
Committee indicated that 13¢ a ton mile costs were possible by
obtaining full southbound loads.

ATA had 51 persons depending upon the company for employment
during the last three months. $43,000.00 was paid out in direct
payrolls. Indirect payrolls made possible by ATA are at least
double this figure. It is our sincere desire to continue building
the safest and most efficient operation to Alaska. In spite of
the unfortunate accident now being investigated, ATA's safety
record does not compare unfavorably with that of the three scheduled carriers that are serving or have served the Seattle-Alaska
run.

ATA is operating under CAA Operating Certificate No. 7-221
and CAB Letter of Registration No. 1896.

ALASKA AIR FREIGHT
AND PASSENGER SERVICE

THREE HUGE C-46
CURTISS COMMANDOS
TO SERVE YOU!

Appendix 7.
Aircoach Transport Association, Inc., Press Release,
May 4, 1953

• NEWS BUREAU •
AIRCOACH TRANSPORT ASSOCIATION, INC.
Suite 211, Wyatt Bldg., 777 14th St., N. W., Wash., D. C.
MEtropolitan 8-6150

P R E S S   R E L E A S E

FOR IMMEDIATE RELEASE

WASHINGTON- May 4 - Howard J. Hunt, operator of a small airline serving
Alaska from Seattle, Wash., today accused the Civil Aeronautics Board "in
joint conspiracy with the scheduled airlines" of establishing an air transportation "monopoly" at the expense of the people of Alaska.

Hunt told a Senate Small Business Committee hearing that his company, Air
Transport Associates, "the last surviving air transportation service to Alaska
that operates in free enterprise without subsidy" was ordered out of business
by the CAB on April 24.

"After working five years to build a legitimate business in Alaska that was
encouraged by the same government I fought for, I find I am stopped from continuing in business because an agency of the Federal Government says it is a
crime for me to compete with its pet carriers, Sir, if the boys in Korea felt
the shock of this injustice as I do, they would believe as I do, that I was
fighting for Bureaucracy and not the free United States. In a few words, I am
the small American business man who has been forced out of business - because
I made good," he asserted.

Hunt charged that statements by the CAB that Alaska has enough air service
without the independent airlines are "only a smoke screen to conceal the facts
concerning the termination of Air Transport Associates service."

Hunt disclosed that Alaskans are already paying more for air produce and
other fresh foods. He said that the impact of independent airline service to

Continued on next page

Appendix 7, continued
Aircoach Transport Association, Inc., Press Release,
May 4, 1953

- 2 -

Alaska reduced the air freight rates on perishables and fresh milk from 68¢ a pound to 15¢ a pound "but with this competition out of the picture, the 68 cents a pound rate will soon be back and the cost of perishable foods and fresh milk will once again be outside the pocketbooks of Alaskans.

"The action of the CAB is another step in the campaign to put Alaska on ice for another decade or two. Pioneering and the reward of the Frontier certainly are dead. The spoils now go to the boys with the best pipeline into the Federal Treasury, the boys who get the subsidy.

"Gentlemen, look at your map, Alaska is an Island surrounded by oceans of wilderness. In case of enemy attack, shipping by truck and water is easily knocked out and your only supply line is by air. I'm sure that if Uncle Joe were alive today he would be very happy to know that the CAB has killed another nonsked airline operating to Alaska. You just heard General Knerr on that sub-ject.

"Yes, ATA the paradox--last week we paid for our crime against Society by death. Our crime was giving Alaskans too much service too well--a service they voluntarily demanded and we provided under the American Free Enterprise System. Since 1948, it amounted to 55,000 passengers and 12 million pounds of freight.

"Today, because of CAB action, many war veteran employees are out of jobs. Many thousands of dollars worth of airport equipment must be sold. The Territory of Alaska has lost the services of our group--all of us War Veterans with a true pioneer spirit--that has done what it could to settle the new frontier, unless you do something to rectify this injustice. There is no place else to appeal.

"MAY GOD HELP US AND LET NOT THE CAB DESTROY US!!!"

Appendix 8.
Air Transport Associates, Inc., Interoffice Communications,
March 30, 1953

INTER-OFFICE COMMUNICATIONS

DATE_____19____

TO | FROM

PROMPT PRINTERS MAIN 2242

SUBJECT:

ATA TO CONTINUE SERVICE

Duncan Miller, General Manager of Air Transport Associates announced today that after a special board of directors meeting, that ATA will not shut down operations in Alaska or anywhere else as had been announced earlier in the week by H. J. Hunt, Alaska Manager. "We'll never quite. They'll have to drag us out by force! We have a tremendous investment in the future of Alaska and will never voluntarily abandon it", Miller stated.

Miller said that the intense public demand for the continuation of the service of ATA has influenced the company to continue all operations. "We'll never let the Alaskans down who have stood 100% behind us for the past five years", he stated. "We'll fight and fight hard for the right to serve Alaskans with low cost passenger and freight service", said Miller.

Miller expressed the desire that a large number of Alaskans would attend the House Interstate and Foreign Commerce Committee Hearings in Seattle on April 8, 1953. Headed by Chairman James Dolliver this committee is including irregular airlines services to Alaska as an important part of the hearings.

Miller stated "We still have legal appeals to the courts with new evidence which has been brought out by certain Congressional Committees in investigating the strangulation by the CAB of irregular airlines." "We'll never say die", he remarked. "As long as Alaskans are behind us we'll have the courage to fight, and we'll wing Something that is morally right and in the public interest will win. It can't be stamped out by an agency of the Federal Government that has a rough ax to grind", Miller concluded.

Appendix 9.
Air Transport Associates, Inc., Interoffice Communications,
March 30, 1953

INTER-OFFICE COMMUNICATIONS

DATE _____ 19 ___

TO

FROM

PROMPT PRINTERS MAIN 2242

SUBJECT:

Air Transport Associates, Inc. announced today it was ceasing operations immediately as a result of the CAB order of March 24, 1953.

Howard J. Hunt, Alaska Manager of ATA, revealed in Anchorage today that the large carrier had been given it's final death certificate, "Under the terms of the order we are allowed thirty days to put our affairs in order, pack our bags and go home. We have already ceased all air cargo operations and as soon as certain contract obligations are fulfilled on passenger transportation we will cease all operations."

"We hope this action will work no hardship on grocery stores and the many Alaskans who have depended on our carrying fresh produce into the Territory. We have carried on our thriving business since 1948 despite constant harrassment by the CAB, however, according to the CAB we gave too much service to Alaskans and flew too frequently. Our service has been one of demand rather than schedule. We ran our flights whenever Alaskans demanded it."

"ATA last year carried over three million pounds of freight and about 21,000 passengers to and from the Territory. That's a pretty large business just to walk away from. Certainly Alaskans needed that service or they would not have used it."

"ATA has always attempted to bring the lowest cost passenger fares and freight rates to Alaskans. We believed that the biggest market in air transportation was in the low cost transportation and not in the luxury transportation. Our savings were your savings in providing this low cost service. We have tried to serve Alaska's need by running planes as frequently as Alaskan's demanded.

Again I want to thank the many thousand of Alaskans who have supported us by letters and telegrams throughout our long fight with the CAB for survival. It is evident that Alaskans have a hard time making themselves heard behind the Bureaucratic Barrier in Washington, D. C. This is also evidenced by the shelving of Alaska Statehood.

We will fight with all our strength for a scheduled certificate in the States-Alaska certificate case to be heard in June. If successfull we could again serve you, but in the interim we must stop all service to Alaskans as per the orders of the CAB or be held in contempt of court.

We sincerely hope that our successors, the scheduled airlines, can supply a comparable service at comparable air freight rates as we have endeavored to do in the past.

ATA employs over 165 people in it's operations which stretch all the way from Alaska to New York City, serving the great need that exists today for the low cost air transportation."

Appendix 10.
Air Transport Associates, Inc., Interoffice Communications, March 31, 1953

INTER-OFFICE COMMUNICATIONS

DATE____3/31/_____19_53_

TO   Duncan Miller

FROM

H. J. Hunt

PROMPT PRINTERS MAIN 3342

SUBJECT:

I see little salvage of our Alaska business through other carriers—mainly because the first thing you lose is economic control of the carrier. They will run anytime they feel like it and you will immediately lose all the ATA good will. I favor only a very temporary deal until such time as all equipment and facilities can be liquidated, or ACE and SDAT can operate full steam.

Frankly, this is the last year twin *engine* stuff is going to fly the coast. People not only want four engines now but also want pressurized cabins. Unless we can procure four engine equipment we will be through as Alaska carriers after this year. Your figures on commission profits are completely too high, actually I think you are going to find yourself doing a lot less business than you did the year before and I also forecast the same for south bound traffic.

As far as selling maintenanee to the other carriers —it's not in the cards — only on a basis that guarantees wages of mechanics whether used or not.

I would suggest you sell the DC-4 junk pile for $140,000.00. That wipes off most of your money problems as well as taking care of what to do with the pile.

Yes, to your question on Airline Services BFI __ reduce them to a minimum, we'll worry later about expansion if it should ever bless us again.

As you can read from the newspapers and the enclosed press releases, ATA is through. However, Alaskans don't seem aroused, the wolf call has been sounded so many times it has no effects anymore.

All personell have been laid off except caretakers at Fairbanks and Anchorage. The only way to cut overhead is to do it now and not wait until overhead consumes you. No operation can be carried on with hope alone. I suggest you cut your own personell to the bare and forget about these rabbit in the hat hopes.

Participating carriers are not the answer unless we have economic control. I am convinced that a cooperative would last about one week and make money only for the attorneys to defend us. Frankly, I'd rather sell our layout in Anchorage and Fairbanks to a responsible carrier. Otherwise, you're just goin to fade away leaving a bad taste in everybodys mouth. I'm not getting any younger, I'm wanting to devote my time and energy to a business with a visible future.

Appendix 11.

Air Transport Associates, Inc., Interoffice Communications, April 22, 1953

INTER-OFFICE COMMUNICATIONS

DATE ___April 22,___ ___19 53___

TO   Vickie and Givens   FROM   Hunt – Seattle

PROMPT PRINTERS MAIN 2242

SUBJECT:

Consider this your unemployment notice as of May 15, 1953. You shall be a C.A.B. casualty.

Collect all accounts, pull in all tickets and prepare for an audit some-time early in May. NSF checks and bad accounts should be turned over to a Collection Agency or attorney and a record made of such.

I am open for purchase or lease of the trucks and etc. The office I am interested in sub-leasing in the neighorhood of $700.00 per month or whatever deals I can make.

Thursday afternoon NB is the last flite. The scheduled airlines and the C.A.B. have finally won — there are no more non-scheduled airlines serving Alaska. I'll be going back to D.C. for a plea before the Senate, but very little hope is held from such. Shall be early May before I return so any questions you have communicate with Seattle.

Press releases are being forwarded for you to release.

Appendix 12.
Howard Hunt Resume, April 2, 1959

Howard Hunt

Resume

1939 Earned solo pilot license by working at airport and other odd
jobs.

1941 Iowa State College, three years, mechanical engineering.

1942 Iowa State College, primary and secondary civilian pilot
training.

1943 Graduated from Army Air Corps Flying School as twin engine
pilot.

1943 Graduated from Instrument Flying School, St. Joseph, Missouri.

1944 Graduated from Instrument Flying School, Homestead, Florida.

1945 Assigned to four engine transport squad on, Wilmington,
Delaware, flying support of B-29 in India. Also transporting wounded
troops and supplies to combat area of the United Kingdom, North
Africa and India. Assigned as route check pilot to instruct pilots in
safe and proper operations procedures.

1945 Assigned four engine transport squadron, Fairfield-Suisan,
California, flying support for invasion and occupation of Tokyo and
transporting wounded troops and supplies in Tokyo. Was assigned check
pilot and instructor pilot. Checked competency of pilots and gave
instruction in proper operations in C-54 and C-47. My duties also
consisted of instructing pilots in acquiring civilian ATRs in DC-4.

1947 Released from active duty as Captain after logging 3,750 hours
as plane commander.

1948 Helped organize and promote aviation business of Northern
Pacific Aero Trading and Transportation Company in Honolulu, whose
purpose was to acquire three C-46s and start an airline to Alaska.
The company liquidated after running out of money. I supervised the
rebuilding of three C-46s and two PBYs from Guam, ferried them to
California and sold to Slick.

1949 Helped organize and promote Air Transport Associates, Inc., an
airline to Alaska with six C-46s. I was the secretary-treasurer and
the Alaskan Manager of the corporation. I supervised and directed
the operation, developing passenger and freight business. I flew
occasionally as duty pilot to keep up my competency. Also served as
check pilot and gave instruction as to proper airline operations.
I dispatched and controlled movements of all Alaskan flight. I
supervised all Alaskan personnel, numbering approximately fifty. The
corporation developed into a $2.5 million yearly gross business, and
was very successful until put out of business in 1953 because it
violated economic regulations of CAB as to the frequency of service
that an irregular carrier could give.

1950 Alaskan Manager and Secretary-Treasurer of Airline Services,
Inc., supplying aircraft maintenance and repairs to transient air
carries at Anchorage, Seattle, Oakland and Baltimore. Successful in
engineering improvements to C-46, salvaging and rebuilding. Also
added a certified electronics section.

1951 Helped organize and promote ATA Sales Co., Inc., promoting and
developing air freight and passenger business to Alaska. I became
Alaskan manager. CAB revocation order in 1953 caused financial ruin of
ATA and all subsidiary companies.

Appendix 12, continued.
Howard Hunt Resume, April 2, 1959

1953 Manager of seventy house housing project. I left eight months later to get back into aviation.
1954 Acquired control of Air Cargo Express, Inc. President, reorganized the company and started another operation to Alaska.
1954 Organized and managed Aircraft Investors, Inc., which was successful in salvaging, engineering and rebuild of a wrecked C-46 in Georgia.
1955 Pilot for United States Overseas Airline, Inc., flying C-54s in trans-Atlantic and Pacific operations. Supervised the successful salvage of a C-54 from the ice in Hudson Bay.
1956 Chief Pilot and President for Air Cargo Express, Inc., flying passengers and freight in connection with the Canadian DEW line. Showed Canadian carrier how to "bush" with large transport aircraft – C-46 and C-54. Also did flying on White Alice construction in Alaska. Supervised operations, maintenance competency and scheduling of crews.
1956 Manager of Barter Island Co., in successful salvage and rebuild of C-46 that went down in the Arctic.
1957 Pilot for Cordova Airlines, flying freight and passengers into mountain top sites construction of White Alice in Alaska.
1958 Chief Pilot and pilot for Interior Airways, flying support of DEW line out of Fairbanks, Alaska, flying C-46, DC-3 and bush aircraft. Supervised scheduling and kept up competency of all pilots. Drew up instrument let-down procedures for DEW line, approved by CAA and distributed to the Air Force or any carrier traveling the DEW line. Instructed bush pilots in instrument flying procedures so as to operate the DEW line in all weather.
1958 Chief Pilot and pilot for Ghezzi, Inc., flying freight in a DC-4 into White Alice and CAA sites in Alaska. Supervised maintenance, kept up competency of other pilots. Was responsible for all flight operations.
1959 Am looking for an aviation challenge in Alaska where I can put my wealth of aviation experience to work.
Aeronautical flying experience as pilot:
    RATINGS:
      a. Military Pilot of

C-54	B-17	AT-9	C-60	B-25
C-46	B-24	P-39	B-26	T-33
C-47	A-20	P-63	BT-13	AT-10

      b. Holder of green instrument card.
      c. Civilian Airline Transport Pilot rating in DC-4, DC-3, C-46.

Pilot flying hours:	Total Hours
Approx total pilot hours	6,450
Military Pilot	3,750
Twin Engine	3,015
Four Engine	3,010
Night Time	1,882
Instructor time	850
Actual Instrument	720
Arctic and Alaska	2,050

Appendix 13.
CBI Hump Pilots Association, Inc., Press Release, 1989

PRESS RELEASE   FOR FURTHER INFORMATION:
                                     CBI Hump Pilots Association, Inc.
For Local Media   808 Lester Street
                                   Poplar Bluff, Missouri 63901
                                   (314) 785-2420

NAME Howard J. Hunt   YOUR PHONE 333-5714

ADDRESS 6924 E. 6th Avenue, Anchorage, AK 99504

COMMENTS:

    ....was awarded the China War Memorial Medal by the Government of the Republic of China.

    Known as the "lost" decoration of WW-II, this Medal commemorates service in China with our Chinese allies in the defeat of the Empire of Japan. The decoration was authorized by the Chinese Government at the end of WW-II, and Circular No. 166, U. S. Forces, China Theater, dated 29 September 1945, was prepared for distribution to provide for issuance of the award. The hasty demobilization of our armed forces and the general confusion then existing in China resulted in the documentation being misplaced. It was noted on some discharge documents and service records, but no one ever saw the decoration or received it. It was generally considered to be a myth by those who had heard the rumors about it.

    But one persistent individual, Graham K. Kidd of Florida, who had served in the 14th Air Force Headquarters in Kunming, China, kept on investigating. After 29 years he succeeded in locating a copy of Circular No. 166.

    Description of Medal: In the center is the Lu Ku Bridge near Peiping, China, where the war broke out. Behind the bridge, and Generalissimo Chiang Kai-shek, there are factories with smoke stacks indicating the victory and the prosperous future of China.

    The Hump Pilots Association is composed of over 5,000 air crew members and support personnel who were engaged in the China-Burma-India Theater of operation during WW-II. A major portion of the flying provided the entire supplies for the American and Chinese Armies and Air Forces in China--the first time such a massive airlift was ever attempted. The November 19, 1945 issue of TIME magazine reported on page 26: "Unofficial estimates were that 3,000 Allied transport and tactical aircraft had been lost among those jagged peaks (Himalaya Mountains). But for this price, the U. S. had backed China, and U.S. units in China, with invaluable aid: 78,000 tons went over the Hump in the peak month of July." These downed aircraft made an "aluminum trail" over the "Hump," as the Himalayas were called. The terrible weather and rugged terrain posed as constant a danger as the Japanese fighters and bombers.

    A two-volume set of books, CHINA AIRLIFT - THE HUMP records a first hand "history" of the CBI Theater during WW-II and are available through the Association. HPA erected a Memorial to those who flew the "Hump" which is located at the Air Force Museum, Wright-Patterson Air Force Base, Dayton, Ohio.

    Receiving the China War Memorial Medal will long be remembered, and is evidence that the successful efforts to keep an entire nation alive under the greatest of odds, enabling us to achieve victory, has not been forgotten!

Appendix 14.
Chinese Air Force Award, August 21, 1990

Translation   Serial No. 79 (A)-302

Chinese Air Force

Be It Known That

Mr. Howard J. Hunt
The China-Burma-India. Hump Pilots Association, Inc.

Is Awarded

A Pair of Pilot Wings No. 129

of

The Chinese Air Force

In Recognition of Outstanding

Personal And Professional Achievements

In Military Aviation

Given This Date   21 August 1990

(SIGNED)
LIN WEN-LI
General, ROCAF
Commander-in-Chief

Taipei

Appendix 15.
2006 Commemorative Air Force Award, February 17, 2007

COMMEMORATIVE AIR FORCE

NATIONAL PATRIOTIC RALLY
MEET ME IN VEGAS

To: Colonel Howard J. Hunt

Date: 17 February 2007

Subject: Commemorative Air Force Aircraft Acquisition Award

Under the provisions of Commemorative Air Force Regulation 900-1, the above named individual is presented the Commemorative Air Force Aircraft Acquisition Award.

CITATION

COLONEL HOWARD J. HUNT IS HEREBY COMMENDED FOR EXCEPTIONAL SUPPORT FOR THE GOALS AND OBJECTIVES OF THE COMMEMORATIVE AIR FORCE. HIS EXCEPTIONAL ENTHUSIASM AND EFFORTS HAVE RESULTED IN THE ADDITION OF ANOTHER AIRCRAFT TO THE COMMEMORATIVE AIR FORCE'S GHOST SQUADRON.

THE GENEROUS DONATION TO THE AMERICAN AIRPOWER HERITAGE FLYING MUSEUM OF THE HARVARD MK- 4, N-421QB BY COLONEL HOWARD J. HUNT, IS AN OUTSTANDING EXAMPLE OF COLONEL HUNT'S SINCERE COMMITMENT TO THE COMMEMORATIVE AIR FORCE'S OBJECTIVES OF PRESERVING AND FLYING WARBIRDS.   THE ADDITION OF THIS AIRCRAFT WILL ADD STRENGTH TO THE ALASKA WING AND VARIETY AND INTEREST TO THE IMPRESSIVE FLEET OF AIRCRAFT OPERATED AND MAINTAINED BY THE ORGANIZATION. THE COMMEMORATIVE AIR FORCE'S ABILITY TO SUPPORT ITS PATRIOTIC AND EDUCATIONAL GOALS HAS BEEN ENHANCED BY THIS GENEROUS DONATION.

COLONEL HOWARD J. HUNT IS BY PRESENTED THE COMMEMORATIVE AIR FORCE AIRCRAFT ACQUISITION AWARD FOR 2006.

BY ORDER OF:

Jethro E. Culpeper

JETHRO E. CULPEPER
COLONEL, CAF
COMMANDER

Honoring America's Legacy of Freedom
CAF Headquarters ❂ P.O. Box 62000 ❂ Midland, Texas 79711-2000
(432) 563-1000 ❂ Fax (432) 563-8046 ❂ www.commemorativeairforce.org

Appendix 16.
Department of Transportation, Federal Aviation Administration,
The Wright Brothers "Master Pilot" Award, July 13, 2007

DEPARTMENT OF TRANSPORTATION
FEDERAL AVIATION ADMINISTRATION

**The Wright Brothers
"Master Pilot" Award**

presented to

Howard "Mike" Hunt

*in appreciation for your dedicated
service, technical expertise, professionalism,
and many outstanding contributions that
further the cause of aviation safety.*

Administrator

July 13, 2007

Date

Appendix 17.
Alaska Legislature, Honoring Howard Hunt,
Alaska Aviation Museum Hall of Fame, 2018

THE ALASKA LEGISLATURE

* HONORING *

* HOWARD "MIKE" HUNT *
* ALASKA AVIATION MUSEUM HALL OF FAME *

The members of the Thirtieth Alaska State Legislature honor Colonel Howard "Mike" Hunt, 96 years young, who on March 24, 2018, will be inducted into the Alaska Aviation Museum's Hall of Fame in recognition of his many years of pioneering aviation in Alaska with the "Lifetime Achievement Award."

Howard was born January 16, 1922, on a farm near Polk City, Iowa, and came to Alaska in 1942 with the Army Air Corps. Hunt and other young pilots flew hundreds of U.S. planes from Great Falls, Montana to Ladd Field in Fairbanks on the Lend-Lease program providing fighter and bomber aircraft for the Russians to use during World War II. He flew both the A-20 fighter bomber and the P-39 Airacobra.

As part of Hunt's Army Air Corp career, he flew the Memphis Belle from Florida to Spokane, Washington on a War Bond tour. Col. Hunt is the last living WWII pilot to have flown as Pilot-in-Command of the B-17 bomber.

With Jack O'Neill, Hunt started Northern Pacific Aero Trading and Transportation Company. After the war, Hunt connected Alaska to the Lower 48 with a fleet of C-46 aircraft as Air Transport Associates (ATA). ATA's first flight was in August of 1948.

In 1954, Hunt was elected president of Air Cargo Express; an aircraft salvage, engineering and operations company rebuilding C-46 aircraft. He was responsible for retrieving a DC-4 that had landed on the ice in Hudson Bay, 40 miles east of Fort Churchill, Canada. Using bay ice under the four-engine airplane and pontoons, the aircraft was pulled by a canoe and two whaling boats across the bay and up the Churchill River to shore.

In November of 1959, the Civil Aeronautics Administration hired Mike to work in Anchorage as a flight inspection pilot with the mission to maintain, commission and flight check all the navigational aids in Alaska. During this era, four course ranges were being decommissioned and the new navigational systems were being built. Mike and pilots Tom Wardleigh, Slim Walters and Don Hood were tasked with overseeing the aviation infrastructure buildout in the newly-minted State of Alaska.

Mike began the Barter Island Company and also flew for Cordova Airlines and Air Cargo Express on Alaska's DEW Line White Alice construction project. After retiring, Mike learned to fly a helicopter, purchased an Enstrom helicopter, and continued flying while staking mining claims throughout Alaska.

In June, 2013, during the 100 Years of Flight in Alaska anniversary, Mike helped launch the Alaska Wing of the Commemorative Air Force (CAF) with the donation of his Harvard IV and BT-13 trainers. He also donated his L-2 Grasshopper to the CAF Wing in 2018.

Col. Hunt's aviation exploits have been featured in magazines, books and television interviews. He received the China War Memorial Medal, the FAA Wright Brothers Award for 50 years of safe flying, and was recognized by the Alaska Air Carriers Association as an Alaska Legend of Aviation. Over his lifetime, he accumulated more than 19,000 hours as Pilot-in-Command in the aircraft he flew.

The members of the Thirtieth Alaska State Legislature and the Alaska Aviation Museum greatly appreciate the contribution and lifetime effort that Col. Mike Hunt has given to Alaska's aviation industry and welcome him into the Hall of Fame.

BRYCE EDGMON
SPEAKER OF THE HOUSE

PETE KELLY
PRESIDENT OF THE SENATE

SEN. JOHN COGHILL
PRIME SPONSOR

REP. GABREILLE LEDOUX
PRIME SPONSOR

Date: March 14, 2018

Cosponsors: Senators Costello, Kelly, Begich, Bishop, Egan, Gardner, Giessel, Hoffman, Hughes, MacKinnon, Meyer, Micciche, Olson, Shower, Stedman, Stevens, von Imhof, Wielechowski, Wilson; Representatives Edgmon, Birch, Chenault, Claman, Drummond, Eastman, Foster, Gara, Grenn, Guttenberg, Johnson, Johnston, Josephson, Kawasaki, Kito, Kreiss-Tomkins, Lincoln, Millett, Neuman, Ortiz, Parish, Pruitt, Rauscher, Saddler, Seaton, Spohnholz, Stutes, Talerico, Tarr, Thompson, Tilton, Tuck, Wilson, Wool

Appendix 18.
Happy Victory Day letter from the Russian Ambassador thanking the American allies for their participation in the victory in World War II, received in 2019

Happy Victory Day!

74 years ago the people of our countries triumphed over the greatest enemy of humankind — fascism. Representatives of the allied armies accepted the unconditional surrender of the Nazi army in Berlin. The bloodiest war in Europe's history was finally over.

The world must not forget the courage and heroism of the soldiers of our armies, members of partisan units, underground anti-fascist networks, and the selflessness of home front workers and all those who defied Hitlerism.

We commemorate the heroic deed of the nations of the Soviet Union in the Great Patriotic War of 1941-1945 and remember the support the allies provided to each other. We remember the military fraternity that stopped the annihilation of nations. It is an example for us even today, when the world faces a new global threat of international terrorism.

Our nations suffered tremendous losses in this war — around 27 million lives that were lost on the fronts, from wounds, in Nazi captivity, death camps, and as a result of punitive operations. This memory is sacred for us. It is necessary to strongly oppose its desecration and prevent the destruction and abuse of military graves and monuments.

We are grateful to all those who keep this memory alive in the U.S. by making efforts to erect monuments to pay tribute to our alliance during those years, participating in commemorative events.

On this Victory Day we congratulate the veterans of the Red Army living in the U.S. and our American allies! We wish you many joyful years to come! Thank you for your sacrifice!

Anatoly Antonov, Ambassador of the Russian Federation
Erzhan Kazykhanov Ambassador of Kazakhstan
Varuzhan Nersesyan, Ambassador of the Republic of Armenia
Meret Orazov, Ambassador of Turkmenistan
Bolot Otunbaev, Ambassador of Kyrgyzstan
Farhod Salim, Ambassador of Tajikistan
Pavel Shidlovsky, Charge d'Affaires of Belarus
Javlon Vakhabov, Ambassador of Uzbekistan

Glossary

Azores, Portugal: An archipelago in the mid-Atlantic and is an autonomous region of Portugal with dramatic landscapes, fishing villages and vineyards.

Barrel Bung: 55-gallon barrel drums have a hole at the top, known as the bung. The bung allows the contents of the barrel to be extracted with a drum pump or another dispensing system. The bung usually measures two inches in diameter, has a screw-type opening, which allows a pump to be screwed to the barrel for safe and secure dispensing.

Berlin Airlift: In response to the Soviet blockade of land routes into West Berlin, the United States began a massive airlift of food, water, and medicine to the citizens of the besieged city. For nearly a year, supplies from American planes sustained the over two million people in West Berlin.

Boonies: Short for boondocks. A sparsely populated rural area.

Boxcar C-82: Manufactured by Fairchild from 1944 to 1948, the C-82 Packet is a twin-engine cargo aircraft. The Boxcar C-82 was used by the Army Air Forces and then the successor United States Air Force, during World War II. Immediately after the C-82 was considered surplus to the United States Air Force, few of these planes were sold to civilian operators in Chile, United States, Mexico and Brazil. They were used for many years as rugged aircraft for hauling heavy freight

Celestial Navigation: Also known as astronavigation, is the ancient and continuing modern practice of position fixing using stars and other celestial bodies that enables a navigator to accurately determine his or her actual current physical position in space without having to rely solely on estimated positional calculations commonly known as dead reckoning.

China-Burma-India Theater: June 22, 1942 the China-Burma-Theater (CBI) was officially established. It is often referred to as The Forgotten Theater of World War II. Of the 12,300,000 Americans under arms at the height of WWII mobilization, only about 250,000 were assigned to the CBI Theater. CBI was important to the Allied war effort because of plans to invade Japan from the Chinese mainland. It then became an effort to keep China supplied and in the war. America's role in CBI was to support China by providing war materials and the manpower to get it to where it was needed.

Collective: In a helicopter, the collective pitch control is a control stick located on the left side of the pilot's seat with an adjustable friction control.

The collective is used to make changes to the pitch angle of the main rotor blades.

Crescent Caravan: Second Ferrying Group, flying C-54 type aircraft from New Castle, Delaware to Calcutta, India during World War II.

Dead Man's Spiral: In aviation, a dead man's spiral is a dangerous spiral dive entered into accidentally by a pilot who is not trained or not proficient in flying in instrument meteorological conditions. This occurs more often at night or in bad weather conditions when a pilot cannot see the horizon.

DEW Line: Back in the early 1950s, the U.S. government determined that they needed a series of radar stations across the Arctic that could detect enemy bombers crossing the North Pole. The Distant Early Warning Line was built. It consisted of a series of radar stations across the arctic, from Alaska through Canada over Greenland to Iceland. Canada had already built two lines and wasn't inclined to build another. In the end, Canada agreed that a third line was necessary and allowed the Americans to build it across Canadian territory, as long as the Americans bore the construction costs. The DEW line was shut down in the late 1980s because the technology was obsolete.

Dory: A small, shallow draft boat, 16 to 23 feet long with high sides, a flat bottom and sharp bows.

Dryland Dredge: Is a gas powered, high pressure suction dredge with a nozzle capable of sending water under pressure from the suction dredge pump to the tip of the nozzle to send water and gravel through a sluice box to extract gold.

Geiger Counter: An instrument used for detecting and measuring ionizing radiation.

Gosport: A flexible speaking tube for communication between separate cockpits or compartments of an aircraft.

Gougler Seat: Metal structured rigid seat.

Greywacke Rock: A variation of sandstone generally characterized by its hardness, dark color and poorly sorted angular grains of quartz and feldspar.

Ground Controlled Approach: GCA is a system in which a ground observer monitors the course and descent angle of an aircraft via radar, which enables pilots to land under extremely adverse weather conditions.

Grubstake: An amount of material, provisions, or money supplied to an enterprise, originally a prospector for ore, in return for a share in the resulting profits.

Gust Lock: A gust lock on an aircraft is a mechanism that locks control surfaces and open aircraft doors in place while the aircraft is parked on the ground. Gust locks prevent wind from causing unexpected movements of the control surfaces and their linked controls inside the aircraft. Some gust locks are external devices attached directly to the aircraft's control surfaces, while others are attached to the flight controls inside the cockpit.

Harvard MK IV: Airplane built by Canadian Car and Foundry in Ontario, Canada. Introduced into RCAF service in 1951. The American equivalent is an AT-6 aircraft.

Hillman Minx: British made, 4-speed manual, rear wheel drive, 37-horse power automobile. Manufactured from 1931 to 1970.

"The Hump":   Flying "the Hump" refers to flying over the Himalaya Mountains, the tallest mountain range in the world, located in Asia. The Hump airlift route went over the top of the Himalayas between China-Burma-India (CBI). The airlift began after the Japanese attack on Pearl Harbor in 1942. The U.S. military flew supplies to isolated Chinese forces after the Japanese cut off the only land-based route through Burma. The airlift eventually expanded to include supplying allied troops in Burma, China and India. The supply flights routinely hauled troops, basic supplies, light weapons and 55-gallon fuel barrels. The pilots who crossed over the Himalayas flew in constant adverse weather conditions in aircraft not designed to fly at that extreme altitude and were heavily overloaded. The success of the massive airlift was due in large part to the courage and imagination of the military pilots. Throughout WWII, many military aircraft were used to fly The Hump, including C-47s, C-46s, C-54s, P-38s, and P-40s. The airlift route continued to play a critical role until the war ended in 1945.

Igneous Rock: One of the three main rock types, the other two being sedimentary and metamorphic. Igneous rock is formed through the cooling and solidification of magma or lava.

Lamiflex: A carbon fiber type of manufactured material used in aircraft parts such as helicopter bearings and blades.

Landing Craft: Small or medium sized seagoing watercraft used to convey cargo or personnel from the water to the shore.

Lend-Lease Act: The Lend-Lease Act of 1941 stated that the U.S. government could lend or lease (rather than sell) war supplies such as ammunition, tanks, airplanes, trucks, and food to any nation deemed "vital to the defense of the United States." Under this policy, the United States was able to supply military aid to its foreign allies during World War II while still remaining officially neutral.

Loran Navigation: Long Range Navigation. A hyperbolic radio navigation system developed during World War II. The radio signals operated at a low frequency and provided long-range navigation for ship convoys and aircraft operating in the Pacific theater.

Metamorphic Rock: Rocks that arise from the transformation of existing rock to new types of rock. The process is called metamorphism. The original rock is subjected to temperatures greater than 200 degrees Celsius and elevated pressure causing physical or chemical changes.

Nacelles: The outer casing of an aircraft engine.

Navaids: Navigation device in an aircraft, ship or other vehicle.

Nodwell: A multipurpose, enclosed cab, two-tracked vehicle capable of traversing adverse terrain conditions such as swamp, muskeg, sand and snow.

Non-Skeds: A large number of independent airlines that came into being at the end of World War II when surplus airplanes became available to purchase. Non-skeds operated without the restrictions of scheduled airlines so were able to offer lower cost service to customers.

Otter: A two-track amphibious cargo carrier designed to carry cargo or troops over shallow rivers or swampy terrains. Otter is smaller than a Nodwell and has a small propeller on the back end of the vehicle.

Pontoon Boat: Large, sturdy, rubberized, inflatable boats used by the military to transport troops or equipment across bodies of water.

Purple Project: On August 15, 1945, the Air Transport Command issued orders to fly to Okinawa to haul occupation troops to Tokyo. Three hundred C-54s were assembled at Okinawa for the airlift.

Quonset Hut: is a lightweight prefabricated structure of corrugated galvanized iron having a semicircular cross-section. The standard sized Quonset hut is a 20' x 40' building weighing 3.5 tons. Between 150,000 and 170,000 Quonset huts were manufactured during WWII. After the war, the U.S. military sold the surplus Quonset huts to the public for $1,000 each.

Revetment: A barricade of earth or sandbags set up to provide protection from blast or to prevent planes from overrunning when landing.

Saxon Car Engine: Four-cylinder, twelve-horse-power engine built by Saxon Motor Car Company. Cars were manufactured from 1913–1923.

Scintillation counter: An instrument for detecting and measuring ionizing radiation by using the excitation effect of incident radiation on a scintillating material, and detecting the resulting light pulses.

Sedimentary Rock: Types of rock that are formed by the accumulation of mineral or organic particles at Earth's surface, followed by cementation. Organic sedimentary rocks form from the accumulation of plant or animal debris. Examples include: chalk, coal, diatomite and some limestone.

Set Net Fishing: Fishing nets anchored on shore above high tide and the opposite end extending perpendicular to the shore and anchored offshore. Set nets are staked and buoyed.

Spar: In fixed wing aircraft, the spar is the main structural member of the wing running perpendicular to the fuselage. The spar carries the load of the wings while on the ground. There may be more than one spar in a wing. Where a single spar carries most of the force, it is referred to as the main spar.

Subsidized Carriers: Subsidization of air carriers came about when the federal government contracted air carriers to carry mail. For many years, the issue of subsidy payments to airlines was among the most controversial of all transportation issues considered by Congress. Long-term arguments about subsidies and what they meant continued throughout the 1940s, 1950s and into the 1960s.

Stoneboat: Sometimes called a stone drag is a type of low sled or toboggan for moving heavy objects. Originally they were for animal-powered transport used with horses or oxen to clear fields of stones or large tree stumps without having to lift them. Stoneboats are quick and easy to set up, load, transport and dump.

Sywash: Temporary campsite without a tent.

Tailplane Stall: This occurs when the critical angle of attack is exceeded. Since the horizontal stabilizer counters the natural nose down tendency caused by the center of lift of the main wing, the airplane will react by pitching down, sometimes uncontrollably, when the tailplane is stalled.

Third Class Medical: Third class medical certificate is required for student pilots, recreational pilots and private pilots who fly for pleasure, but not for hire.

Trapper Nelson: Patented in 1924, a Trapper Nelson is a stabilizing rigid external wooden pack frame with a removable canvas pack sack. The Trapper Nelson is still recognized as an icon of the "old days."

V Numbers: The "V" stands for velocity and is used to define airspeeds important to the operation of all aircraft. These speeds are derived from data obtained by aircraft manufacturers during flight testing.

> V-1 is the speed by which time the decision to continue flight if an engine fails has been made.

> V-2 is the speed at which the airplane will climb in the event of an engine failure. It is known as the takeoff safety speed.

Variation: The difference in degrees between the magnetic north and the true north. These two poles are about 1,300 miles apart. Magnetic variation is the angle on the horizontal plane between magnetic north and true north. This angle varies depending on position on the earth's surface and changes over time.

Very High Frequency (VHF):   A 30–300 megahertz electromagnetic wave between audio and infrared.

VHF Omni-directional-Range/Tactical Air Navigation (VORTAC):   A radio-based navigational aid for aircraft pilots consisting of a co-located VHF omnidirectional range beacon and a tactical air navigation system beacon.

White Alice: The White Alice Communications System (WACS) was a United States Air Force telecommunication network with eighty radio stations constructed in Alaska during the mid-1950s. It used tropospheric scatter for over-the-horizon links and microwave relay for shorter line-of-sight links. Each White Alice site was capable of receiving radio waves from up to 200 miles away, and transmitting them another 200 miles on down the line. The system also supported military radar site such as the Distant Early Warning (DEW) line that covered the Arctic Circle and would relay notice to the Lower 48 of any impending bombs sent over from Russia.

References

Air Force Magazine
Dec. 1, 1996. Valor: All For One by John L. Frisbee. https://www.airforcemag.com/article/valor-all-for-one/

Anchorage Daily News, Anchorage, Alaska

Anchorage Daily Times, Anchorage, Alaska

Cavalier, Greenwich, Conn., (Fawcett Publications)
Cavalier, March 1958, pages 36-41, 87-92. "The Great Ice Floe Gamble" by George Scullin

The Daily Monitor Leader, Mount Clemens, Michigan
Nov. 16, 1944. Junk 'Lung' Saves Life of Officer. Chronicling America: Historic American Newspapers. Lib. of Congress. <https://chroniclingamerica.loc.gov/lccn/sn96077289/1944-11-16/ed-1/seq-17/>

Daily Sitka Sentinel, Stika, Alaska

Des Moines Tribune, Des Moines, Iowa

Edmonton Journal, Edmonton, Alberta, Canada

Evening Star, Washington, D.C.
Aug. 11,1944. Artificial Respiration saves Officer Hit by Polio in china. Chronicling America: Historic American Newspapers. Lib. of Congress. <https://chroniclingamerica.loc.gov/lccn/sn83045462/1944-08-11/ed-1/seq-10/>

Oct. 8, 1944. Wife Coming Here to Comfort Polio Victim Flown From India. Chronicling America: Historic American Newspapers. Lib. of Congress. https://chroniclingamerica.loc.gov/lccn/sn83045462/1944-10-08/ed-1/seq-37/

Oct. 9,1944. Wife Visits Walter Reed Paient Striken with Polio in Tibet. Chronicling America: Historic American Newspapers. Lib. of Congress. https://chroniclingamerica.loc.gov/lccn/sn83045462/1944-10-09/ed-1/seq-17/

Fairbanks Daily News Miner, Fairbanks, Alaska

Google Books
https://books.google.com

Heros of the Horizon, Flying Adventures of Alaska's Legendary Bush Pilots, Gerry Bruder, Alaska Northwest Books, Anchorage and Seattle, 1991.

Library of Congress Chronicling America

Chronicling America, https://chroniclingamerica.loc.gov/

Life

Life, June 27, 1955, pages 61-62, The Sawdust Airdrop on Hudson Bay, https://books.google.com/books?id=qlYEAAAAMBAJ&pg=PA61

Life, July 18, 1955, pages 34-35, https://books.google.com/books?id=-11YEAAAAMBAJ&pg=PA34

The Nome Nugget, Nome Alaska

The Nome Nugget, https://chroniclingamerica.loc.gov/search/pages/results/?lccn=sn87062011&lccn=sn87062014&lccn=sn84020662&lccn=sn87062013&dateFilterType=yearRange&date1=1949&date2=1953&language=&ortext=&andtext=&phrasetext=&proxtext=&proxdistance=5&rows=20&searchType=advanced

Prop Wash 42H, Sequoia Field, Visalia, California

Edited magazine published the aviation cadets.

United States Senate Hearings

March 31, May 1, 2, 5, 6, 7 and 8, 1953. Hearings before a Subcommittee of the Select Committee on Small Business, United States Senate, Eighty-Third Congress. First Session on Future of Irregular Airlines in United States Air Transportation Industry. https://www.google.com/books/edition/Future_of_Irregular_Airlines_in_United_S/oXf6l8d7ZGEC

Winnipeg Free Press, Winnipeg, Manitoba, Canada

Winnipeg Tribune, Winnipeg, Manitoba, Canada

Index

About the Author

Howard "Mike" John Hunt was an Alaskan pioneer who came to Alaska in 1949 to establish a non-scheduled airline, Air Transport Associates. ATA was formed when Hunt and several pilots who also served in WWII obtained surplus C-46s from the United States Air Force. The goal was to provide inexpensive air cargo and passenger service between the Territory of Alaska and the United States.

He was part of a U.S. Air Force Crescent Caravan's, 2nd Ferry Group, airplane relay team whose sole purpose was to bring home an Army lieutenant, stricken with polio, near the Tibetan border. The 11,000-mile trip took sixty-five hours to travel halfway around the world to Walter Reed Hospital in Washington, D.C. on October 5, 1944.

Hunt was a ferry pilot during World War II flying with the Army Air Corps. He participated in the United States/Russia Lend-Lease program. This program involved ferrying a variety of military airplanes from factories in Wichita, Kansas to Great Falls, Montana. From there, the aircraft were flown across western Canada to Ladd Field in Fairbanks, Alaska. The Russian pilots picked up the airplanes at Ladd Field, and flew them across Russia to the German front, where they successfully defeated the German Army.

In December 1943, he flew the B-17, Memphis Belle, on a ten-day bond drive from Spokane, Washington to Tampa, Florida, to promote the war effort. He was the last known surviving pilot to have flown the Belle.

Flying was everything to him. He soloed at age seventeen and flew everything from a J-3 Super Cub to a Saberliner jet over his lifetime. However, World War II airplanes were his passion. He purchased, restored, flew and then donated three warbirds to the Alaska Wing of the Commemorative Air Force based in Anchorage, Alaska.

Dressed in his original World War II uniform, Howard Hunt poses in his living room with a small collection of replica model airplanes that he flew during his career. Photograph courtesy of Rob Stapleton, Alaskafoto.

Howard "Mike" Hunt was an avid supporter of the Alaska Aviation Museum and the Alaska Wing of the Commemorative Air Force. It was his utmost desire to have revenue from the sale of his autobiography, *Saga of an Aviation Survivor*, support these two entities.

In keeping with his wishes, the Howard Hunt Estate is donating the net proceeds of *Saga of An Aviation Survivor* to the Alaska Aviation Museum and the Col. Howard "Mike" Hunt Wing of the Commemorative Air Force.

Alaska Aviation Museum

The goal of the Alaska Aviation Museum is to preserve, display, educate and honor Alaska's aviation heritage. The Museum is located in the heart of Alaska aviation on the south shore of Lake Hood, Anchorage, Alaska. Lake Hood is the busiest seaplane base in the world with more than 87,000 takeoffs and landings per year. The Ted Stevens International Airport, the air crossroads of the world, is located nearby.

The museum presents one of the finest displays of Alaskan aviation history with interactive displays, memorabilia, photographs, films and artifacts from personal collections of Alaska's pioneer aviators.

Alaska Wing
National Commemorative Air Force

The overall mission of the non-profit National Commemorative Air Force is to restore and preserve military aircraft, as well as showcase the restored aircraft at air shows across the country. The Alaska Wing was established in 2006 with the donation of the Harvard MK-IV.

The Col. Howard "Mike" Hunt Alaska Wing of the Commemorative Air Force takes that original mission of preserving historically significant military aircraft to the Far North of Alaska—the only state to be invaded during World War II.

By preserving these aircraft in flying condition, the Alaska Wing is able to preserve the important connection for Alaskans to that deadly conflict in such a way lest we forget what happened so many years ago.

Your purchase of *Saga of an Aviation Survivor*
helps support these organizations.

CPSIA information can be obtained
at www.ICGtesting.com
Printed in the USA
FSHW011729310122
87989FS